split level

pomes

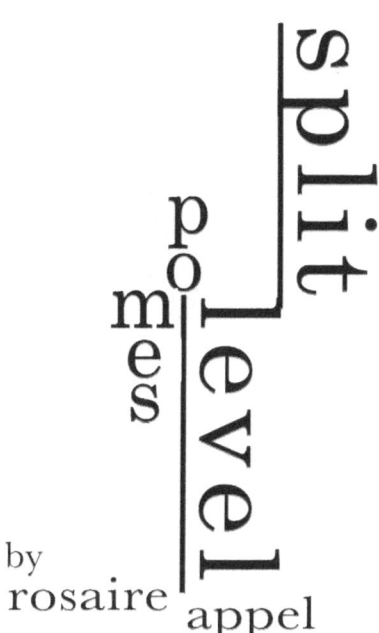

by rosaire appel

press rappel

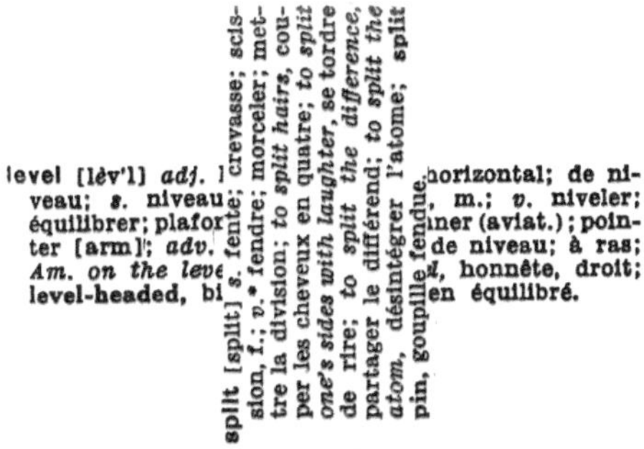
level [lèv'l] adj. l horizontal; de ni-
veau; s. niveau , m.; v. niveler;
équilibrer; plafor ner (aviat.); poin-
ter [arm]; adv. de niveau; à ras;
Am. on the leve d, honnête, droit;
level-headed, bi en équilibré.
split [split] s. fente; crevasse; scis-
sion, f.; v.* fendre; morceler; met-
tre la division; to split hairs, cou-
per les cheveux en quatre; to split
one's sides with laughter, se tordre
de rire; to split the difference,
partager le différend; to split the
atom, désintégrer l'atome; split
pin, goupille fendue.

split-level pomes[1,2]

[1]*POME* :

A dyslectic version of ***poem***.

POEM 1 (pō′ əm), *n.* (The letter "P"; the waving hand denotes rhythm.) The right "P" hand swings back and forth rhythmically over the open left hand, whose palm faces the body. The right hand may also describe a figure-eight movement instead of the back-and-forth movement.

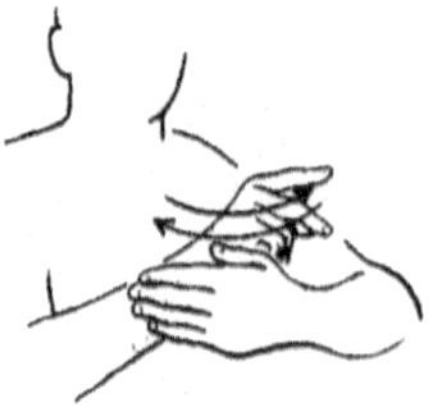

²*POME*

A typographically erroneous version of home.

home (hōm) ▸*n.* **1.** A place where one lives; residence. **2.** A structure or unit for domestic living. **3.** A household. **4.** A place of origin. **5.** The native habitat, as of a plant or animal. **6a.** *Baseball* Home plate. **b.** *Games* Home base. **7.** An institution where people are cared for. ▸*adv.* **1.** At or to the direction of home. **2.** On target: *The arrow struck home.* **3.** To the very center: *Your comment struck home.* ▸*v.* **homed, hom•ing 1.** To go or return home. **2.** To be guided to a target automatically, as by radio waves. **3.** To move toward a goal: *home in on the truth.* —*idiom:* **at home** Comfortable and relaxed. [< OE *hām.*]

home base ▸*n.* **1a.** *Games* An objective toward which players progress. **b.** *Baseball* Home plate. **2.** A base of operations.

home•bod•y (hōm′bŏd′ē) ▸*n., pl.* **-ies.** One whose interests center on the home.

home•boy (hōm′boi′) ▸*n. Slang* **1.** A male friend from one's neighborhood or hometown. **2.** A fellow male gang member.

home•com•ing (hōm′kŭm′ĭng) ▸*n.* **1.** A return home. **2.** An annual event at schools and colleges for visiting graduates.

home economics ▸*n. (takes sing. or pl. v.)* The science and art of home management. —**home economist** *n.*

home front ▸*n.* The civilian population or the civilian activities of a country at war.

home•girl (hōm′gûrl′) ▸*n. Slang* **1.** A female friend from one's neighborhood or hometown. **2.** A fellow female gang member.

home•land (hōm′lănd′) ▸*n.* **1.** One's native land. **2.** A state or region closely identified with a particular people.

home•less (hōm′lĭs) ▸*adj.* Having no home or haven. ▸*n. (takes pl. v.)* People without homes considered as a group.

home•ly (hōm′lē) ▸*adj.* **-li•er, -li•est 1.** Not attractive or good-looking. **2.** Simple or unpretentious; plain: *homely truths.* **3.** Characteristic of the home. —**home′li•ness** *n.*

home•made (hōm′mād′) ▸*adj.* **1.** Made or prepared in the home. **2.** Crudely or simply made.

home•mak•er (hōm′mā′kər) ▸*n.* One who manages a household. —**home′mak′ing** *n.*

nment
Coast

ndell.

·1935.
S Su-

A rel-
nt. At.
lolmia

tirely:

Great
caust
ers by
holo-

dj. Of
uater-
. The

ıe pat-
m that
n pho-

A doc-
of its
′aph′-
ıol′o•

hod of

an ob-
erence
minat-

ıd for-
he Jut-

ı breed

ıhaped
carry

r asso-
Vorthy
itually

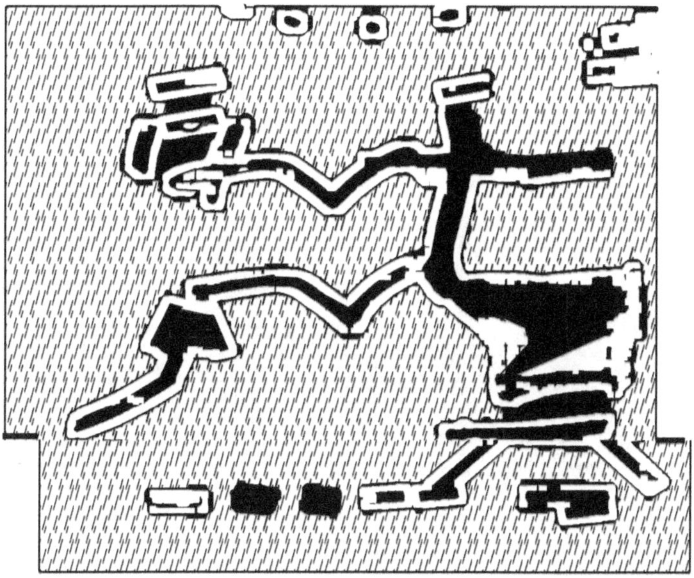

en-
reas
nals
But
Nick
rats,
pro-

the
for-
cial,
be-
top-
qui-
nese
esti-
t ef-
tion
nies,
d to
S.A.
any-
now-

trol ne
ists an
Lon
comm
in per
come
phone
ties he
rif Kou
a polic
as sus
would
witho
expert
tween
Som
radica
er an
Merah
in Tou
ing sol
radica
Sim

error-

roups
often
e be-
tele-
amily
Ché-
lled in
tified
tacks,
verse
cern,
ls be-
ual.
mbers
broth-
mmed
eople
arget-
more

sur-

som
B
wou
Josh
mor
sho
reso
R
inte
the
tute,
he s
the
cros
so t
lowe
T
lone
kille
vik,
in 20
icals
tive,

data.
nitor
t, Mr.
quire
"We
with

tor of
ies at
Insti-
s, and
wn to
yet
cern,
nd, a

e not
gby's
Brei-
Oslo
n rad-
inac-

ism," h
for the
of Hon
his sur
of the
leaked
about
to go
friends
do, Mr.
Man
dramat
memb
ganda
the am
tioned
claime
done in
of the
one of
corded
"He
spoke

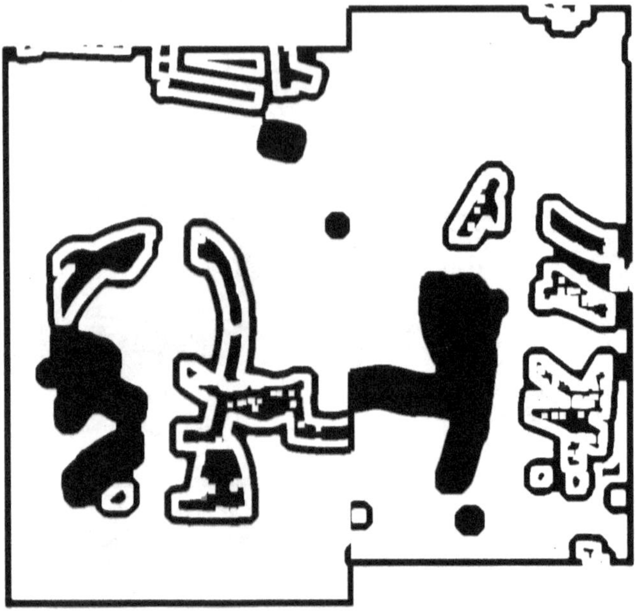

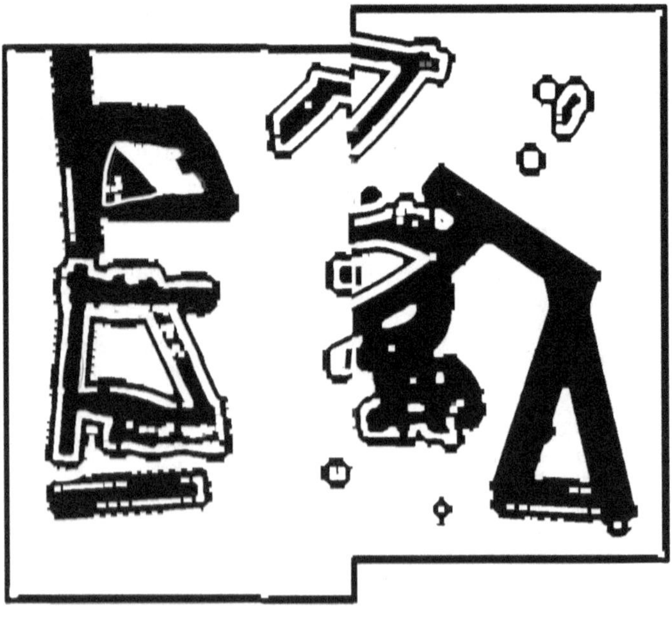

bility to
s intelli-
e of Ed-
he said,
contrac-
Security
ny of its
"The
by ter-
)."
s by in-
s across
e press-
ther in-
eans of
Internet
ia. Ger-
the ID
of trav-

Grand sa
watch lis
act, unles
or what
quisite in
call that
day, you
everyone
Shash
low at th
Institute
lone wolf
as a wolf
formal c
ated enor
The ac
even a
costs les
black ma
and a me

ders
nt an
rror-
mall
s are

ts of
s by
arted
e the
s on
bings
part
erna-
n de-
plots,
harp
e in
Cam-
alled

tial trou
ed, the fo
said, by
track the
gence ca
ward Sn
referring
tor for
Agency
eavesdr
tactics t
rorists m
After
dividual
Europe,
ing for
telligenc
commun
sites, inc

ide to
rmant
ll 'ex-
phone
is the
follow

ch fel-
rvices
that a
known
ithout
d, cre-

pon —
which
n the
knives
e ones

that t
file"
often
their
their
lence.
their
and
"regul
able a
tivitie
group
rorist
Tha
that t
in tar
detect
this p
phone

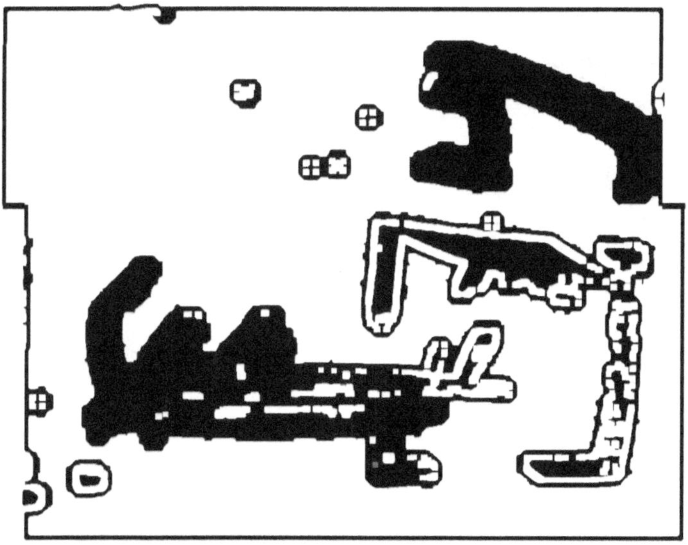

cunt?—Saul Bellow

in one's **wheels** *v phr by 1940s* To waste time; work fruitlessly: *Nobody spun his wheels. I'm proud of them*—Washington Post/ *Stop spinning your wheels, get yourself in gear*—W T Tyler

it *n by 1960s* Nothing; =ZILCH, ZIP: *"What'd she come up with?" "Spit"*—Scott Turow [a euphemism for *shit*]

See HOT SPIT, NOT WORTH A BUCKET OF WARM SPIT, SWAP SPIT

itball 1 *n baseball by 1905* A pitch thrown using a ball wetted with spit or otherwise illegally besmeared 2 *v by 1955* To speculate; propose conclusions or possibilities: *Well, I'm just spit-balling*—Paul Theroux/ *You're just spitballing*—Lawrence Sanders 3 *n by 1970s* A nasty but feeble attack: ... *despite the spitballs he keeps getting from the critical liberal media*—Philadelphia Journal [second and third senses fr the mischievous schoolboy's vice of throwing bits of paper soaked in saliva; second sense fr the notion of tossing such spitballs more or less idly]

it in someone's **eye** *v phr by 1908* To show extreme contempt and ingratitude: *What I hate is when you pay for it and they spit in your eye*—Stan Cutler

it it out *v phr by 1855* To speak out; reveal; disclose: *If you've got any more to tell me, spit it out right now*

itless **See** SCARED SPITLESS, SCARE someone SHITLESS

itter *n baseball by 1908* =SPITBALL

izzerinktum or **spizzerrinctum** *n by 1940s* Vigor; pep; =PIZZAZZ: ... *the fellow who put foresight, science, and spizzerinktum into their business*—H E Babcock [origin unknown; since the earliest meaning is "money," perhaps a coinage fr Latin *specie rectum*, "the right sort"]

lash **See** MAKE A SPLASH

lat 1 *v by 1922* To hit with a smacking sound; slap: *I wouldn't be at all concerned that a tomato would splat me in the face*—Mike Royko 2 *n by 1958* A slap or smack [echoic]

splice *v by 1751* To marry •Most often in the passive: ... *crying to be spliced*—Joseph Auslander

splice the main brace *v phr nautical by 1850* To have a drink of liquor

spliff *n narcotics by 1936* A marijuana cigarette: *Smoking a spliff of high-octane chronic*... —People Weekly [a West Indian term]

splinter **See** KNEE-HIGH TO A GRASSHOPPER

split *v jazz musicians by 1956* To leave; depart; =CUT OUT: *This party is dullsville, let's split*

See HELL TO SPLIT, LICKETY-SPLIT

split a gut *v phr by 1940s* To try very, very hard; make a maximum effort; =BUST one's ASS

◁**split beaver**▷ *n phr by 1972* A photograph or view of a woman's vulva between spread legs; =SPREAD BEAVER: *I can toss off phrases like "split beaver" with almost devil-may-care abandon*—Esquire

splitsville *n by 1980s* A parting or dissolution; separation: ... *teach the little chickadees to fly and then... it's splitsville*—Milwaukee Journal/ *Splitsville... Fergie and Prince Andrew are calling it quits*—Milwaukee Journal

split the difference *v phr by 1750* To compromise, esp when agreement is near: *We're almost agreed, so let's split the difference/ She may have to realize that the philosophical difference between herself and Rome remains one that finally just can't be split*—New Republic

split the scene *v phr black musicians by about 1952* To leave; depart; =CUT OUT, SPLIT: ... *just as I was about to split the scene*—Tennessee Williams

split the sheets *v phr by 1980s* To get a divorce: *They split the sheets*—TV show *Hogan Family* [fr the division of property after a divorce]

split-up 1 *n by 1908* An angry separation: *Me and the old man had a split-up*—W R Burnett 2 *n by 1975* A divorce or legal separation of a married couple provided that the *real-is-positive convention is used. This takes distances to real objects, images, and foci as positive; those to virtual objects, images, and foci as negative. The equation does not always apply if the alternative New Cartesian convention (*see* sign convention) is used.

Lenz's law An induced electric current always flows in such a direction that it opposes the change producing it. This law, first stated by Heinrich Lenz (1804–65) in 1835, is essentially a form of the law of conservation of energy.

lepton Any of a class of *elementary particles that consists of the *electron, muon, tau particle, and three types of *neutrino (one associated with each of the other types of lepton). For each lepton there is an equivalent antiparticle. The antileptons have a charge opposite that of the leptons; the antineutrinos, like the neutrinos, have no charge. The electron, muon, and tau particle all have a charge of –1. These three particles differ from each other only in mass: the muon is 200 times more massive than the electron and the tau particle is 3500 times more massive than the electron. Leptons interact by the electromagnetic interaction and the weak interaction (*see* fundamental interactions).

Leslie's cube A metal box in the shape of a cube in which each of the four vertical sides have different surface finishes. When hot water is placed in the cube, the emissivity of the finishes can be compared. The device was first used by Sir John Leslie (1766–1832).

level An instrument used in *surveying to determine heights. It usually consists of a telescope and attached spirit level mounted on a tripod. The level is set up between a point of known height and a point for which the height is required. Before use it is adjusted until the line of sight is exactly horizontal. Sightings are then made onto a graduated levelling staff at the two points. The difference in elevation between the two points can then be calculated from the readings taken at these points.

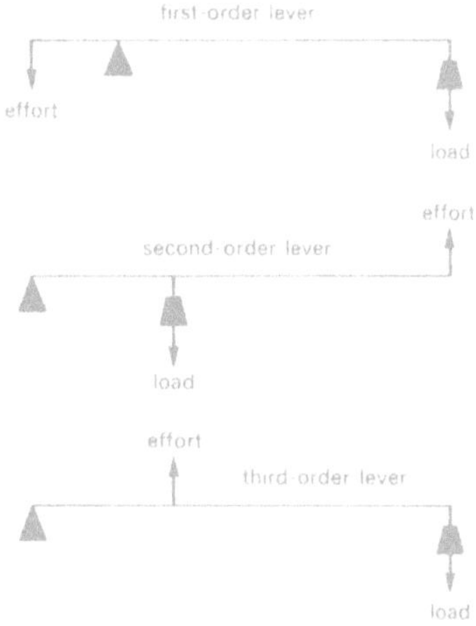

Levers

lever A simple machine consisting of a rigid bar pivoted about a fulcrum. The mechanical advantage or *force ratio of a lever (the ratio of load to effort) is equal to the ratio of the perpendicular distance of the line of action of the effort from the fulcrum to the perpendicular distance of the line of action of the load from the fulcrum. In a first-order lever the fulcrum comes between load and effort. In a second-order lever the load comes between the fulcrum and the effort. In a third-order lever the effort comes between the fulcrum and the load. See illustrations.

Leyden jar An early form of *capacitor consisting of a glass jar with a layer of metal foil on the outside and a similar layer on the inside. Contact to the inner foil is by means of a loose chain hanging inside the jar. It was invented in the Dutch town of Leyden in about 1745.

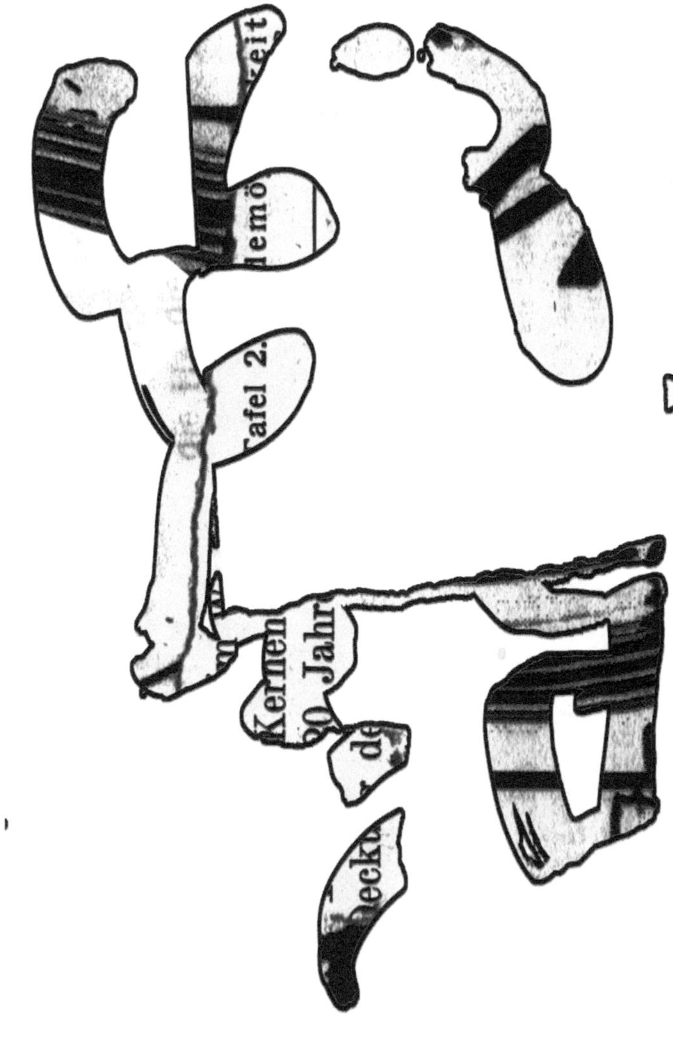

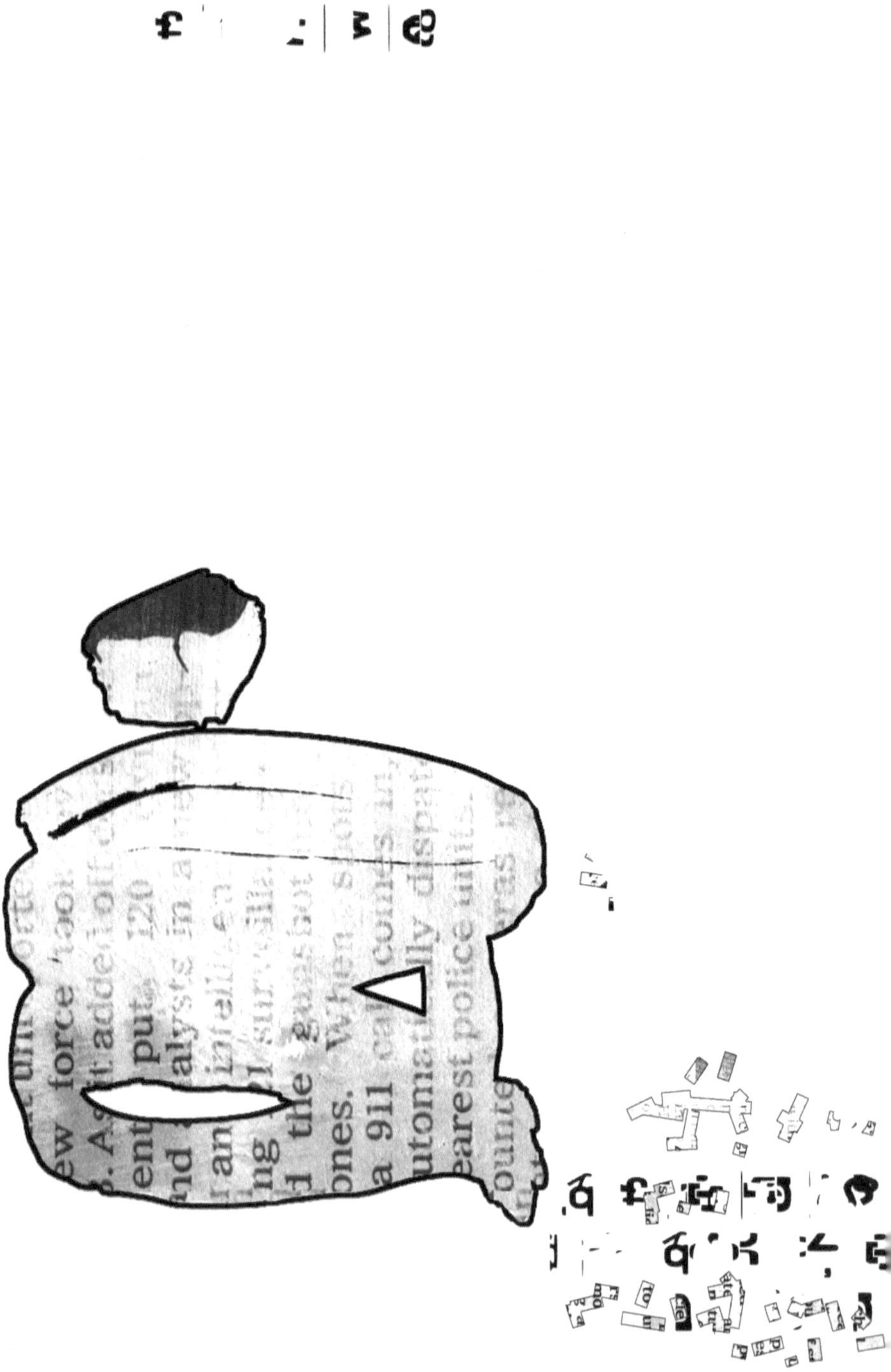

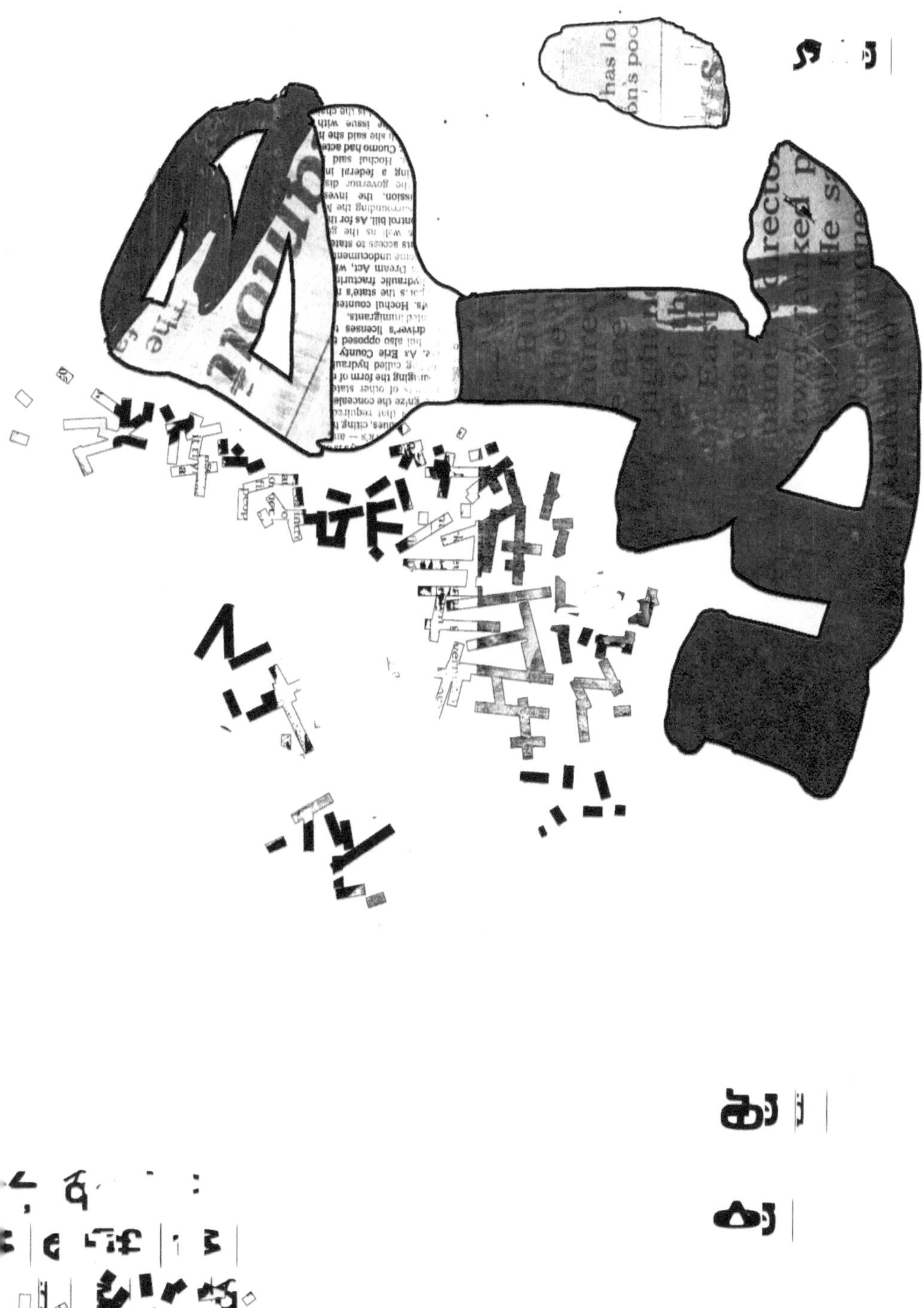

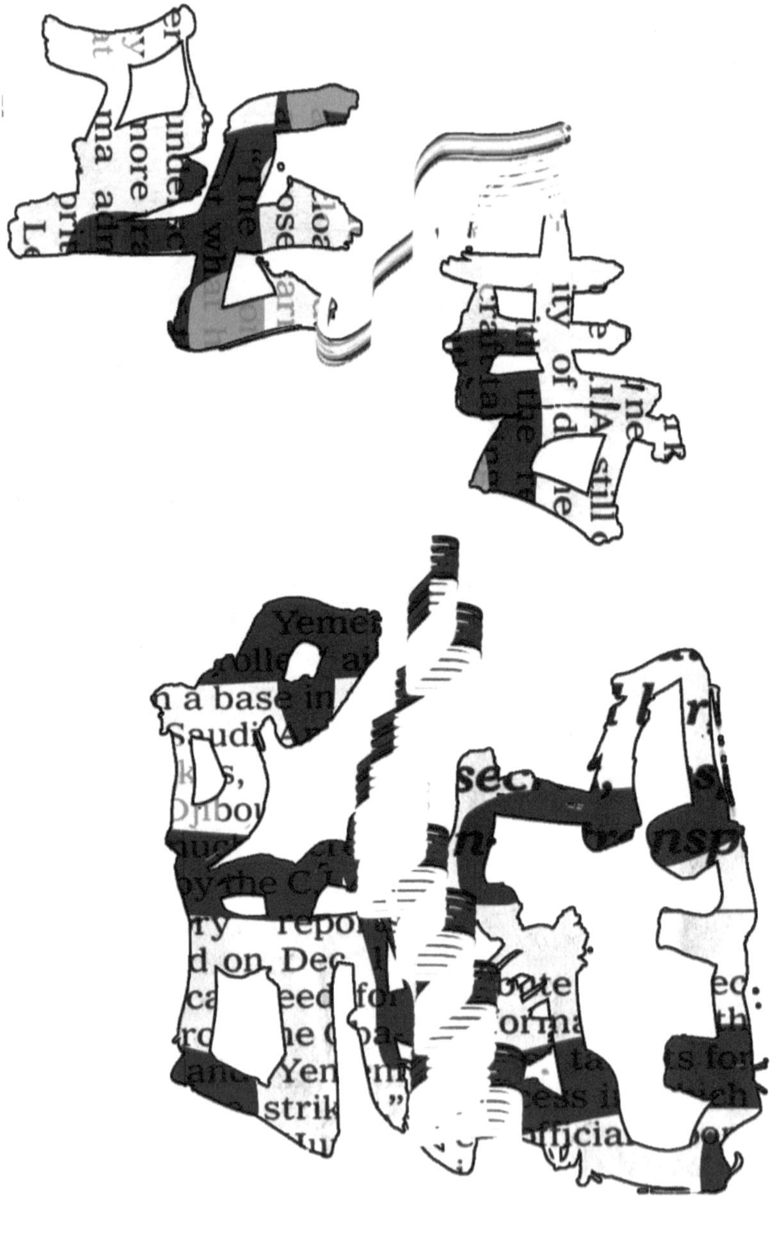

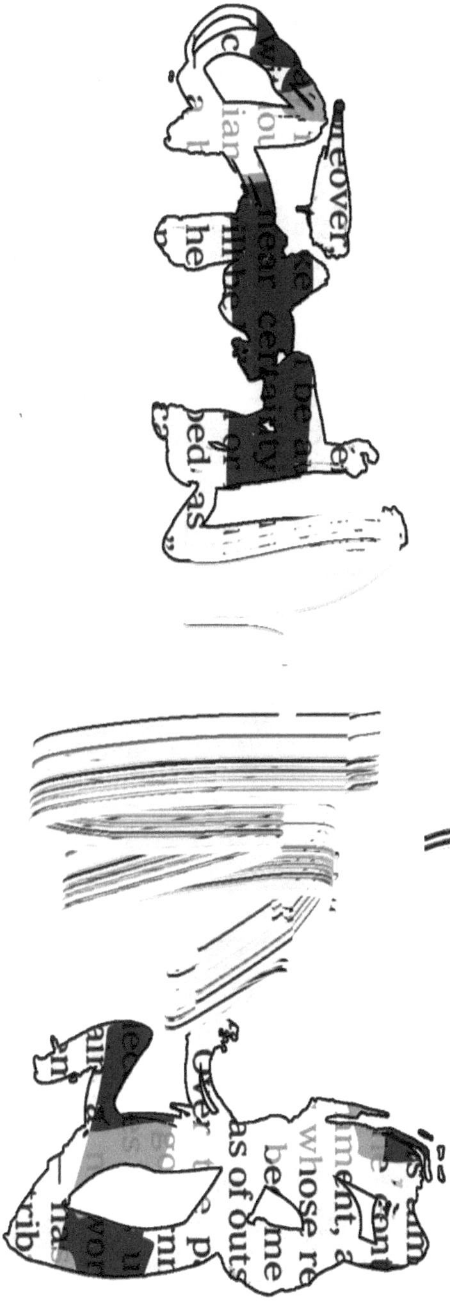

wh h 5 ple
luding en
he min

gnite or
nen's ity es
d aged A
Yemen
up or op
man bect
ther words may
s to ni ulate
befo nd after
.

ne ay
t ts
week. But in the
officials have
o be misin
the accidenta
civilians in

e from g.
ed a 28 ar
pened to hitch a
pec d to
er Ac
mber tnesses
cal officials
Yas bi
ting by a sta
n the re
and Cruise
ve him a ride.

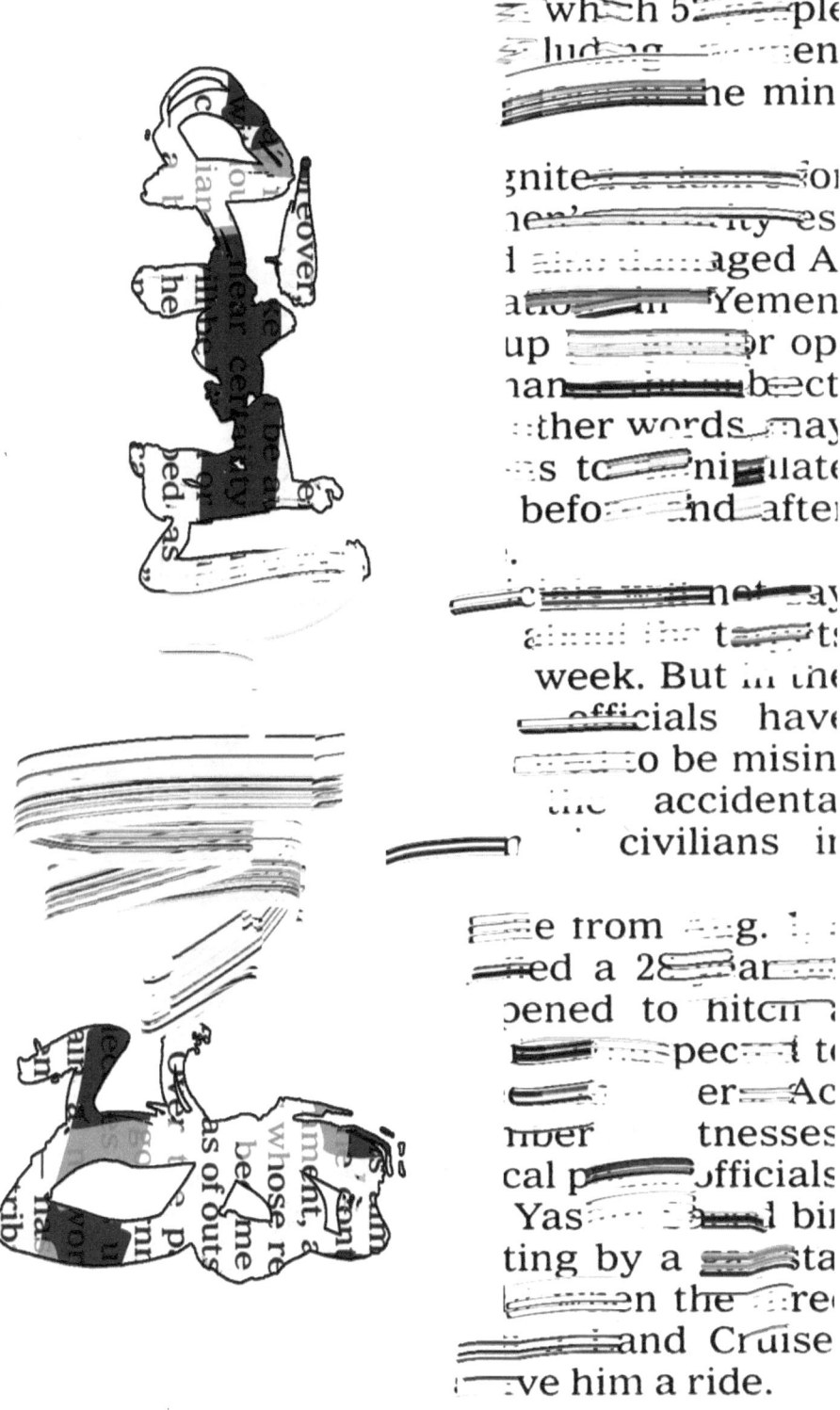

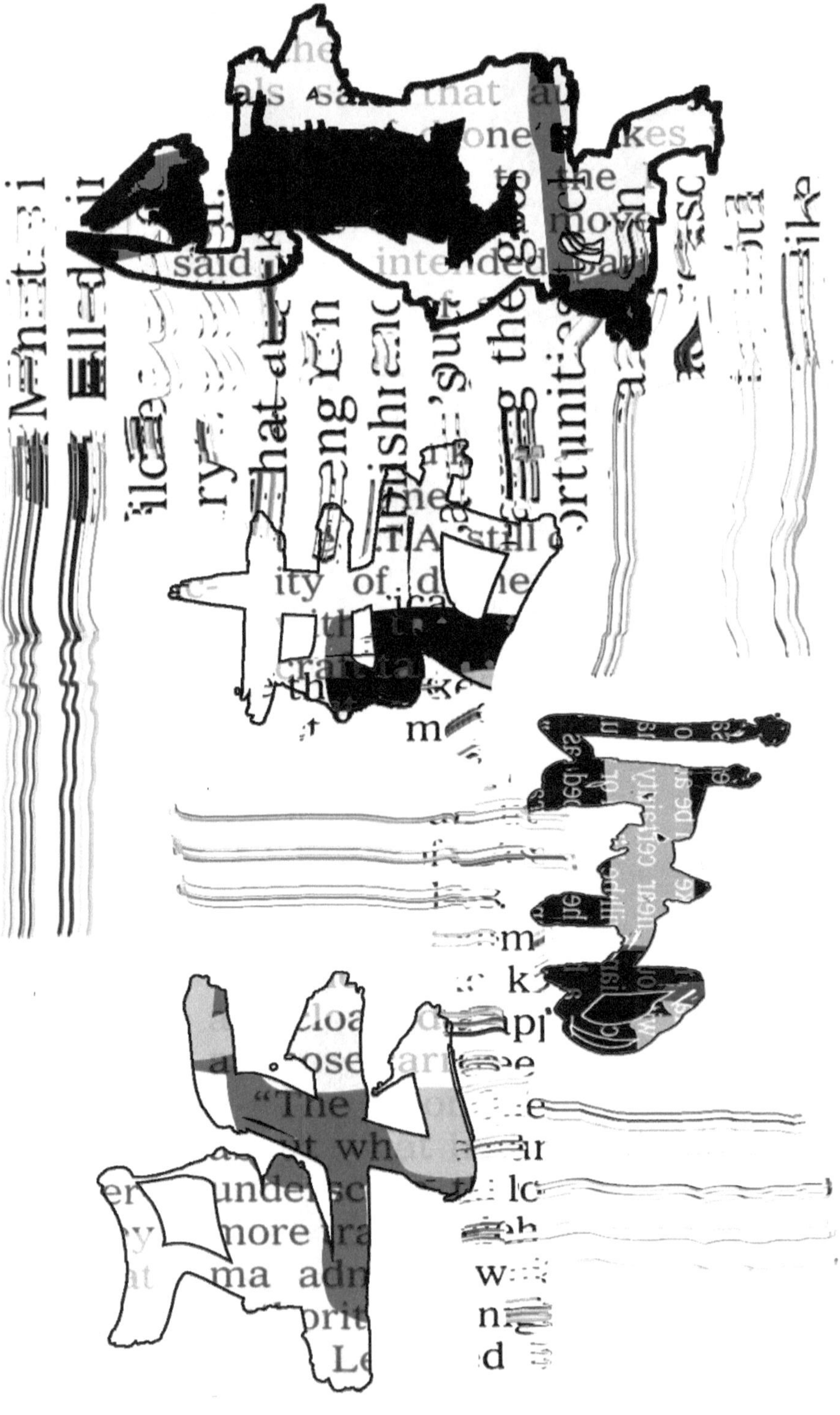

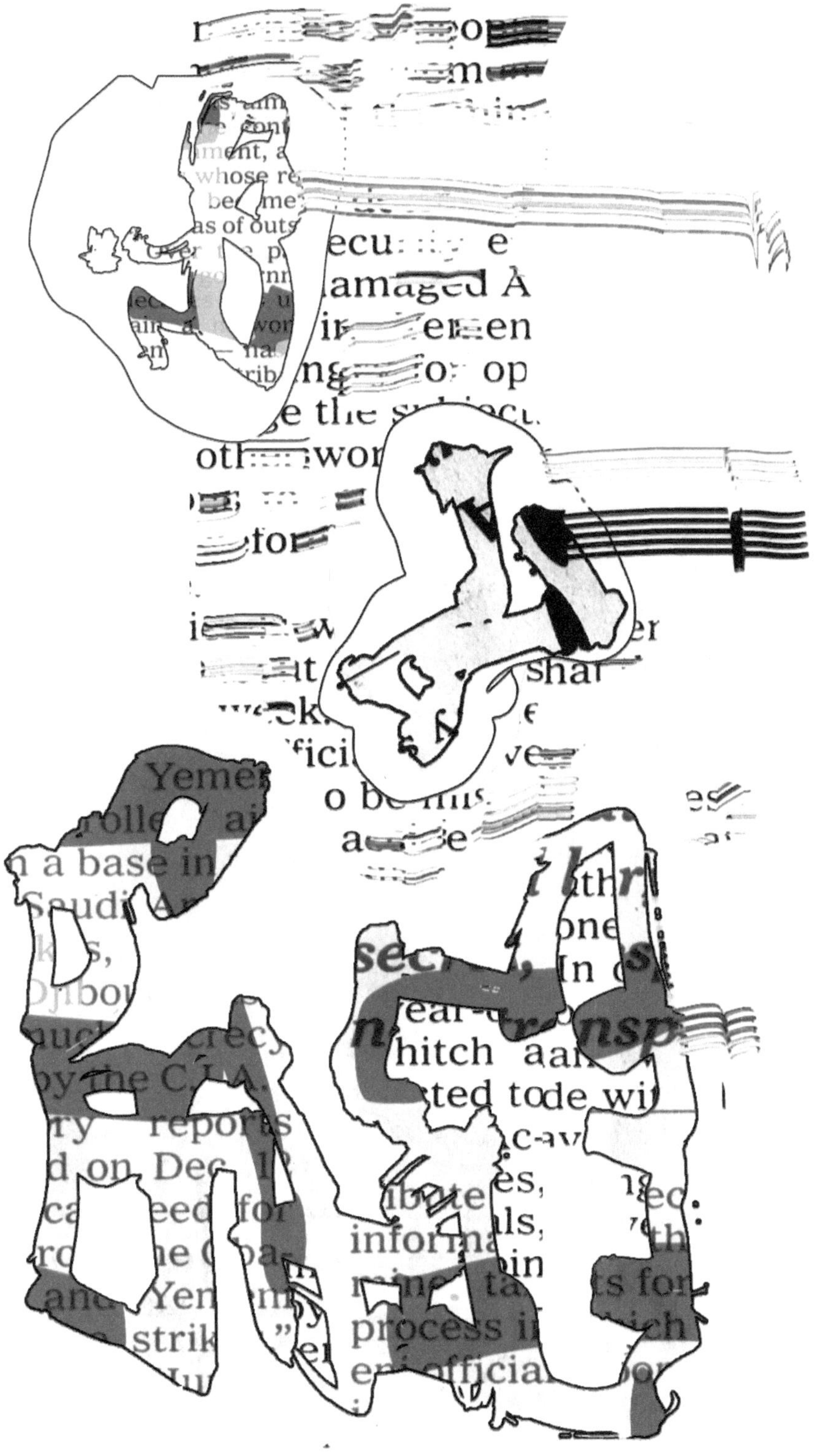
whose re
as of outs
amaged A
e the
for
shar
Yeme
o be
a base in
Saudi A
Djibou
by the C.I.A.
report
d on Dec
strik
hitch
ted tode wit
informa
process i
official

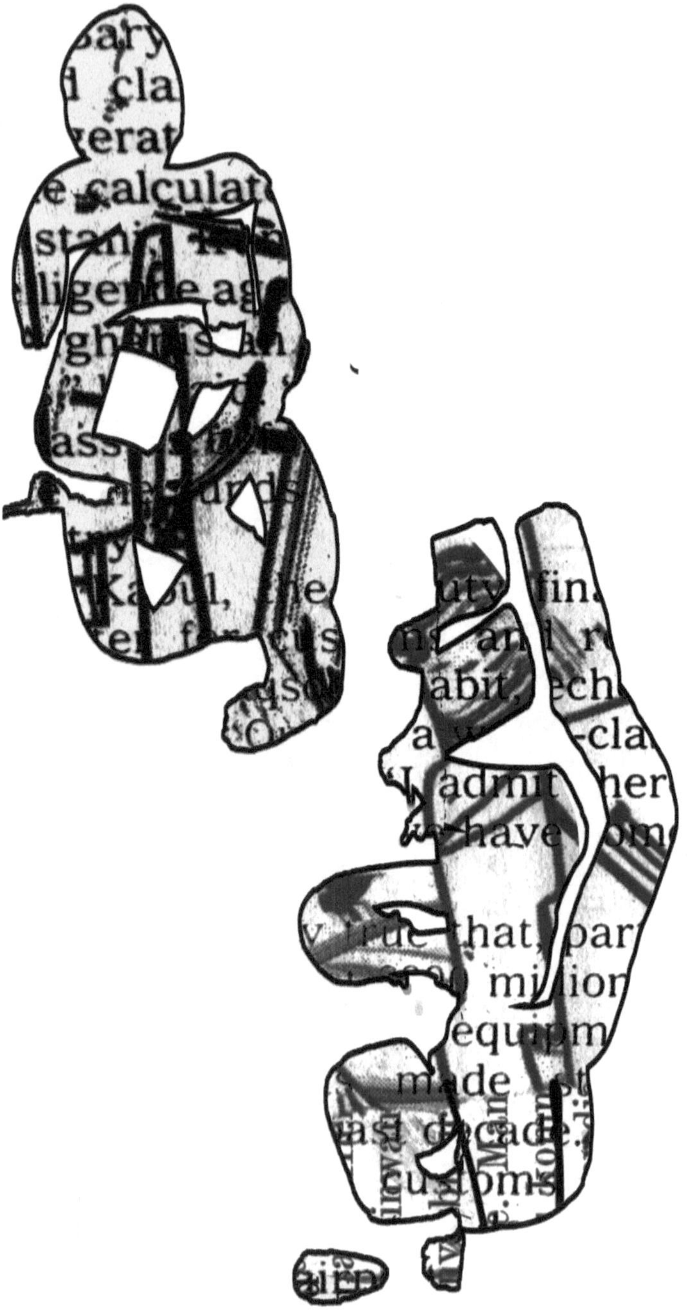
ary
cla
gerat
calculat
stan
ligence ag
Kabul, the
admit
have
true that, par
million
equipm
made
decade.
customs

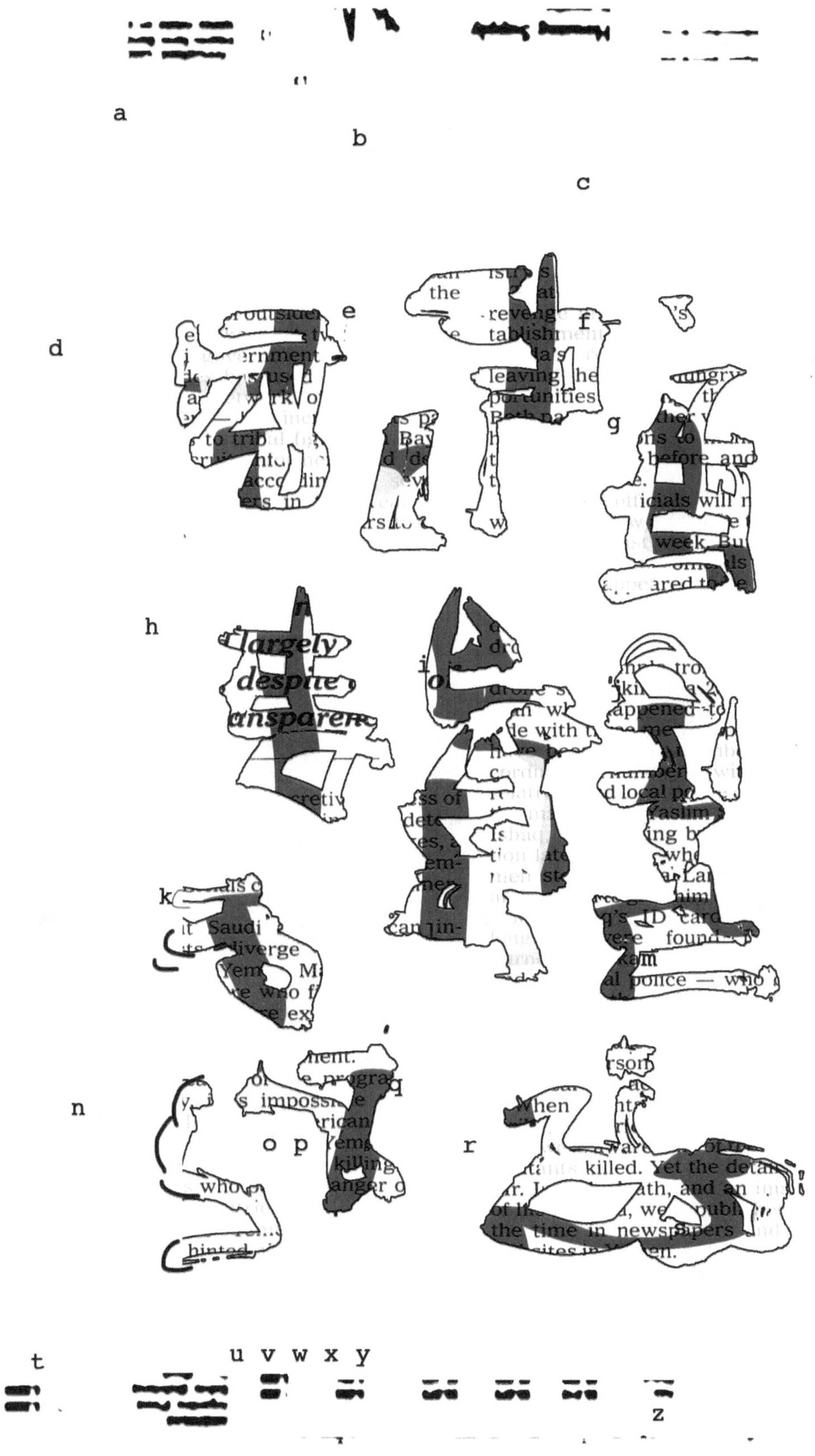

a
b
c
d
e
f
g
h
i
k
n
o p
q
r
t
u v w x y
z

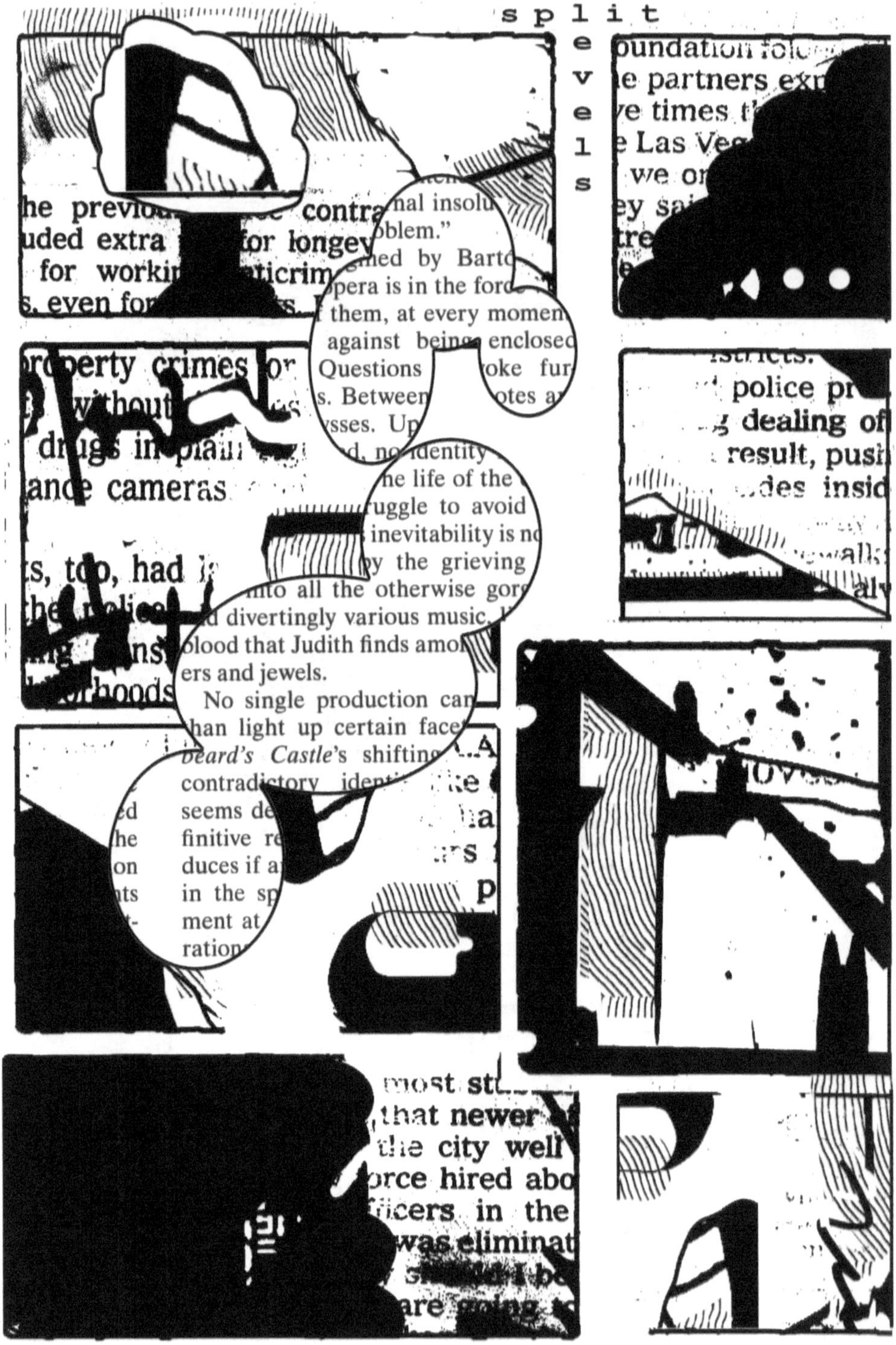
split levels
nal insolu
oblem."
gned by Barto
opera is in the forc
them, at every momen
against being enclosed
Questions oke fur
s. Between otes a
ysses. Up
d, no identity
he life of the
ruggle to avoid
inevitability is no
by the grieving
into all the otherwise gorg
d divertingly various music, b
blood that Judith finds amo
ers and jewels.
No single production can
than light up certain face
beard's Castle's shifting
contradictory
seems de
finitive re
duces if a
in the sp
ment at
ration
he previo contra
uded extra for longev
for worki
property crimes for
without
drugs in plain
ance cameras
s, too, had
police pr
g dealing of
result, push
des insid
oundation fo
e partners ex
ve times t
e Las Ve
we o
most st
that newer
the city well
force hired abo
ficers in the
was eliminat
are going t

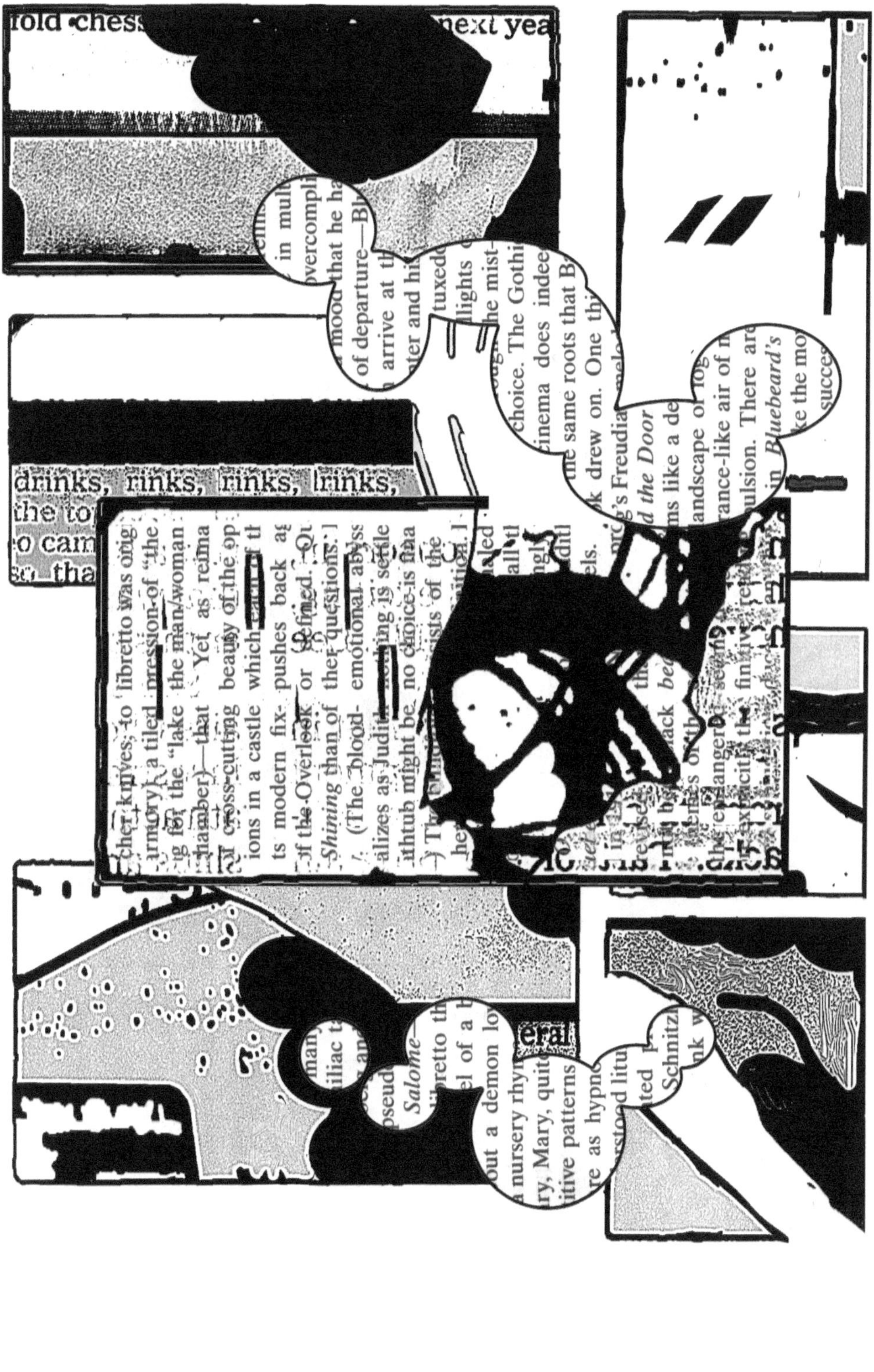
drinks, rinks, rinks, rinks,

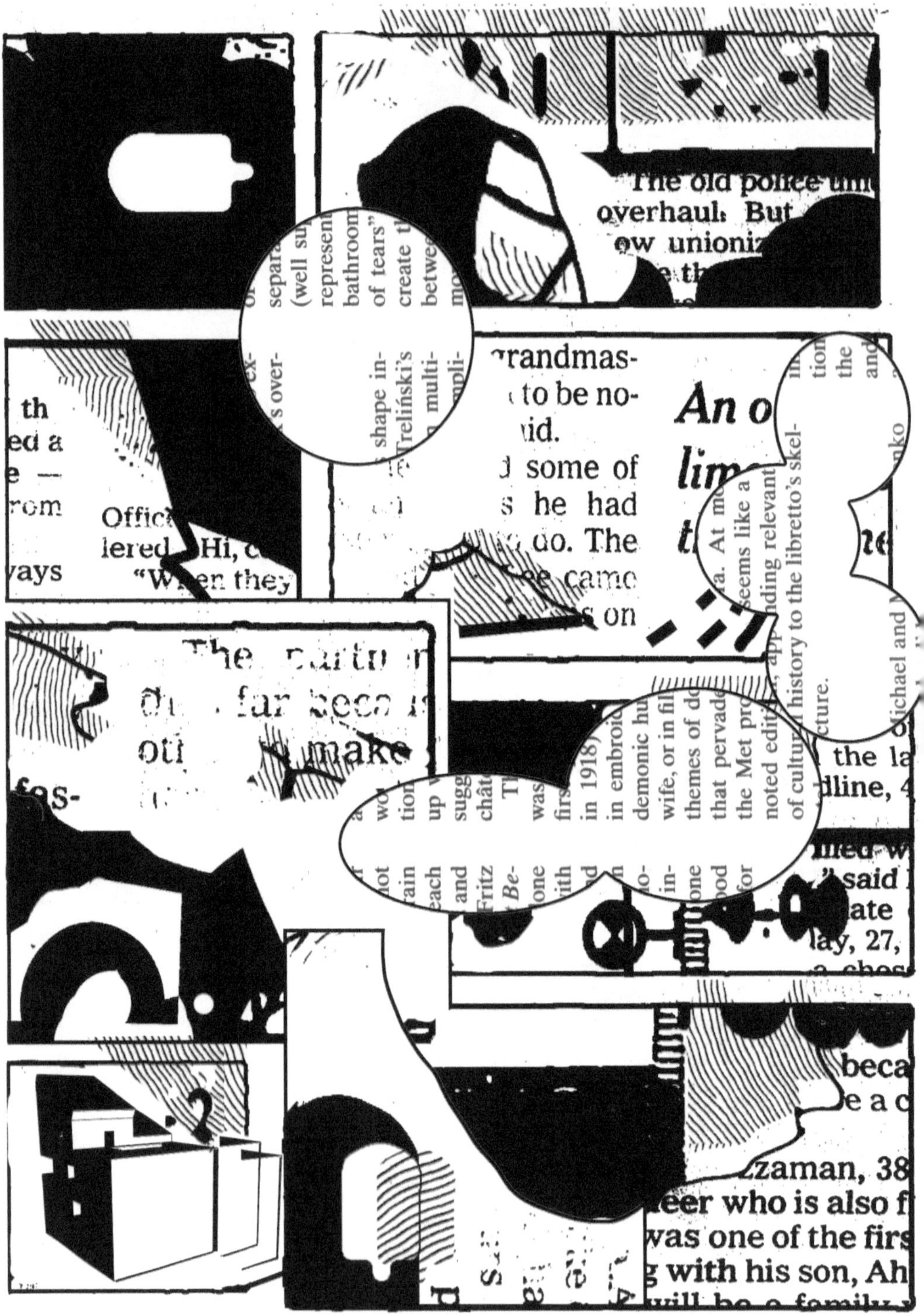

The old police uni
overhaul. But
ow unioniz
grandmas-
to be no-
id.
some of
s he had
do. The
An o
lim
th
ed a
rom
Offic
lered Hi, c
"When they
ays
The partn
far beca
make
fos-
the la
dline, 4
said
ate
ay, 27,
beca
e a c
zaman, 38
eer who is also f
was one of the firs
g with his son, Ah

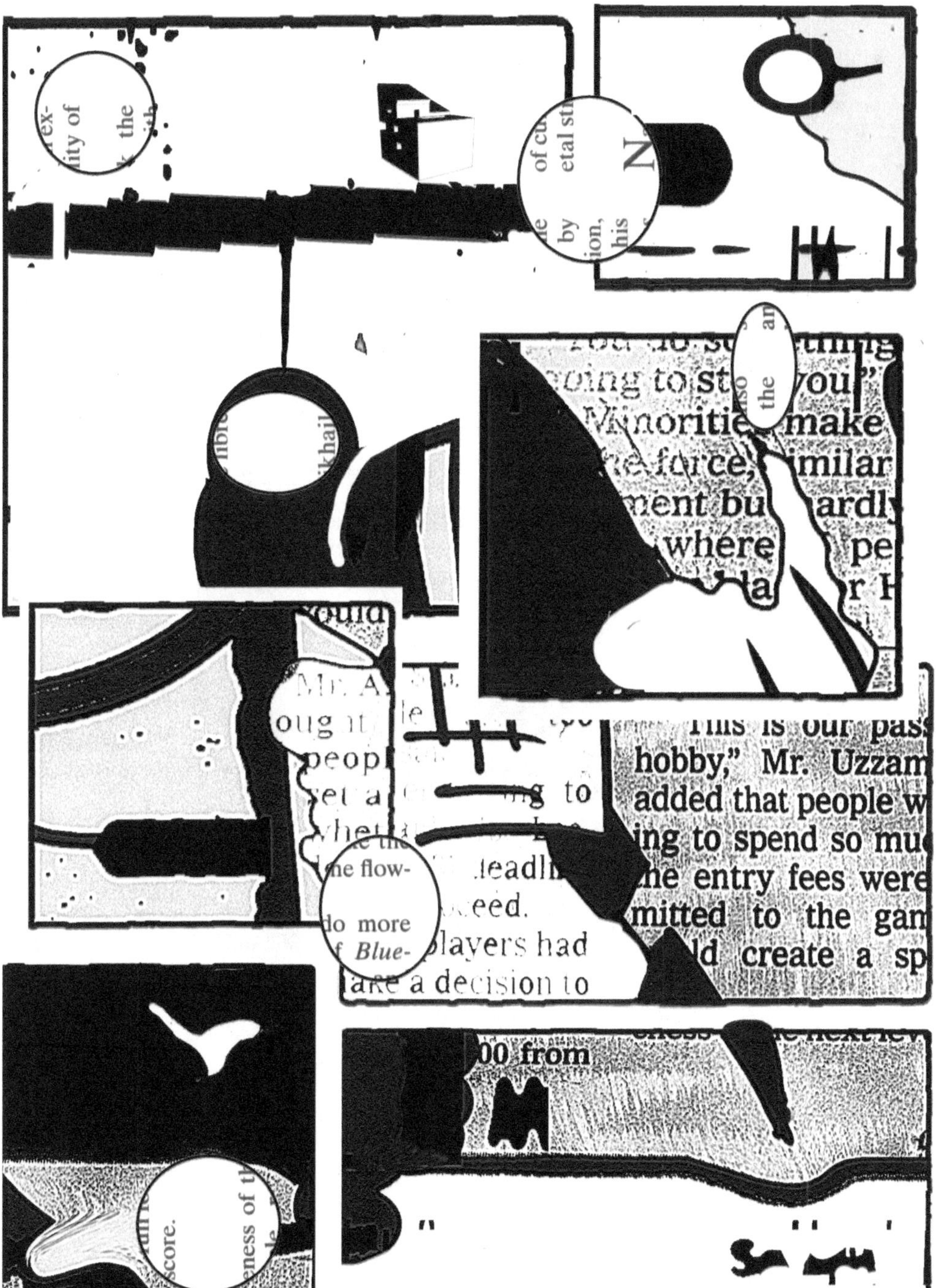

going to st
you"
Minorities make
force, similar
ment bu ardly
where pe
"This is our pass
hobby," Mr. Uzzam
added that people w
ing to spend so mu
he entry fees were
mitted to the gam
ld create a sp
he flow-
do more
Blue-
eed.
players had
take a decision to
00 from

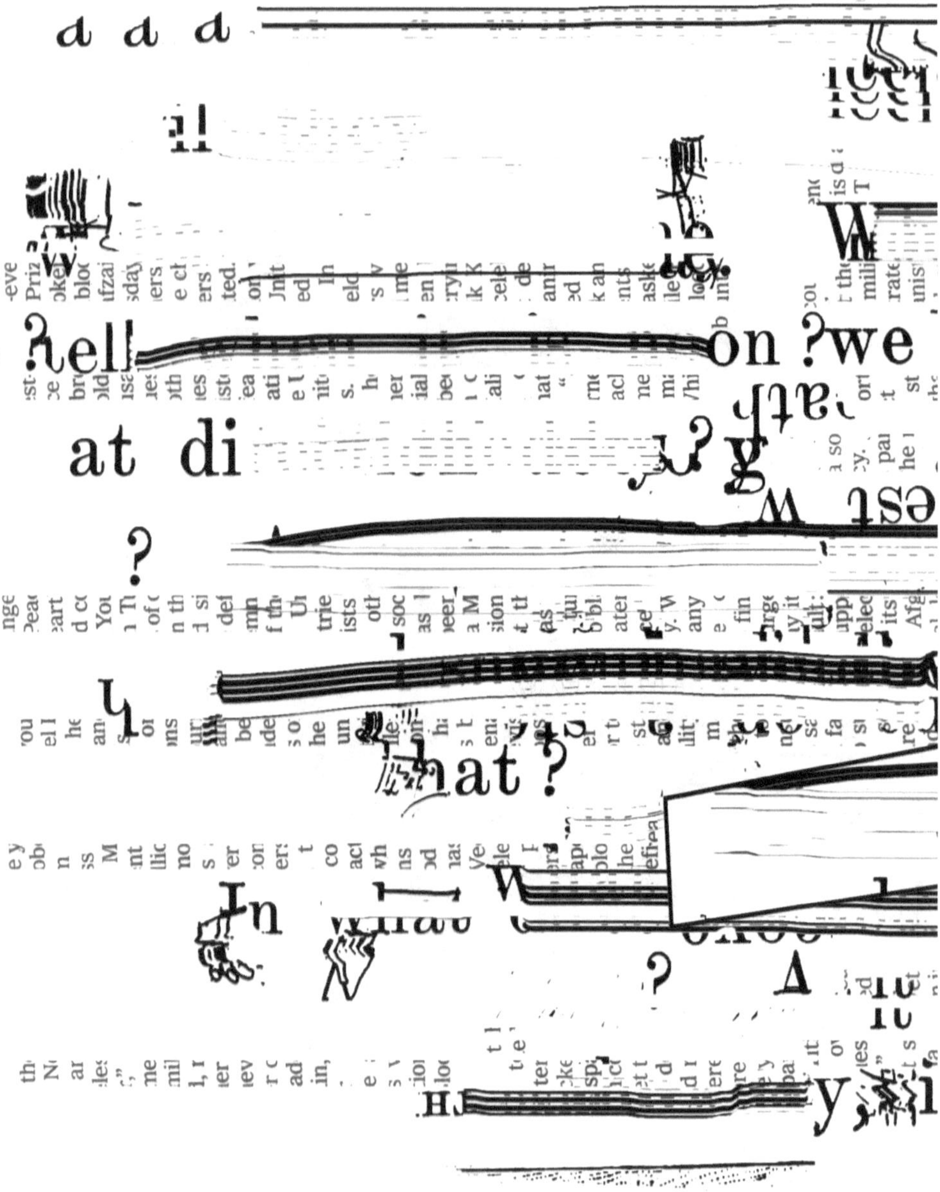
a a a
?hell
on ?we
at di
?
hat?
In

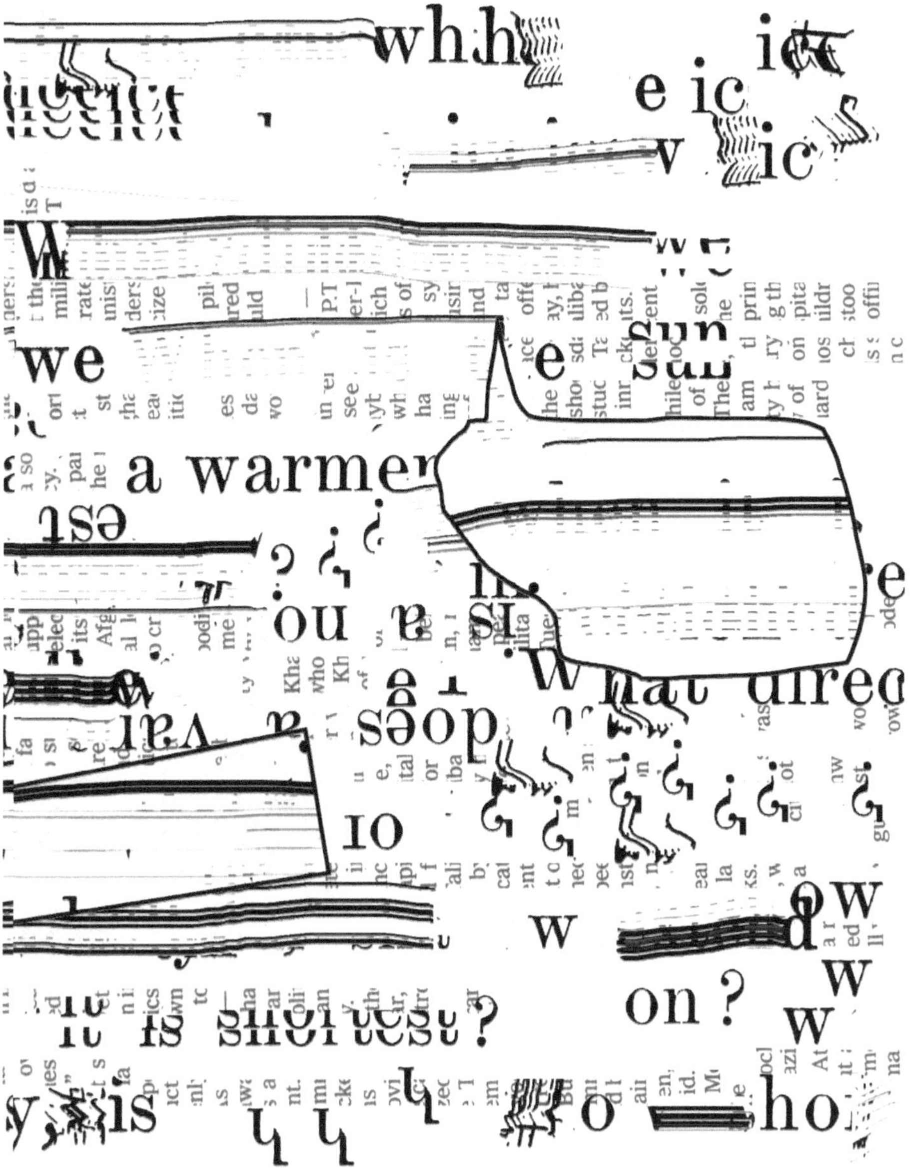
whh
e ic
we
a warmer
What direc
on ?

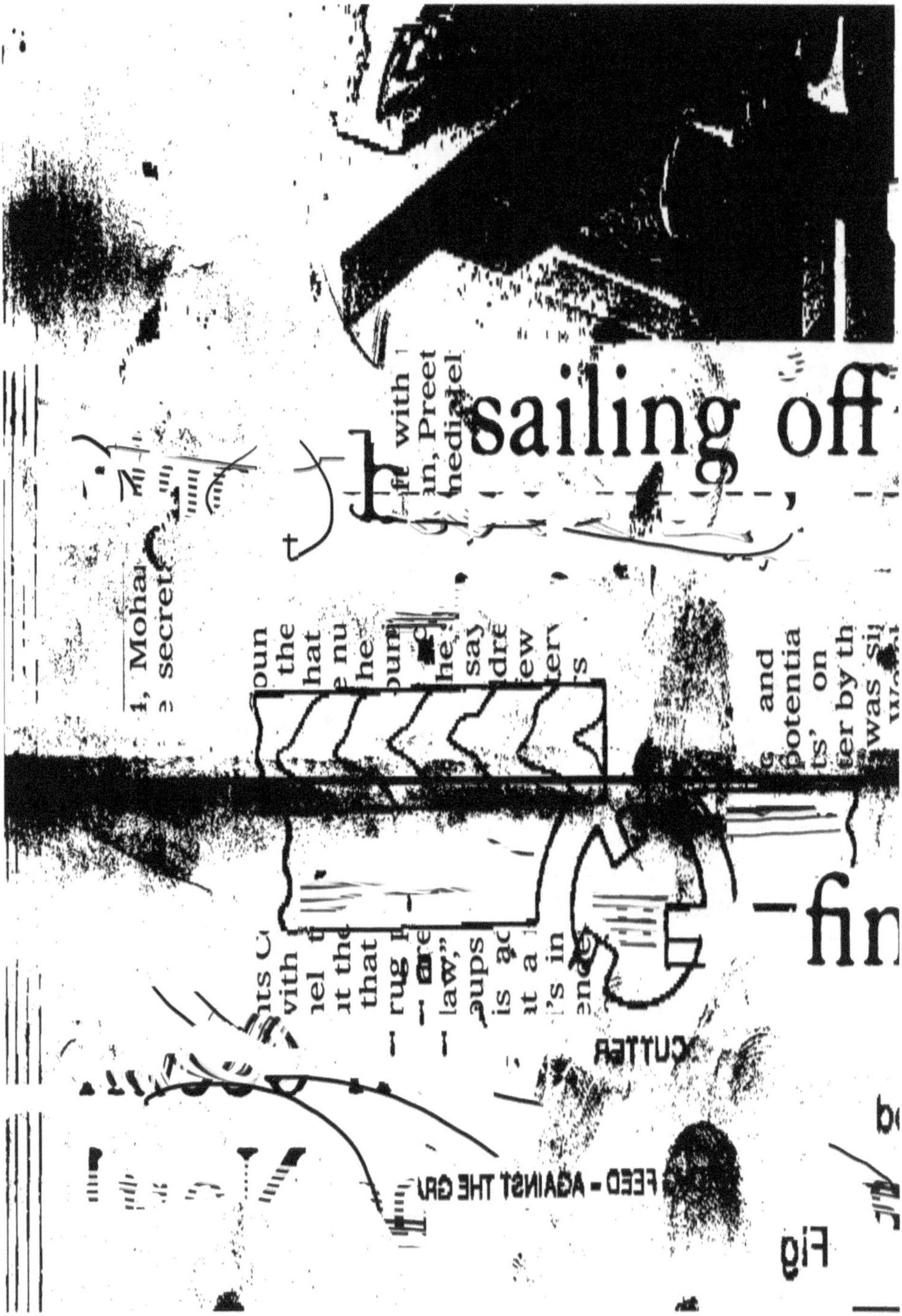
sailing off

and ridges will appear — the finished

MATERIAL WARPED

If the work

across

jointed is cupped or warped,

is flat. Forcing

the material flat against the table will still leave

warped piece after the cuts you've made.

you want

MATERIAL OR THIN JOINTING

material caught into the jointer's throat and be

ding a way

could come

Avoid jointing thin material which

guard.

back

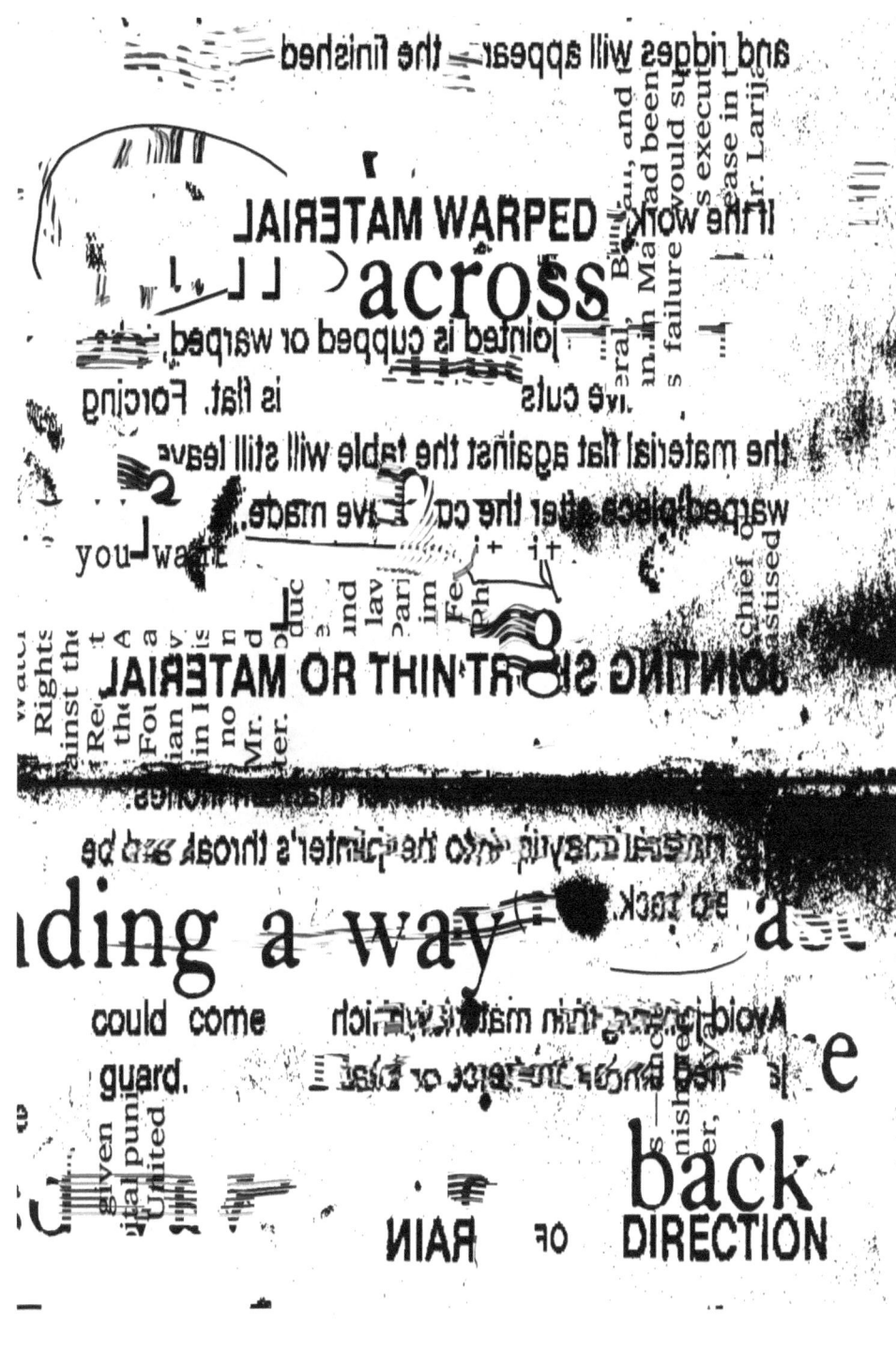

RAIN OF DIRECTION

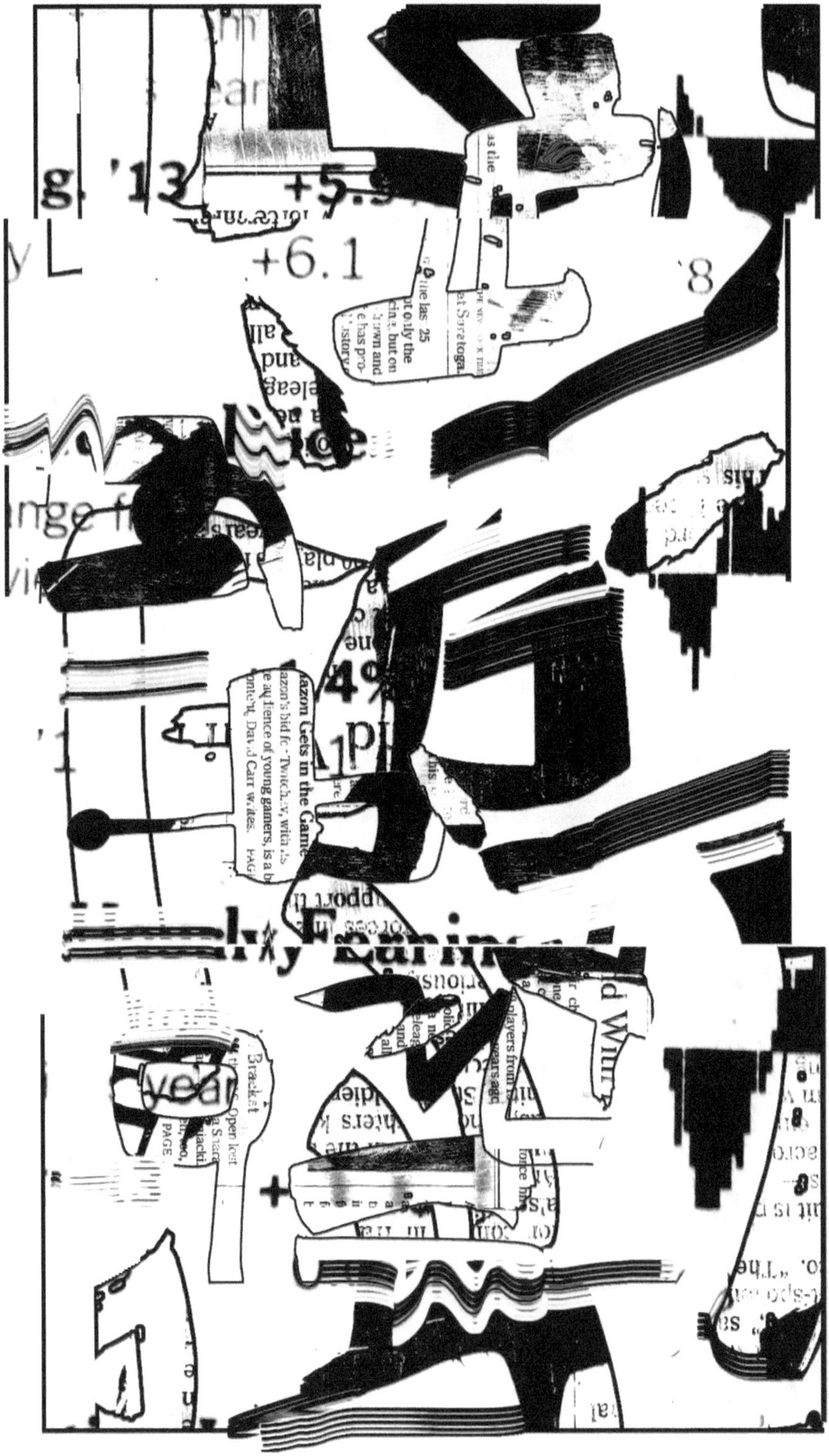
g. '13
+6.1
'8

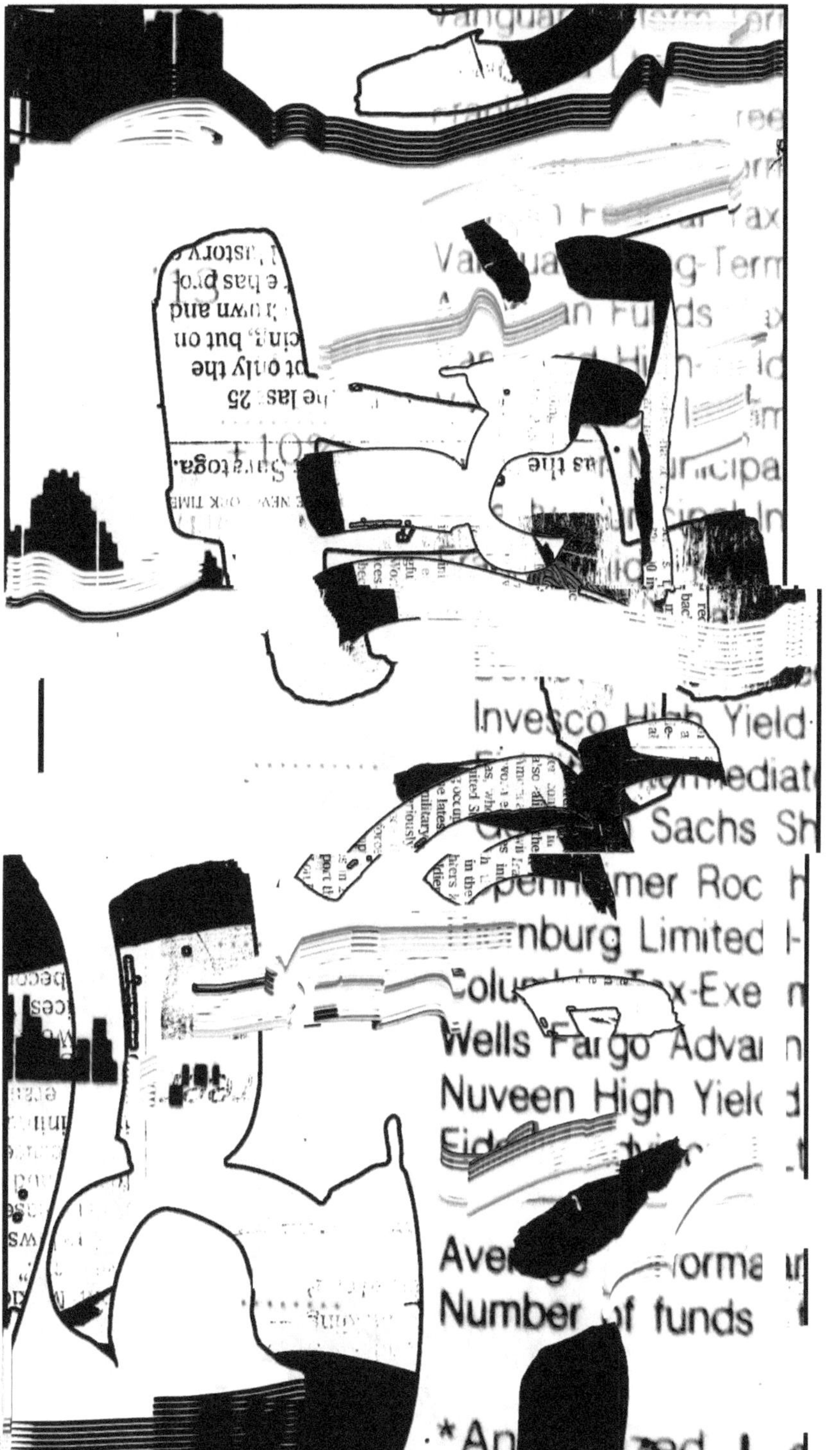
Invesco High Yield
Sachs Sh
nburg Limited
Wells Fargo Advai
Nuveen High Yiel
Number of funds
Saratoga.

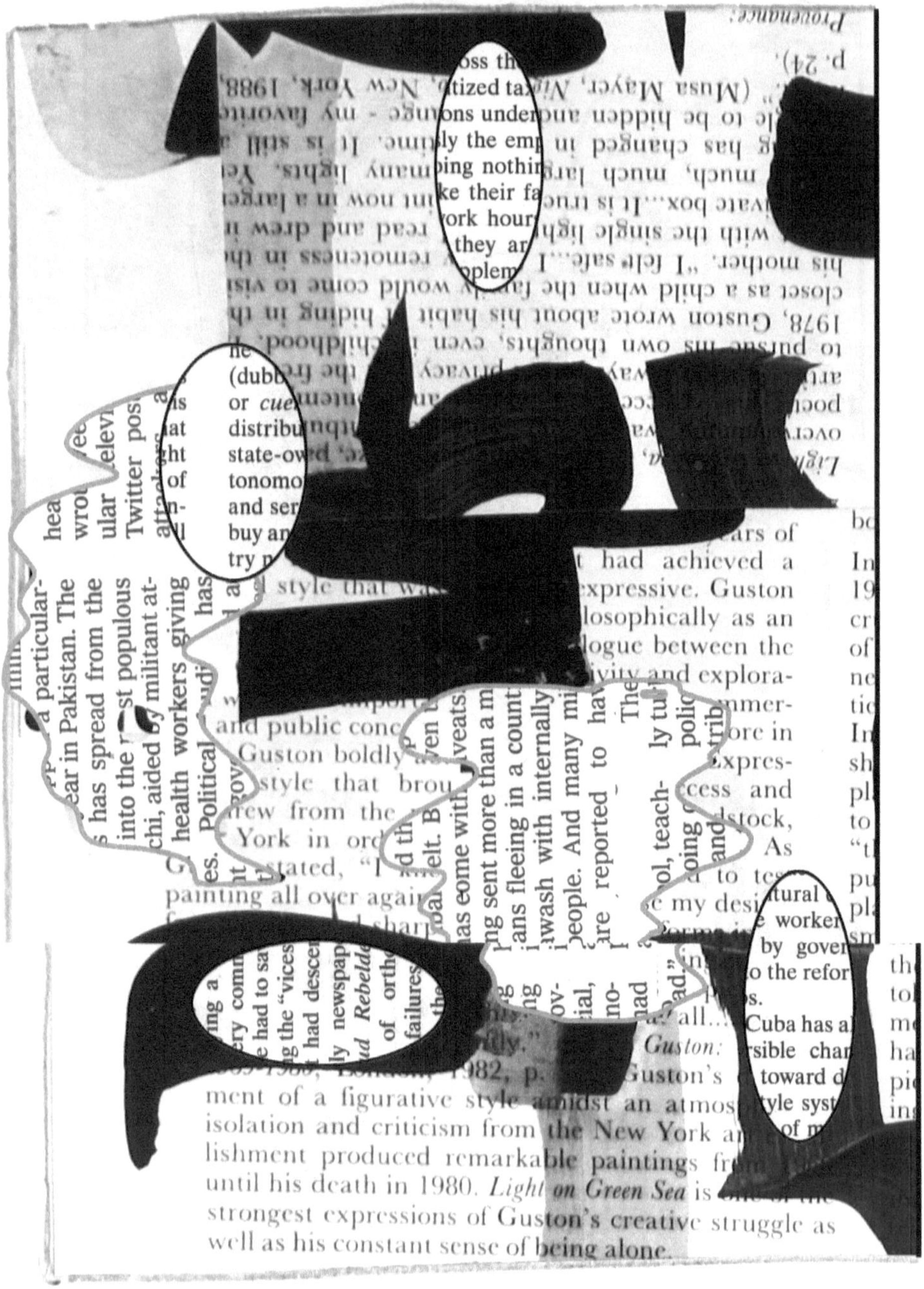
ment of a figurative style amidst an atmos
isolation and criticism from the New York a
lishment produced remarkable paintings fr
until his death in 1980. Light on Green Sea is
strongest expressions of Guston's creative struggle as
well as his constant sense of being alone.

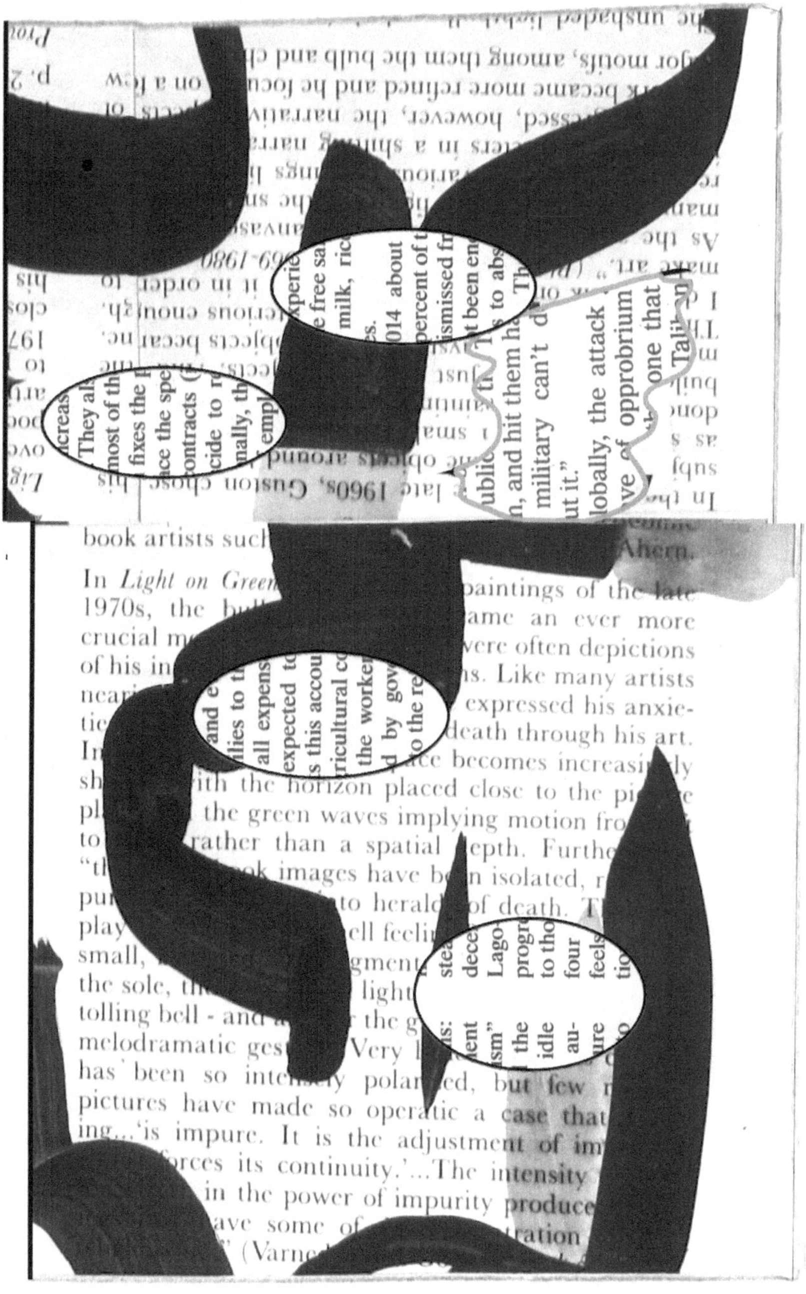
book artists such
In Light on Green
paintings of the late
1970s, the
came an ever more
crucial m
were often depictions
of his in
ns. Like many artists
expressed his anxie-
death through his art.
ce becomes increasi
ith the horizon placed close to the pi
the green waves implying motion fro
rather than a spatial
epth. Furthe
images have b
n isolated, r
to herald
of death.
small,
gment
the sole,
light
tolling bell - and
the g
melodramatic ges
Very
has been so inte
y polar
ed, but few
pictures have made so operatic a case that
ing...'is impure. It is the adjustment of im
rces its continuity.'...The intensity
in the power of impurity produce
ave some of
tration
(Varne

The growing number of poten-
tial troublemakers is compound-
ed, the former intelligence official
said, by a diminished ability to
track th... "We have less intelli-
...the wake of Ed...

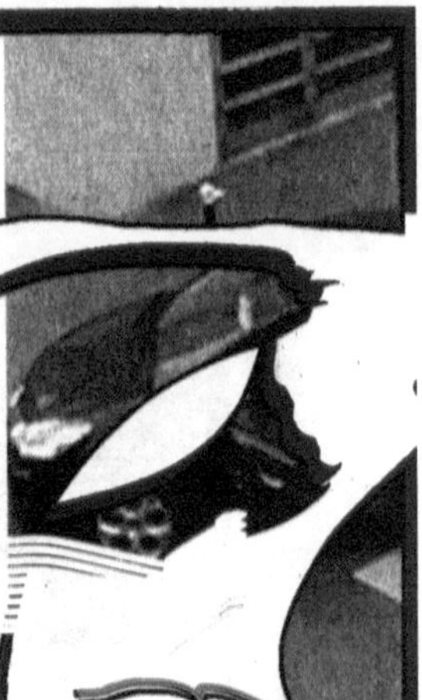

continue to
lly orchestrat... ds by
terrorist gro... tarted
anned from ab... like the
s in the Unite... ates on
1, 2001, and t... mbings
ain on July 7, ... In part
e of the succes... interna-
ntelligence ag... es in de-
such compl... d plots,
r, there has ... a sharp
throughou... rope in
ime Minist... vid Cam-
Britain t... k called
f roving ... terror-
"
cts ... ge and
...-scale

Age... who expos... of its
eav... opping acti... "The
ta... hat are being ... d by ter-
ro... make it hard... so."
a series of ... cks by in-
di... ls or small ... ups across
E... e, governme... are press-
in... more power... to gather inte... nce from mod... rn means of
c... unication li... e Internet
s... including soci... media. Ger-
n... wants to re... ke the ID
... of those susp... d of trav-
... join jihadis... ups. In
... ate
abo...

icant fear and create
propaganda that hel...
ment and fund-raising
ed extremist groups.
scious militants now

online.
"The threats we ...
with recently include trac...
Al Qaeda plans for large-scale at-
tacks, with concerns about explo-
sives hidden in tablets and com-
...itish intelli-
But over the

triot Act.
s the episodes
ying out last T
Parker, direct...
mestic intellig...
called for mor...
nitor comm...
e increasing, he said,

"three U.K. terrorist plots"
that could have led to deaths
were disrupted...
"My ...
Parker s... growing gap
...the increasingly chal-
threat and the ...
bility of capabil...
s it."
s speech adde...
ning debate he...
balance the ri...
n the obligation...
ty for citizens...
ned, as Mr. Ca...
day in Notting...
nce agencies s...
the ... means to inte...
encryp... of

...mer British
who requeste...
cause of the s...
ic, is "what ...
sition,' fi...
people ...

...ry Schw...sky, "Diversion, Oblivion, and the Pur-
...t of New ...jects: Reflections ... Ar... Biennial"
Arts 61, ...e 1987, p. 78, ill...

Literature...
...iennial E...ition, 1987, p. 74, illustrated in color
...w Yor... Whitney Museum of American Art, 1987

what security people call 'ex-
quisite intelligence,' with a phone
call that says

small groups, a...
y about that, to...
ing the proble...
services, the f...
l, is that "mor...
ad direct conta...

intelligence agency, re...
cused ...technology ...

L... er... ssa

...y Return...

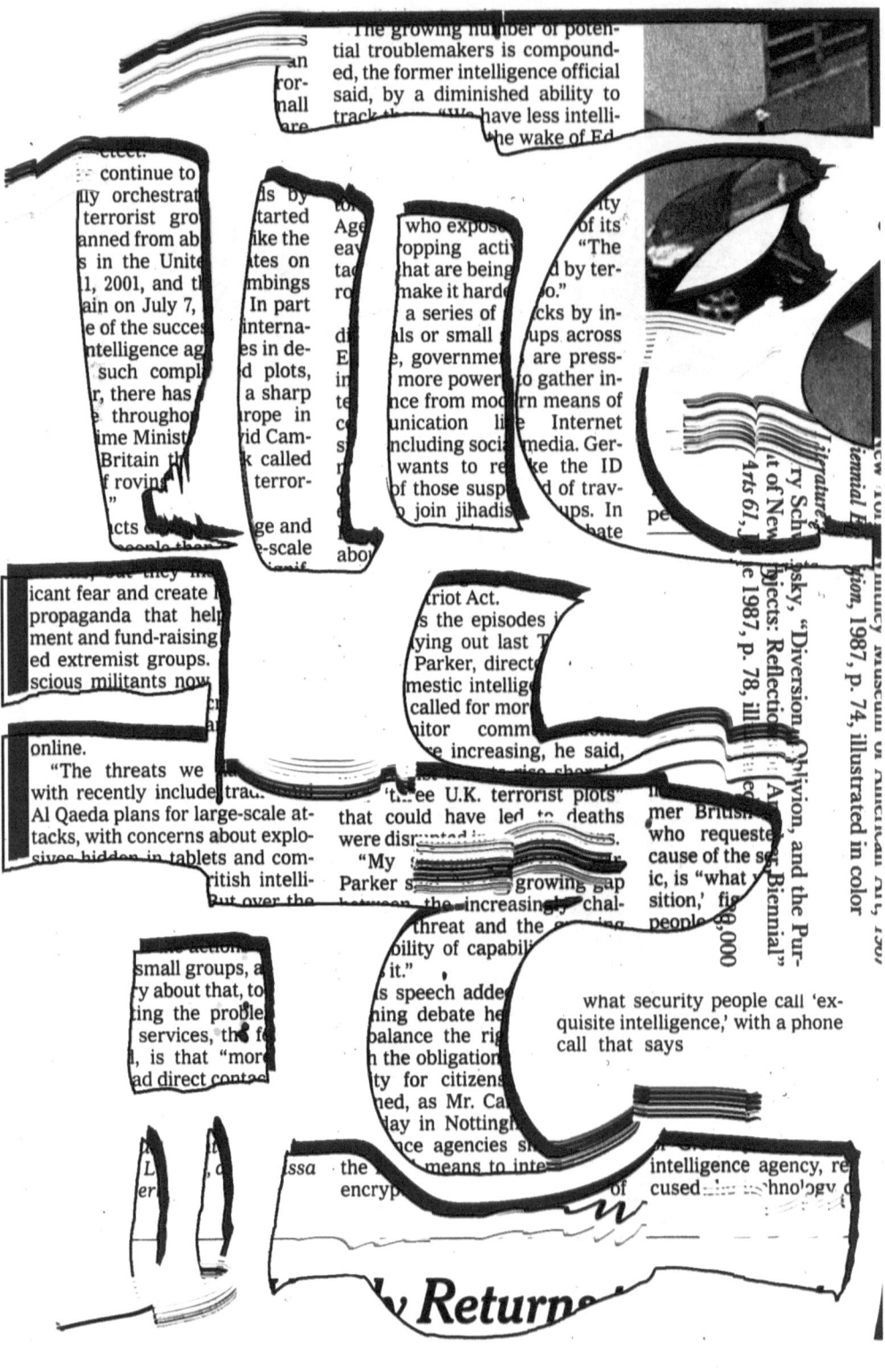

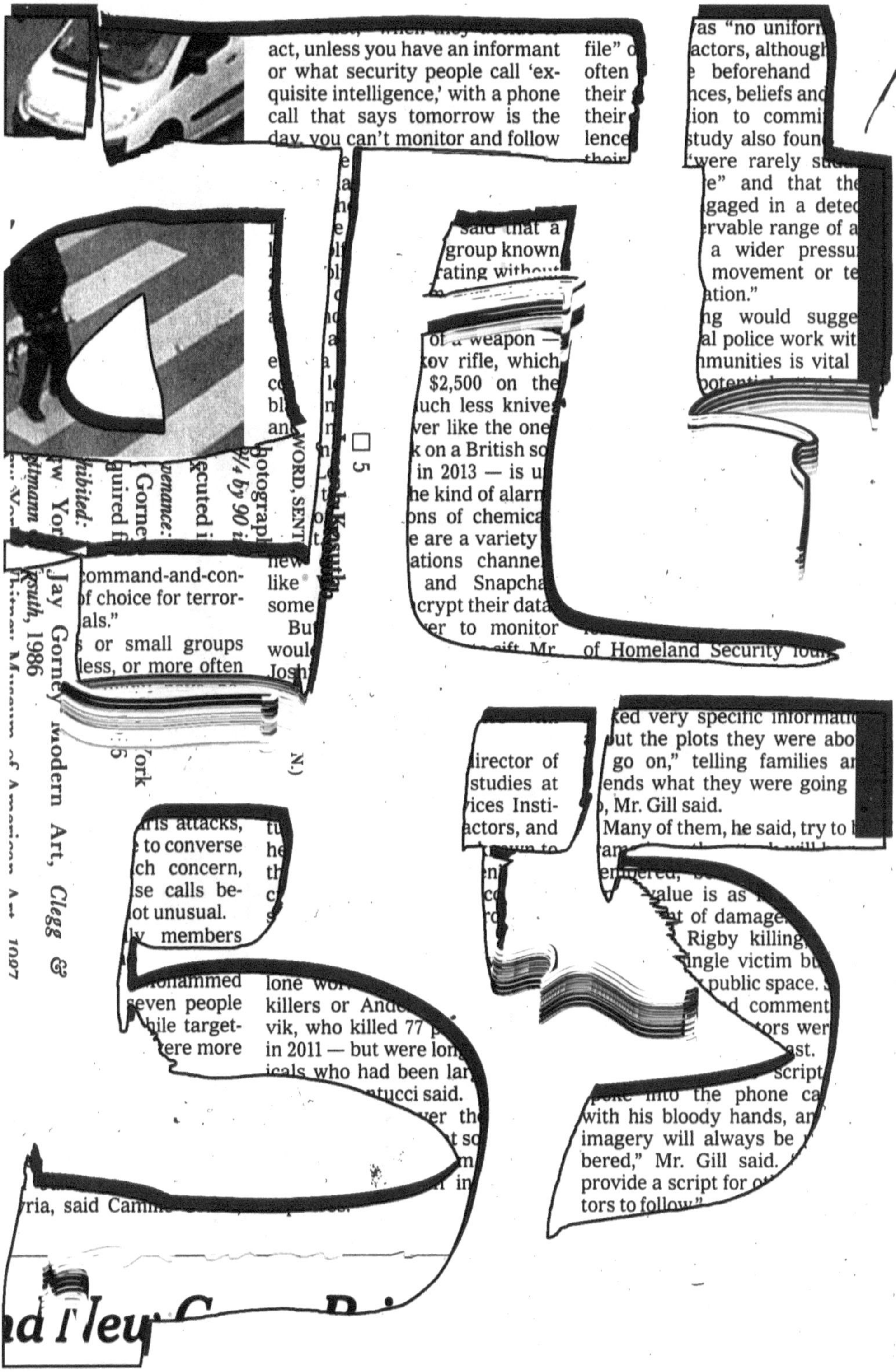
act, unless you have an informant
or what security people call 'ex-
quisite intelligence,' with a phone
call that says tomorrow is the
day, you can't monitor and follow
group known
$2,500 on the
on a British so
in 2013 — is u
he kind of alarm
ons of chemica
e are a variety
ations channe
and Snapcha
crypt their data
er to monitor
of Homeland Security
as "no uniform
actors, although
beforehand
nces, beliefs and
ion to commi
study also foun
"were rarely s
e" and that the
gaged in a detec
rvable range of a
a wider pressu
movement or te
ation."
ng would sugge
al police work wit
mmunities is vital
command-and-con-
of choice for terror-
als."
or small groups
less, or more often
Jay Gorney Modern Art, Clegg &
ut the plots they were abo
go on," telling families an
ends what they were going
, Mr. Gill said.
Many of them, he said, try to
irector of
studies at
vices Insti-
actors, and
to converse
ch concern,
se calls be-
ot unusual.
members
seven people
hile target-
ere more
killers or
vik, who killed 77
in 2011 — but were lon
icals who had been lar
value is as
Rigby killing
ingle victim b
public space.
with his bloody hands, a
imagery will always be
bered," Mr. Gill said.
provide a script for o
tors to follow."
yria, said

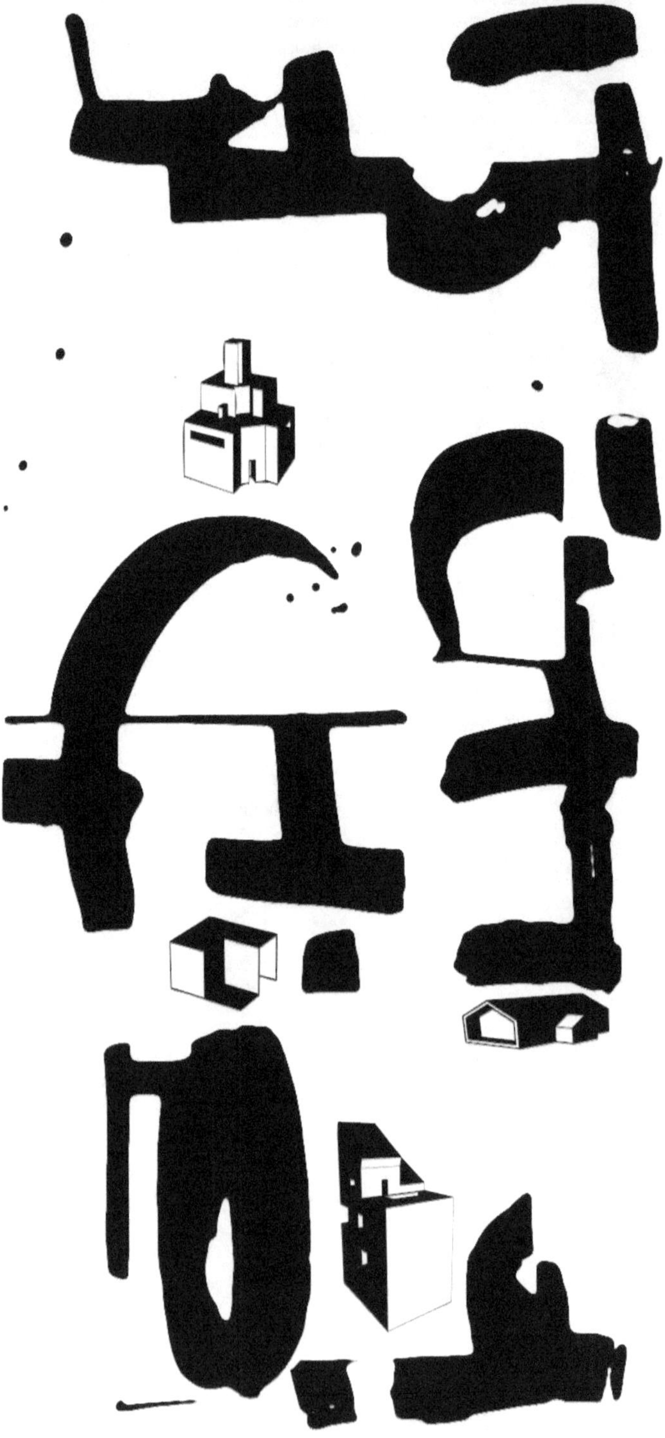

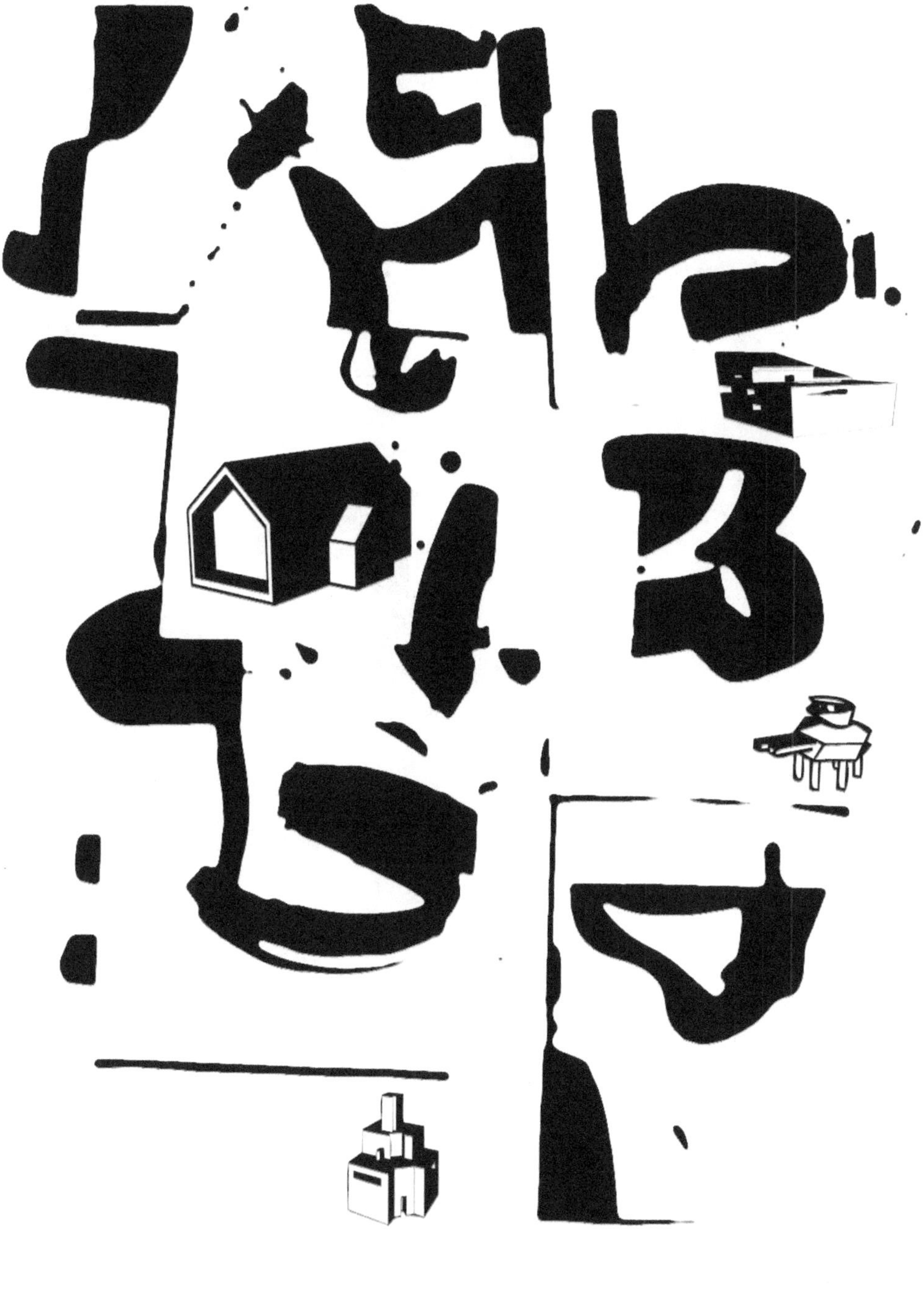

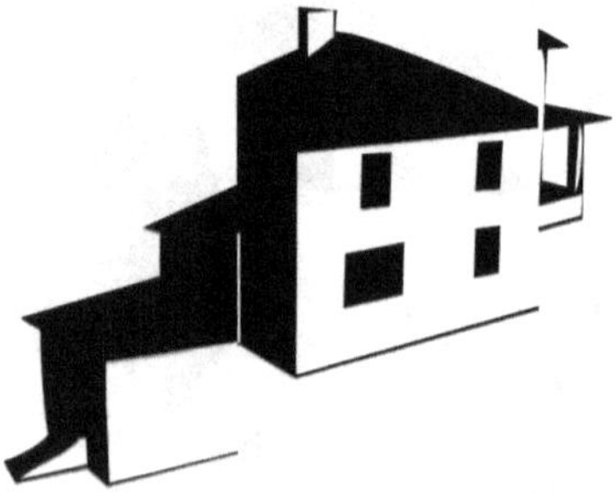

SPEED
at full speed

SPELL
spell something out □ spell trouble

SPEND
tax-and-spend

SPICE
Variety is the spice of life.

SPICK
spick-and-span

SPILL
cry over spilled milk □ spill the beans □ take a spill

SPIN
go into a tailspin □ make someone's head spin □ spin one's wheels □ spin something off

SPINDLE
fold, spindle, or mutilate

SPIRIT
in good spirits

SPIT
be the spit and image of someone □ be the spitting image of someone □ spit (something) up

SPITE
cut off one's nose to spite one's face □ in spite of someone or something

SPLEEN
vent one's spleen

SPLIT
in a split second □ split hairs □ split one's sides (with laughter) □ split people up □ split something fifty-fifty □ split the difference □ split up

SPOIL
To the victors belong the spoils. □ Too many cooks spoil the broth. □ Too many cooks spoil the stew.

SPOKEN
spoken for

SPONGE
throw in the sponge

SPOOK
spook someone or something

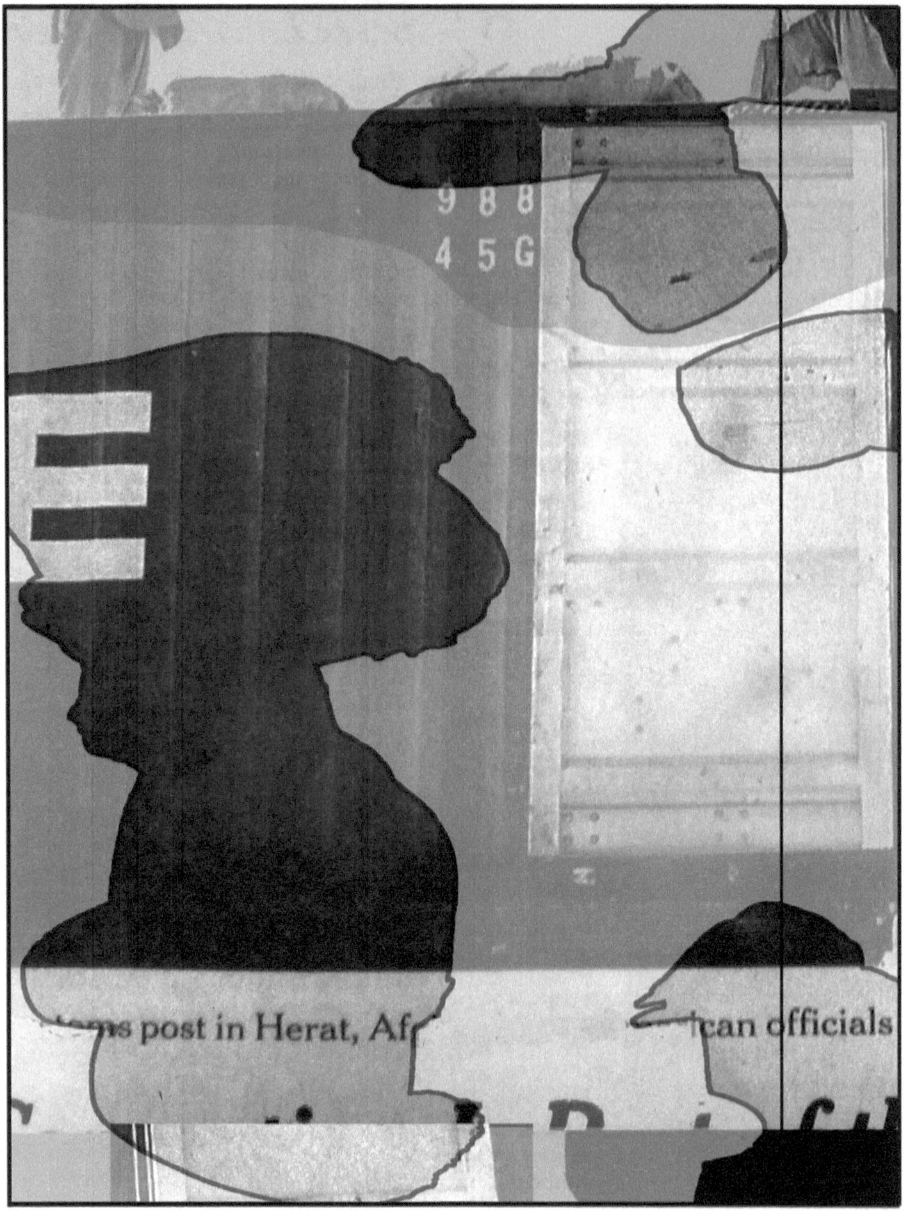
9 8 8
4 5 G
post in Herat, Af
can officials

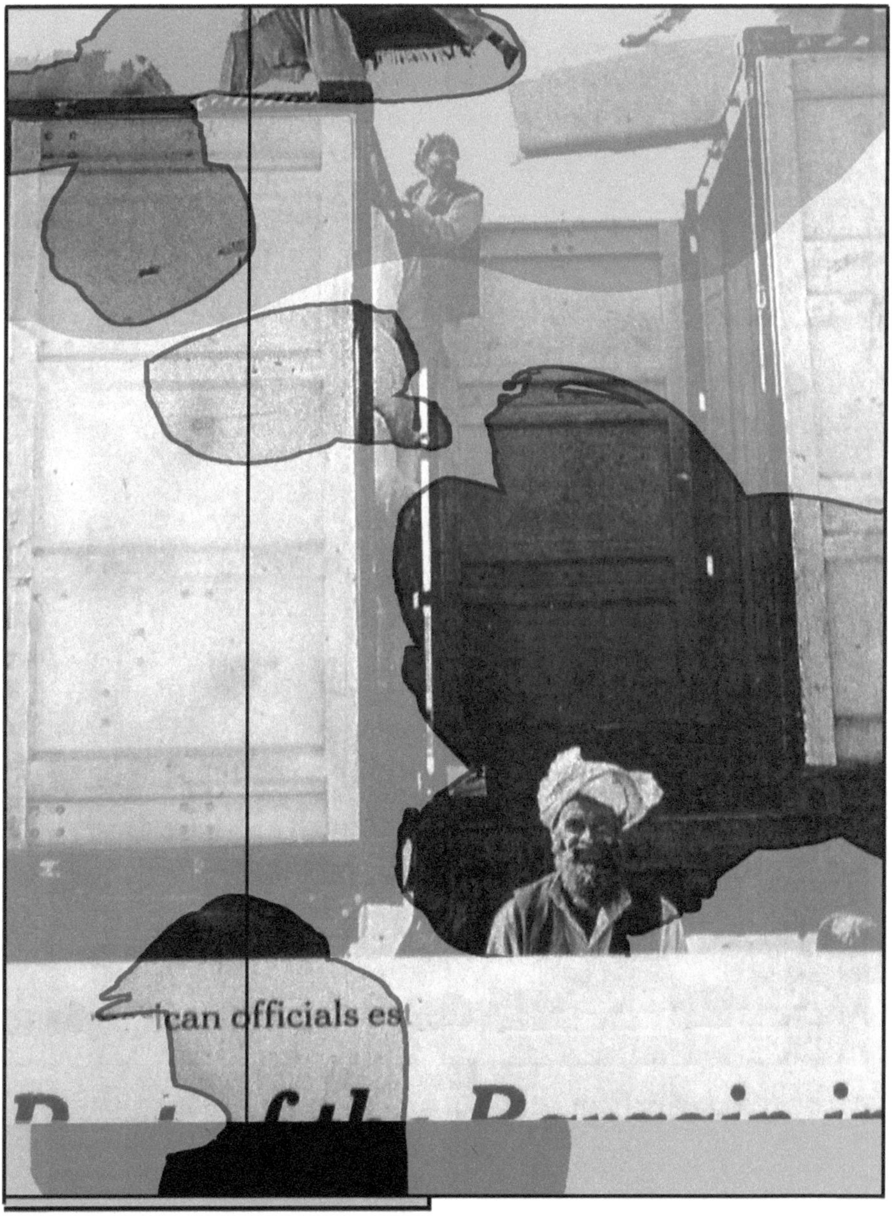
can officials es

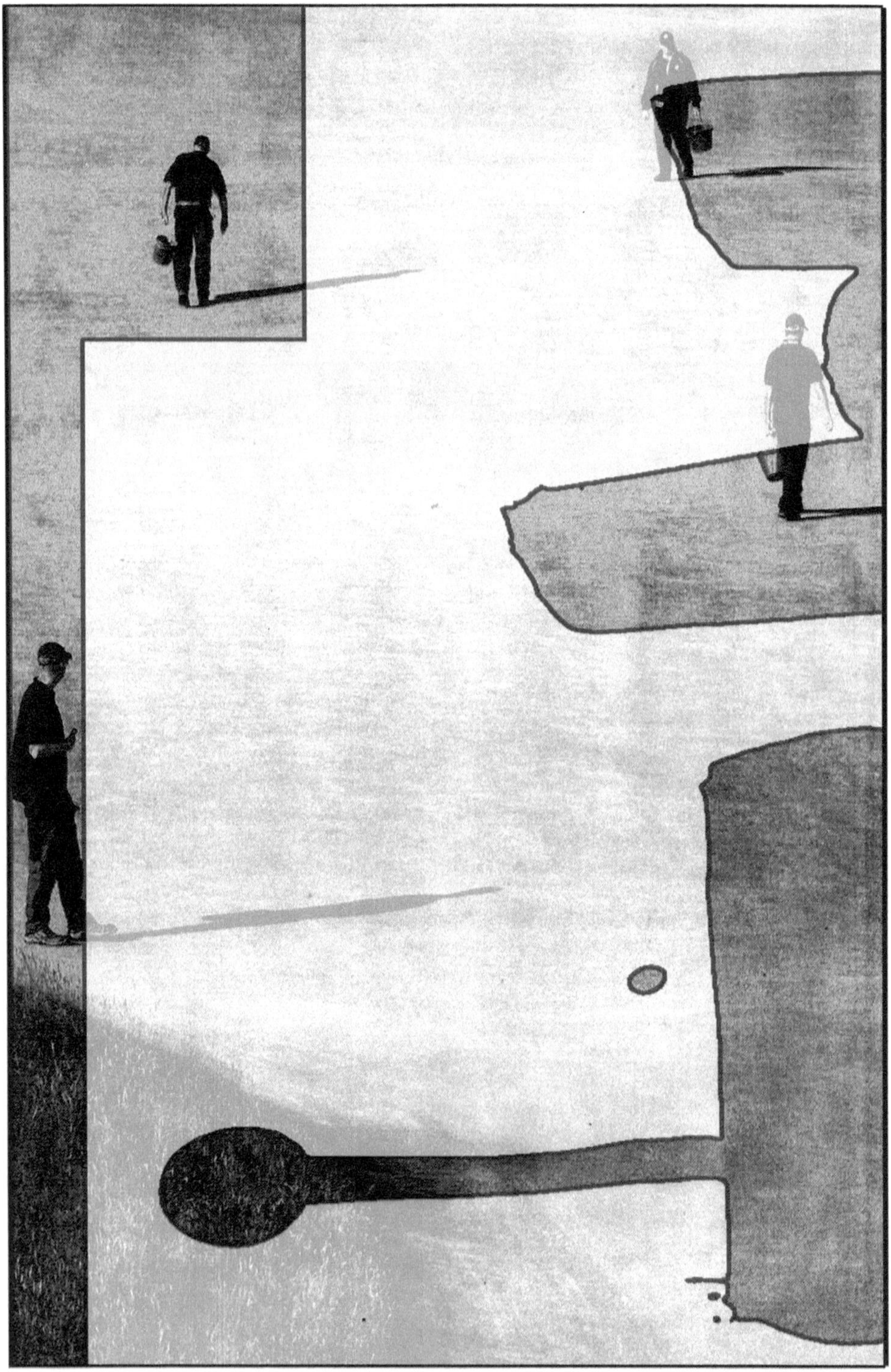

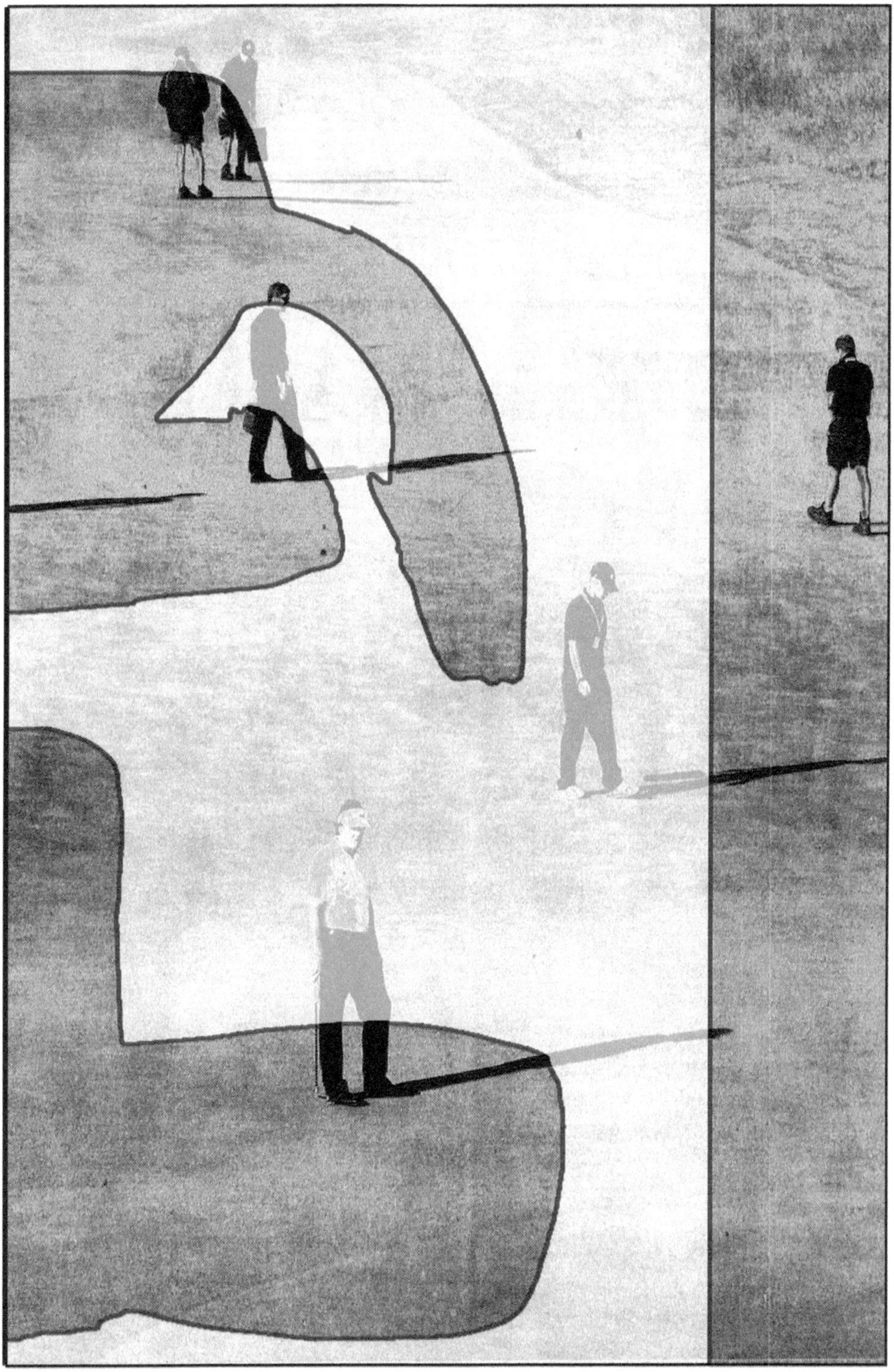

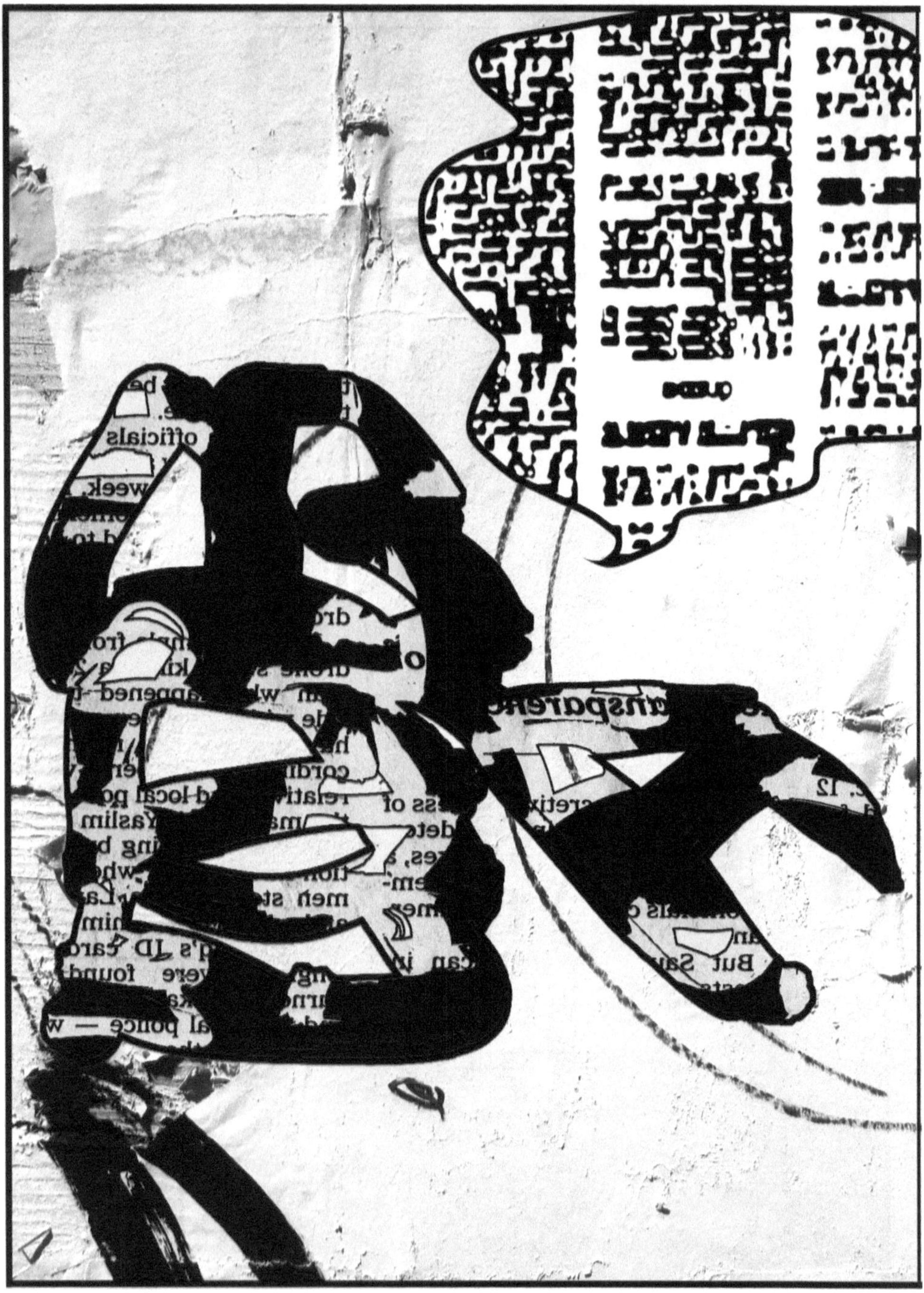

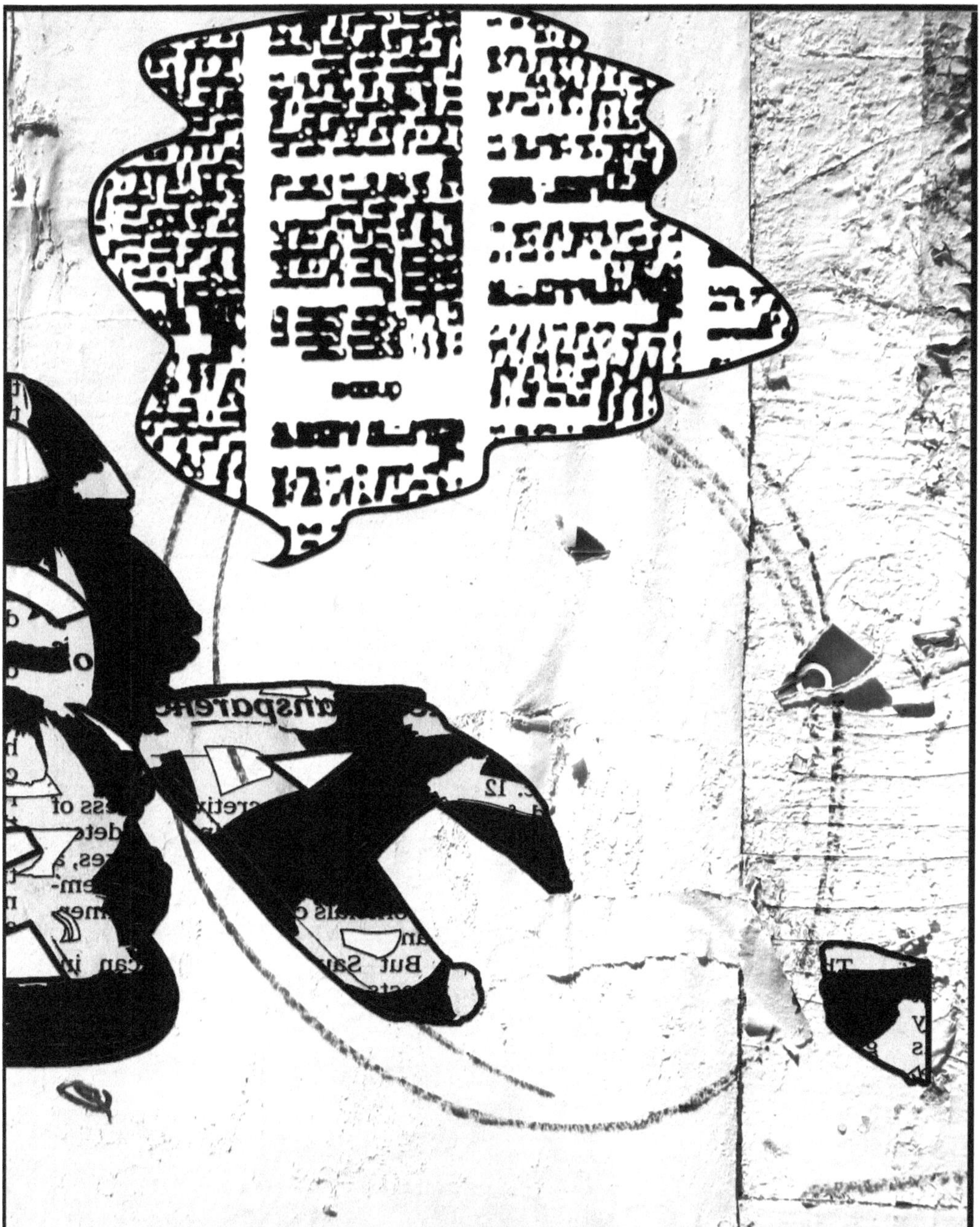

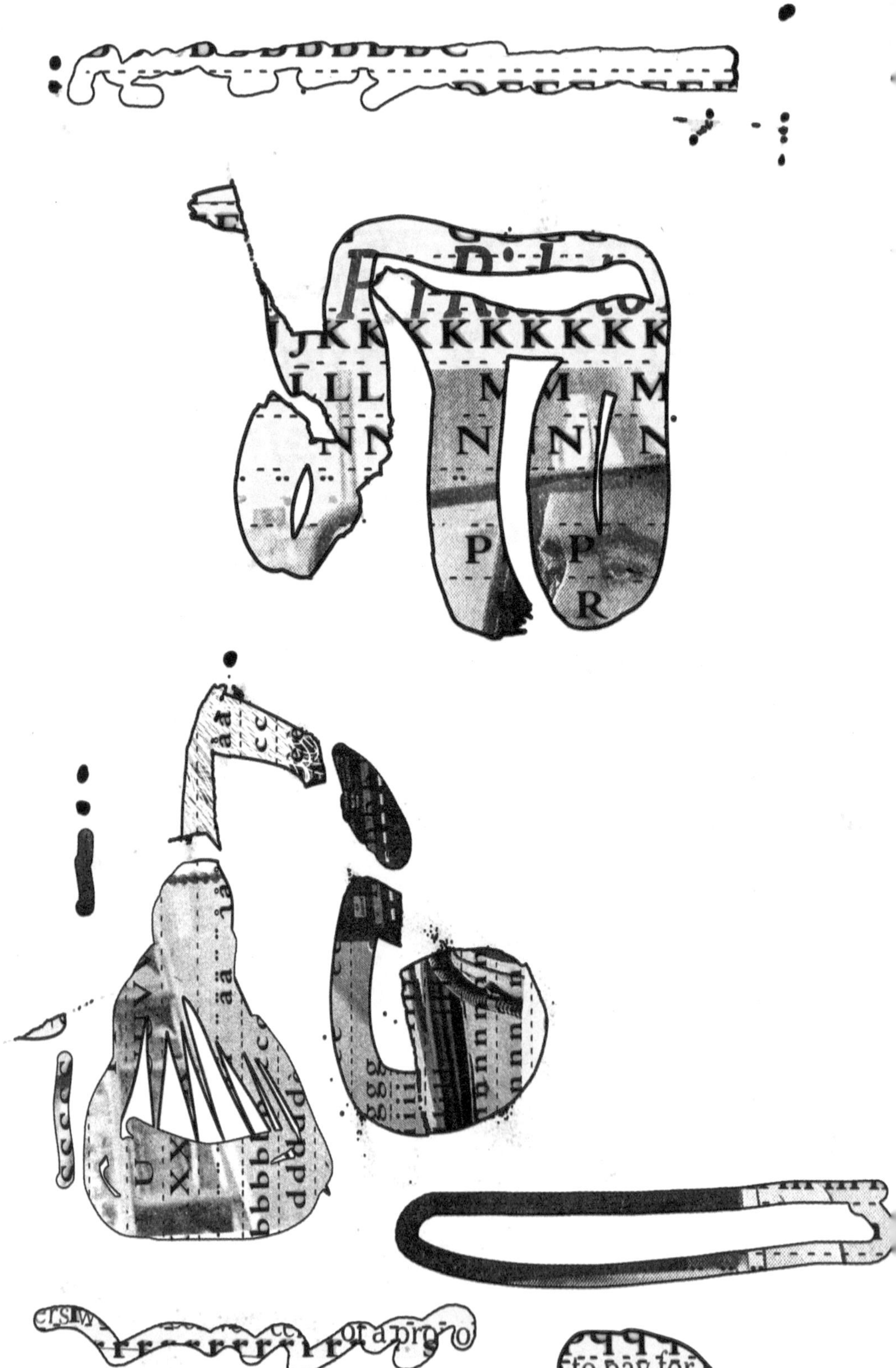
to pay for

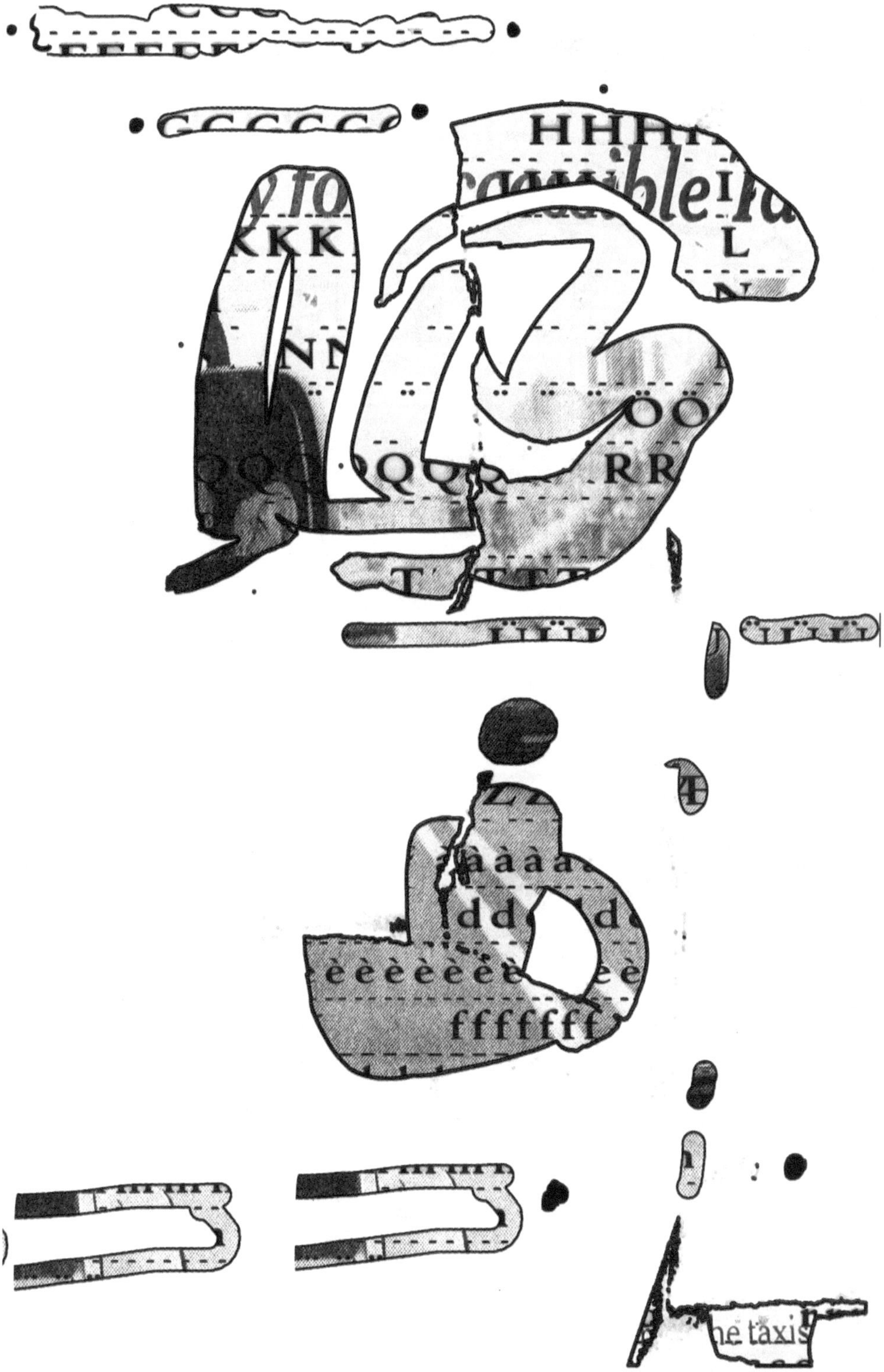

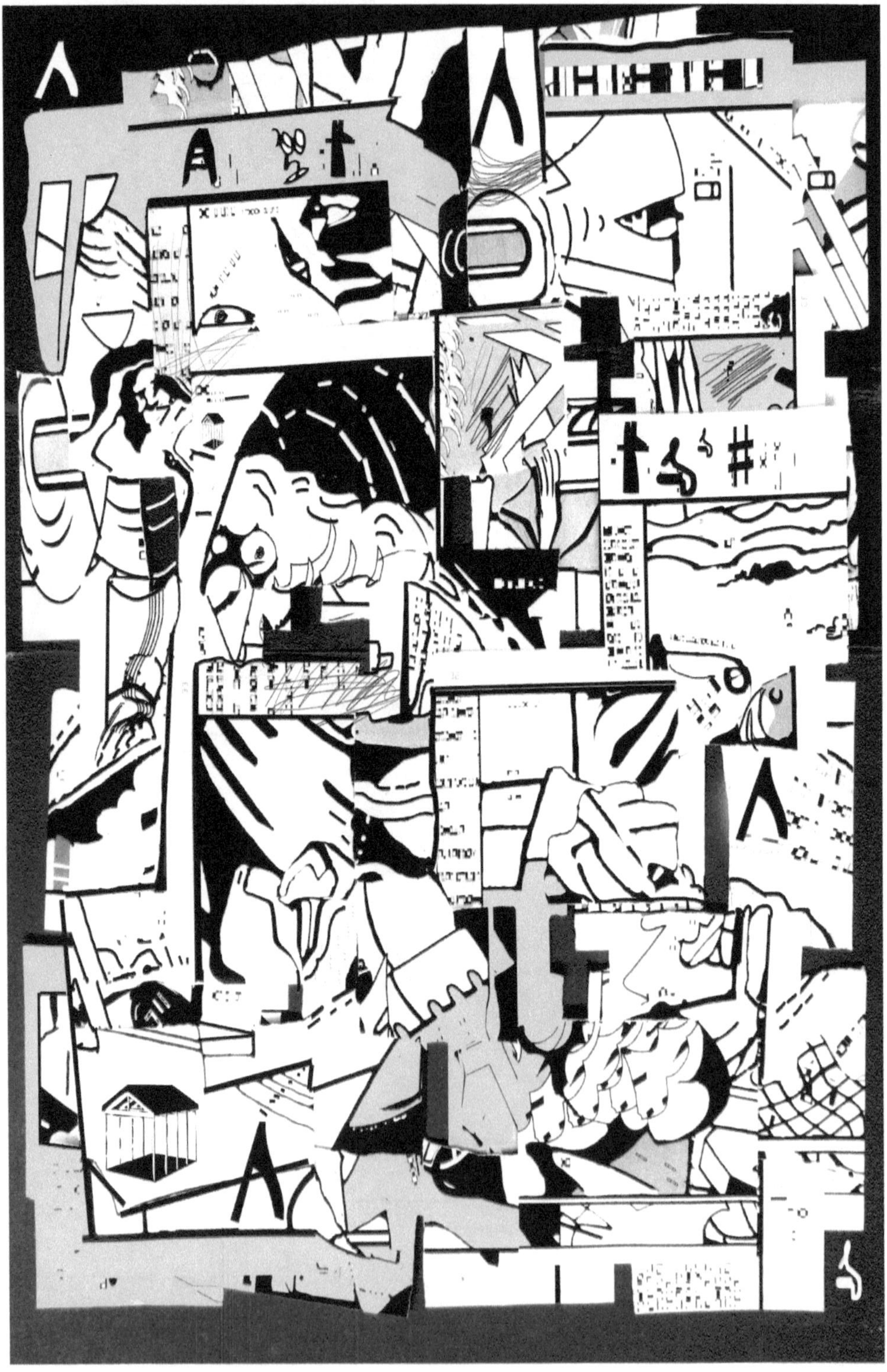

-- you wonder if there IS a level, or are there only splits....

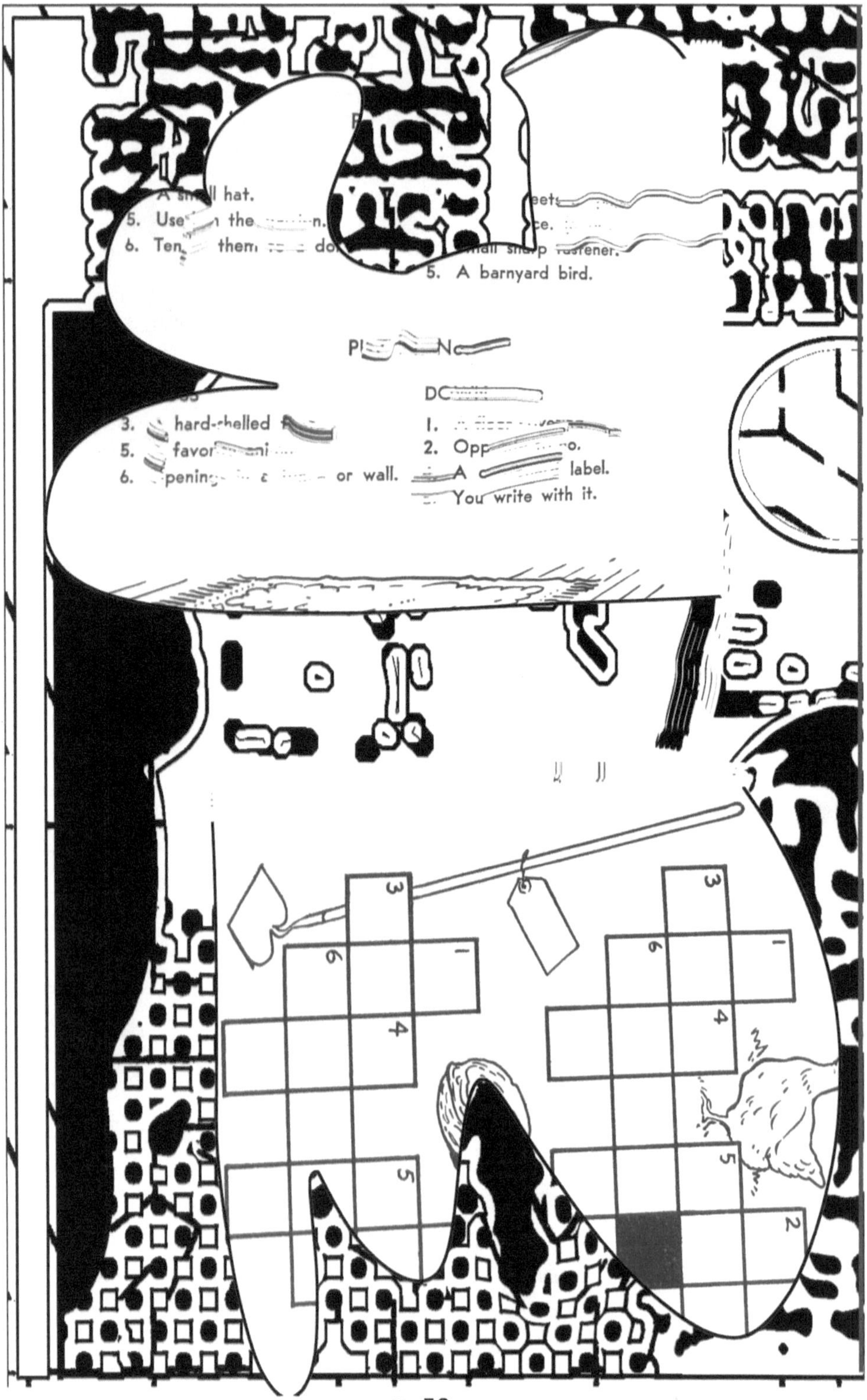
A small hat.
6. Ten them
5. A barnyard bird.
3. hard-shelled
6. or wall.
2. Opp
A label.
You write with it.

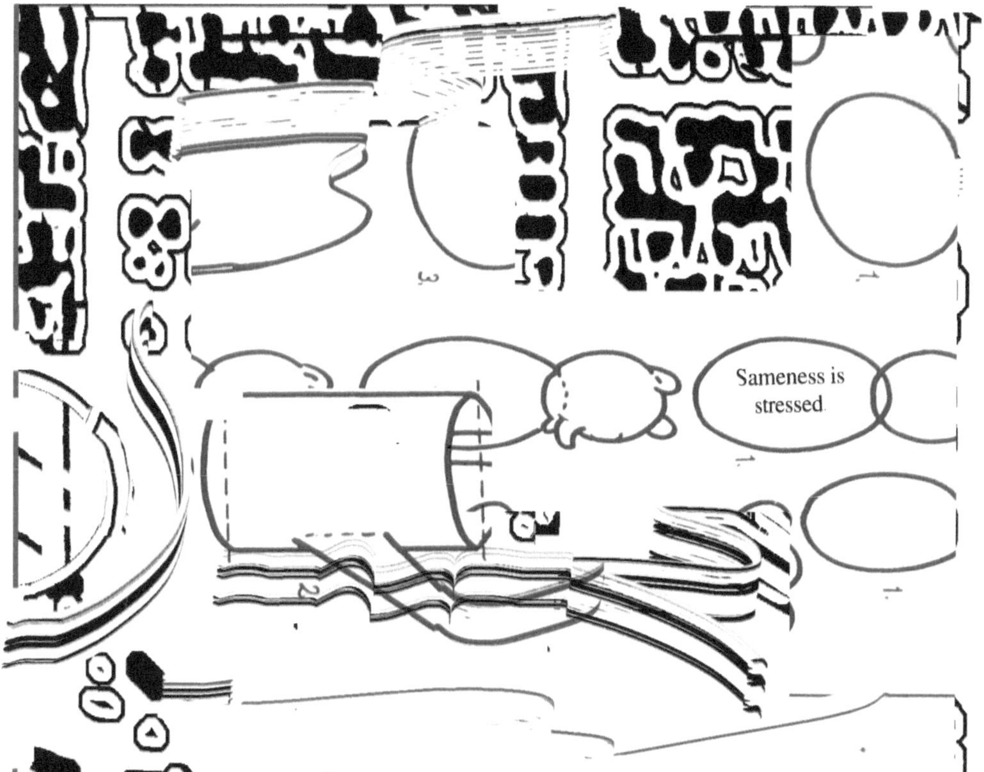

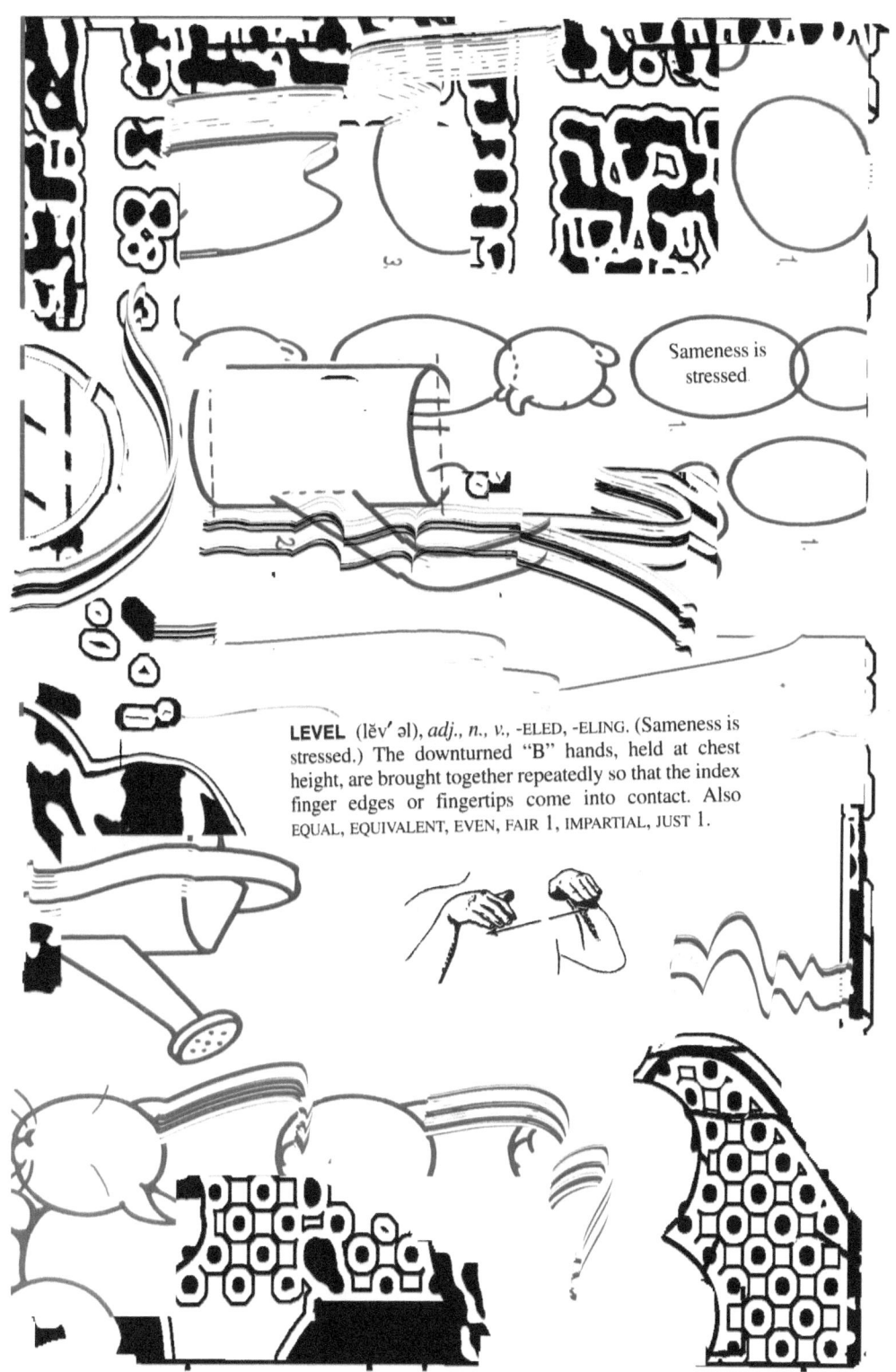

LEVEL (lĕv′ əl), *adj., n., v.,* -ELED, -ELING. (Sameness is stressed.) The downturned "B" hands, held at chest height, are brought together repeatedly so that the index finger edges or fingertips come into contact. Also EQUAL, EQUIVALENT, EVEN, FAIR 1, IMPARTIAL, JUST 1.

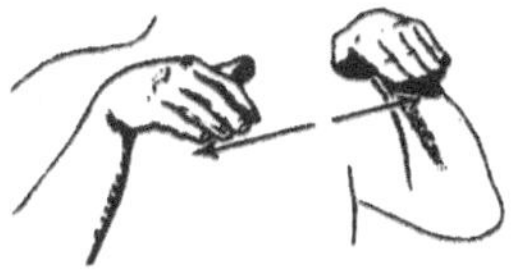

spinner

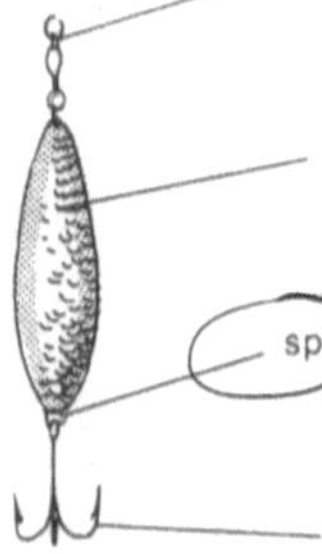

phenomenalist, physio
ist, preferentialist, pro
ist, sacerdotalist, spir
transcendentalist, uni
vivisectionist; arboric
bacteriologist, ceremo
alist, constitutional
conversationalist, edu
talist, individualist,
lectualist, internationa
Also: **-iss** + **-ed** (as ir
st (-īst), Christ, feist; Z
Also: **-ice** + **-ed** (as ir
t, bit, bitt, chit, fit, flit,
mitt, nit, pit, Pitt, qu
spit, split, sprit, tit,

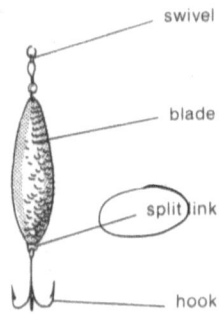

spit, split, sprit, tit,
acquit, admit, armpit
mit, emit, misfit, m
permit, refit, remit, ı
sunlit, titbit, tomtit, tr
benefit, counterfeit, d
ite, hypocrite, infin
perquisite, preterite, r
tch, bitch, ditch, fitch,
pitch, rich, snitch,
which, witch; bewit
unhitch; czarevich.
te (-īt), bight, bite, bli
Dwight, fight, flight,
kite, knight, light, mi

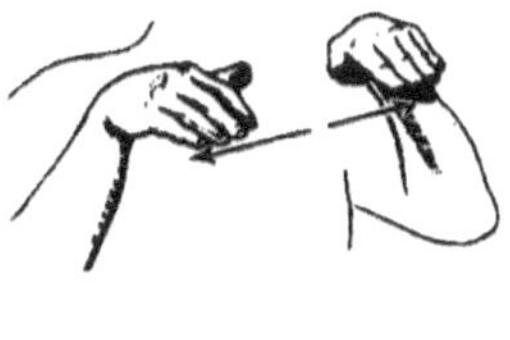

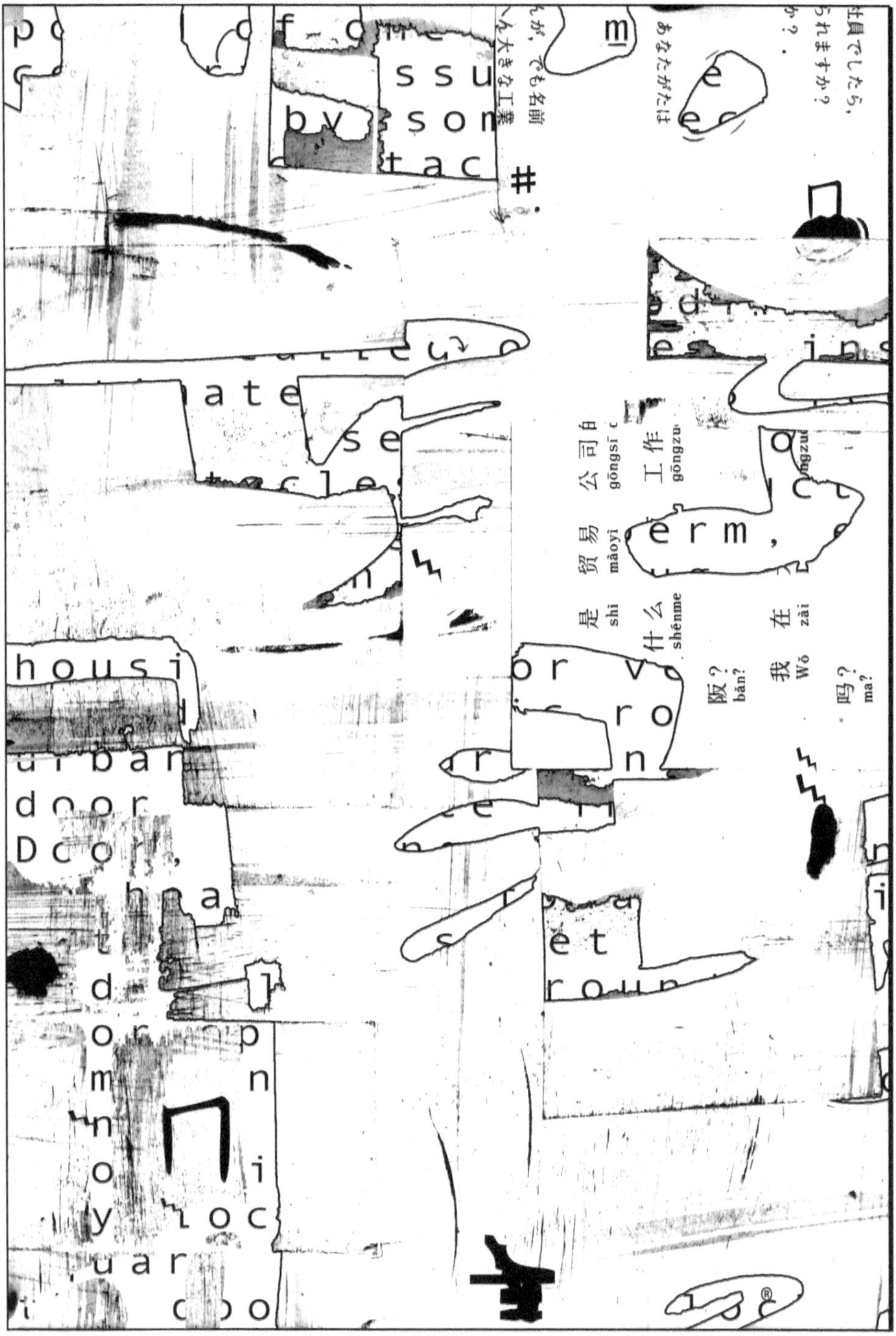

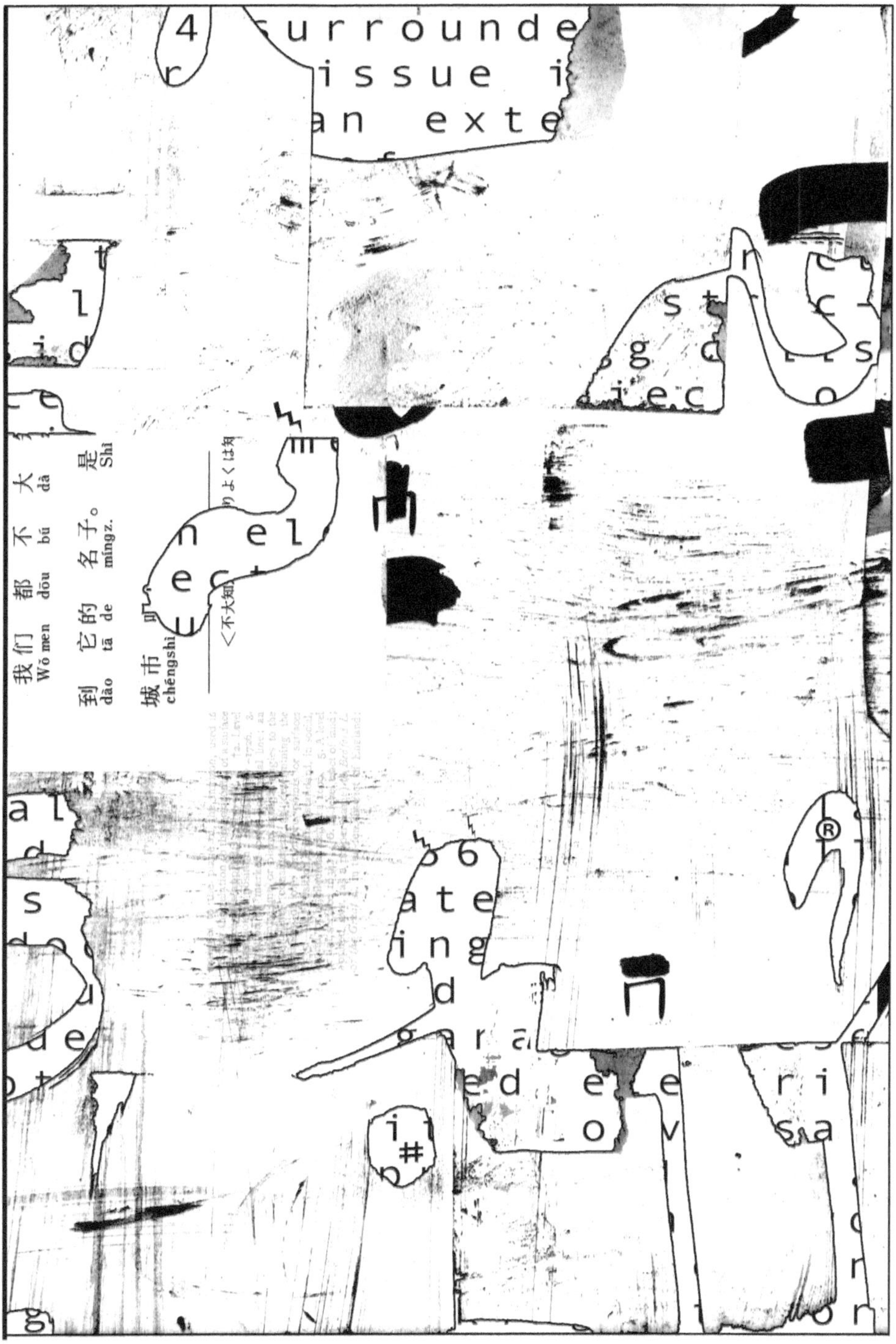
4 surrounde
issue i
an exte

furnished map

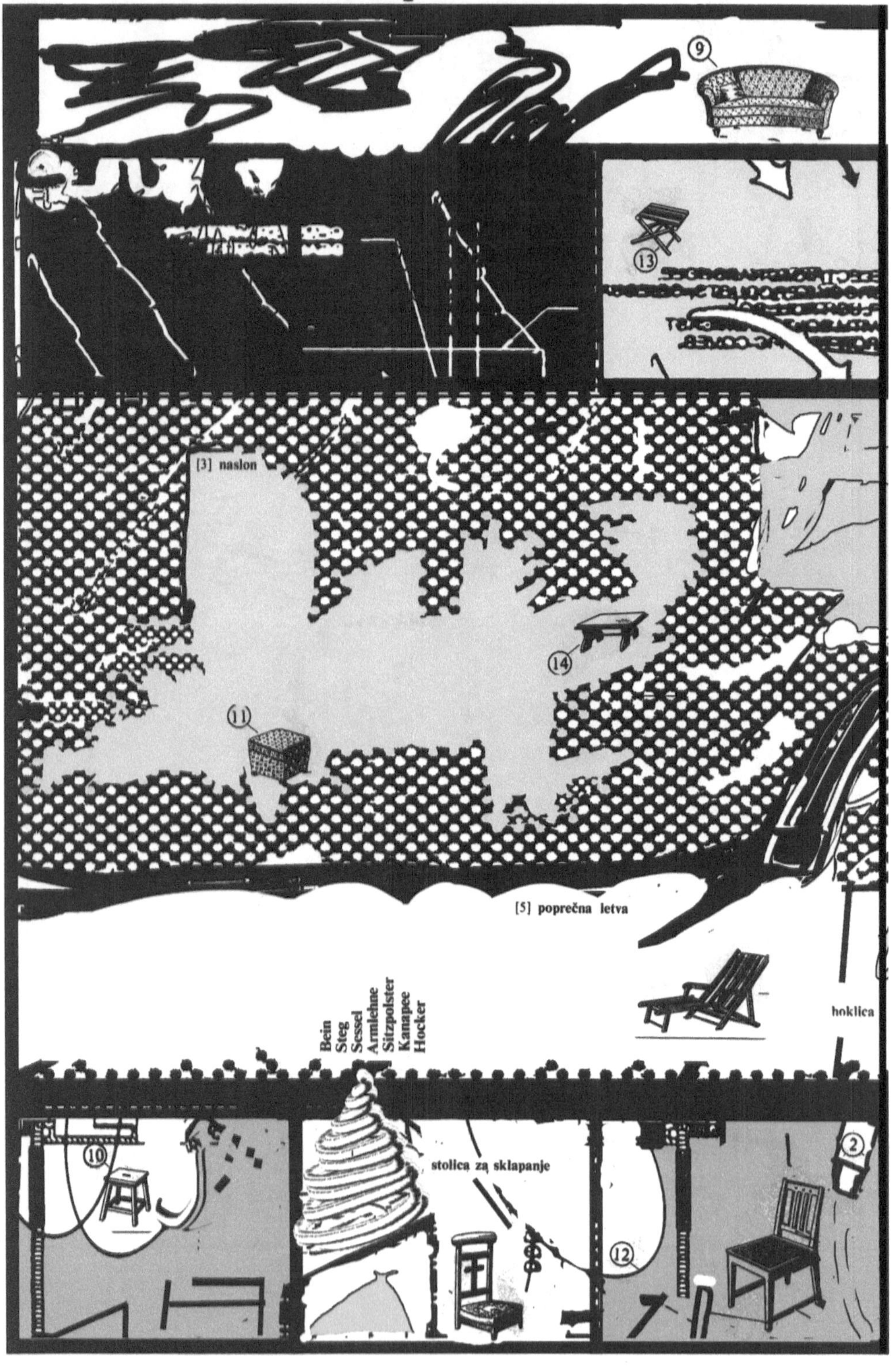

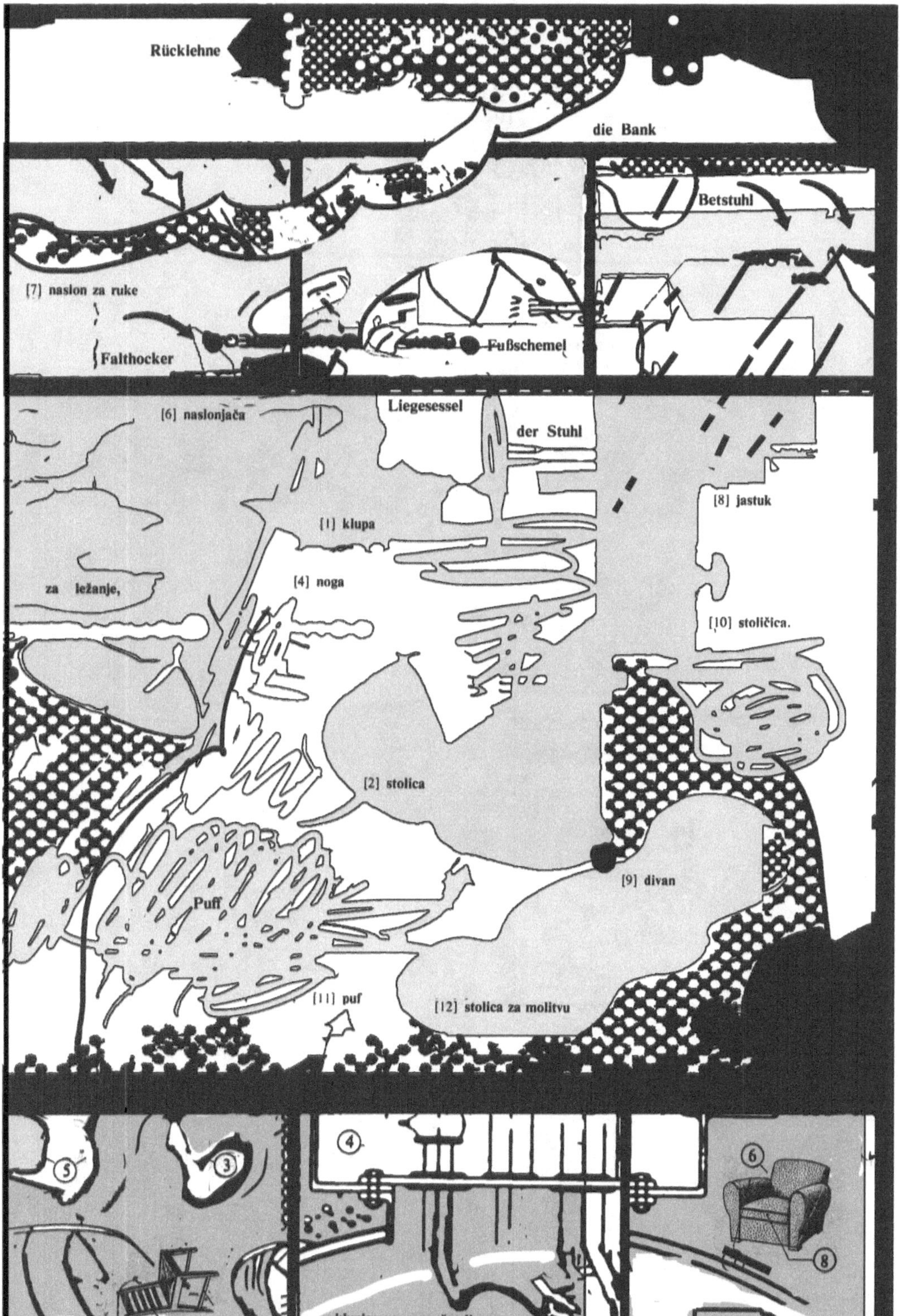
Rücklehne
die Bank
Betstuhl
[7] nasion za ruke
Falthocker
Fußschemel
[6] naslonjača
Liegesessel
der Stuhl
[8] jastuk
[1] klupa
za ležanje,
[4] noga
[10] stoličica.
[2] stolica
Puff
[9] divan
[11] puf
[12] stolica za molitvu
klupica za noge, šamlica

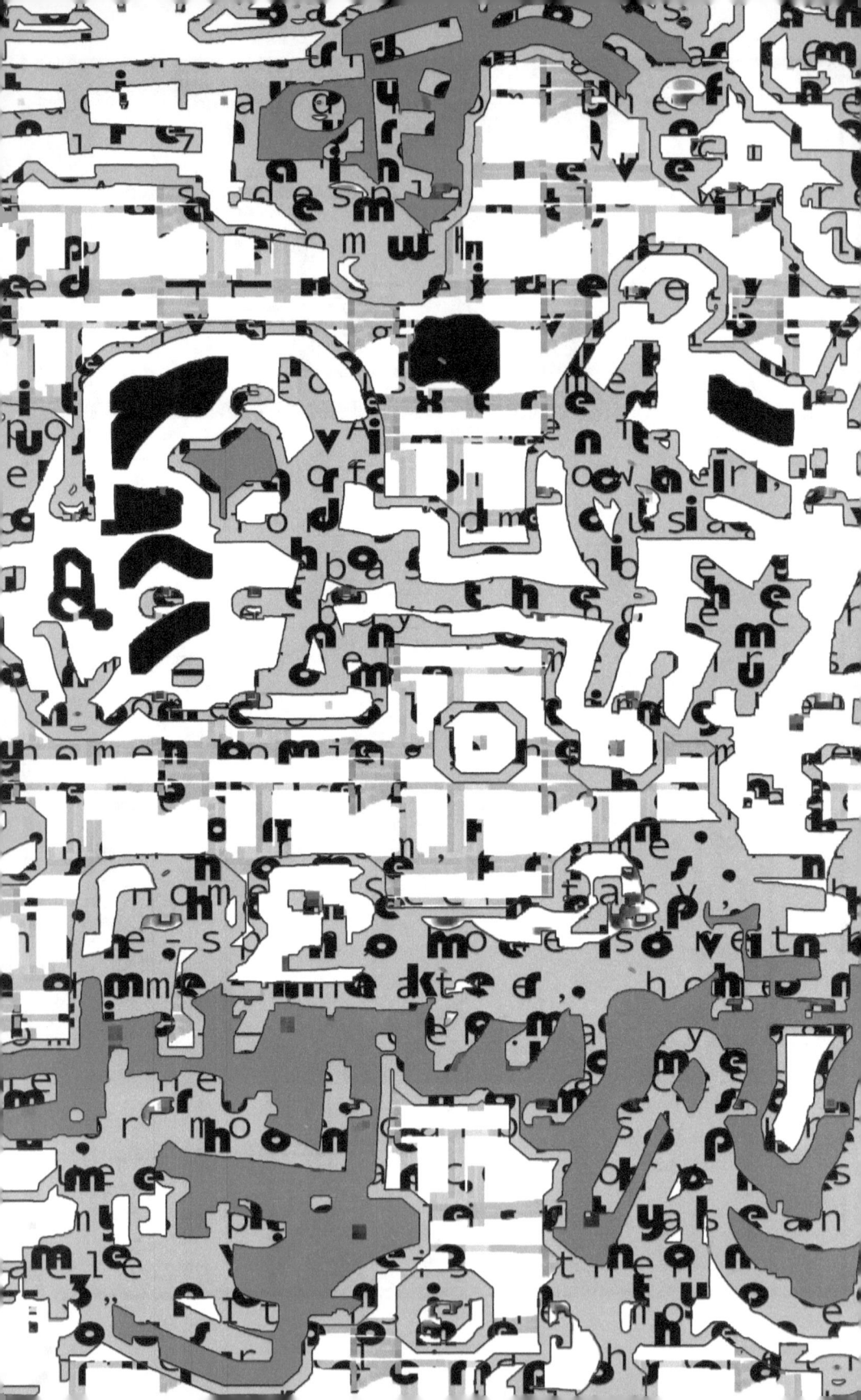

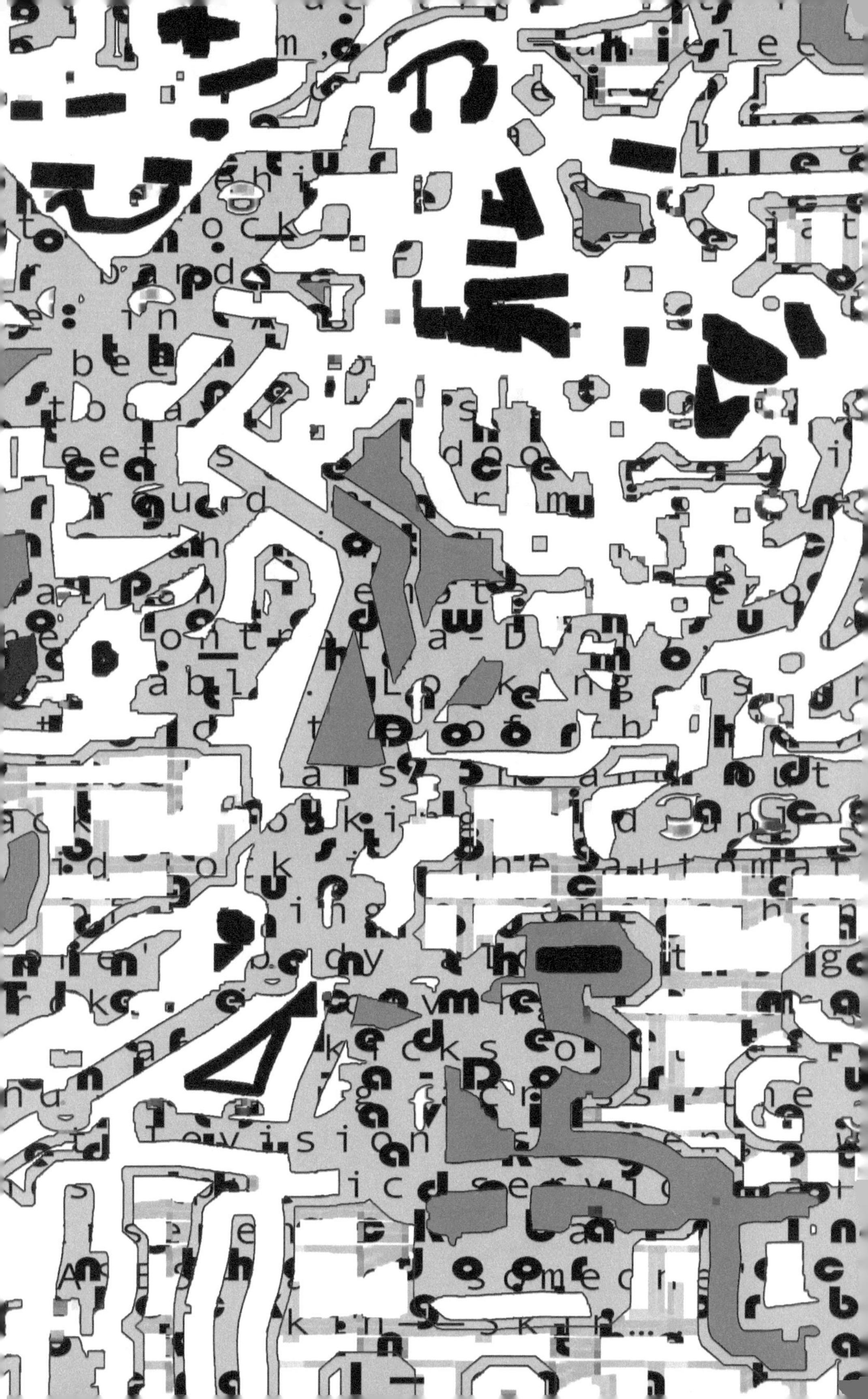

rguard
ontr
able
Looking
airs
automat
evision
icd servi
some

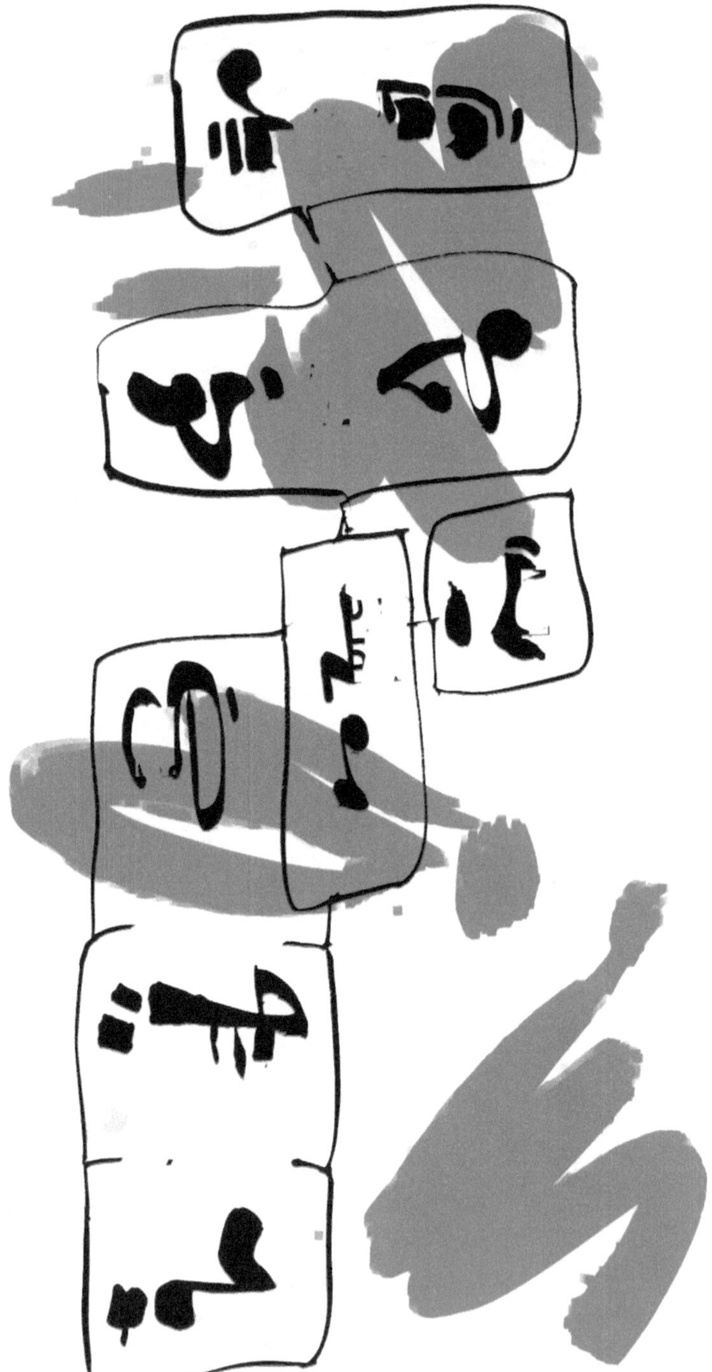

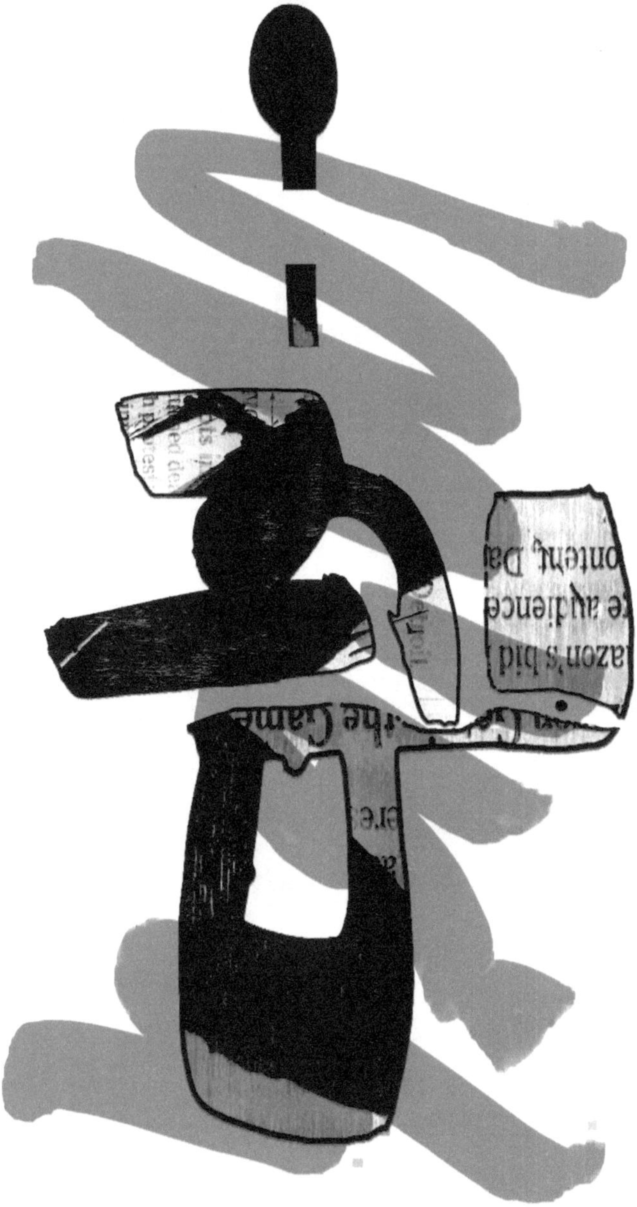

正月建寅					
立春節 雨水氣	清明節 谷雨氣	立秋節 處暑氣	大雪節 冬至氣		

builder, ker, ho arm, home

鐘點算表

每日分為子，丑，寅，卯，辰，巳，午，[illegible]亥十二時辰，每個時辰包括兩小時，惟子時分作兩截，上子時稱[illegible]由零一時。下子時稱為夜子初，由廿三時管至零時。由於[illegible]日子夜零[illegible]中天，為一日之始也。

acle to e the

fied leafy

標準時間

丑	1至3
寅	3至5
卯	5至7
辰	7至9
巳	9至11
未	下午 1至3
申	3至5
亥	9至11
子	上午 11至12

三

歲破

破午山 丑年破未山 寅年破申山

年破戊山 巳年破亥山 午年破子山

年破寅山 酉年破卯山 戌年破辰山

維論歲破，宜看所偏之綫論之。如乾兼亥，壬兼亥，遇巳年為歲破。癸兼[redacted]兼丑，遇未年為歲破。艮兼寅，甲兼寅，遇申年為[redacted]破。乙兼辰，巽兼辰，遇[redacted]歲破。巽兼巳，丙兼巳，遇亥年為歲破，丁兼未，[redacted]兼未，遇丑年為歲[illegible]。兼申[redacted]歲破。

擇日[redacted]以立春起至驚蟄前止，定[redacted]月管事，由驚蟄起至清明前止，定為卯月令，作二月管事，各月類推雨水，春分等為中氣，乃太陽過宮之日，可作查考立命小限

九月建戌 寒露節 霜降氣	[illegible]	正月建寅 立春節 雨水氣
立[illegible]	小暑節 大暑氣	[illegible]
大雪節 冬至氣	七月建申 立秋節 處暑氣	清明節 谷雨氣
[illegible]	[illegible]	[illegible]

通勝擇

九日	[illegible]	[illegible]
[illegible]	[illegible]	[illegible]
[illegible]	七月建申 立秋節 處暑氣	建辰 清明節 谷雨氣
[illegible]	白露節 秋分氣	四 氣

與扶山

三

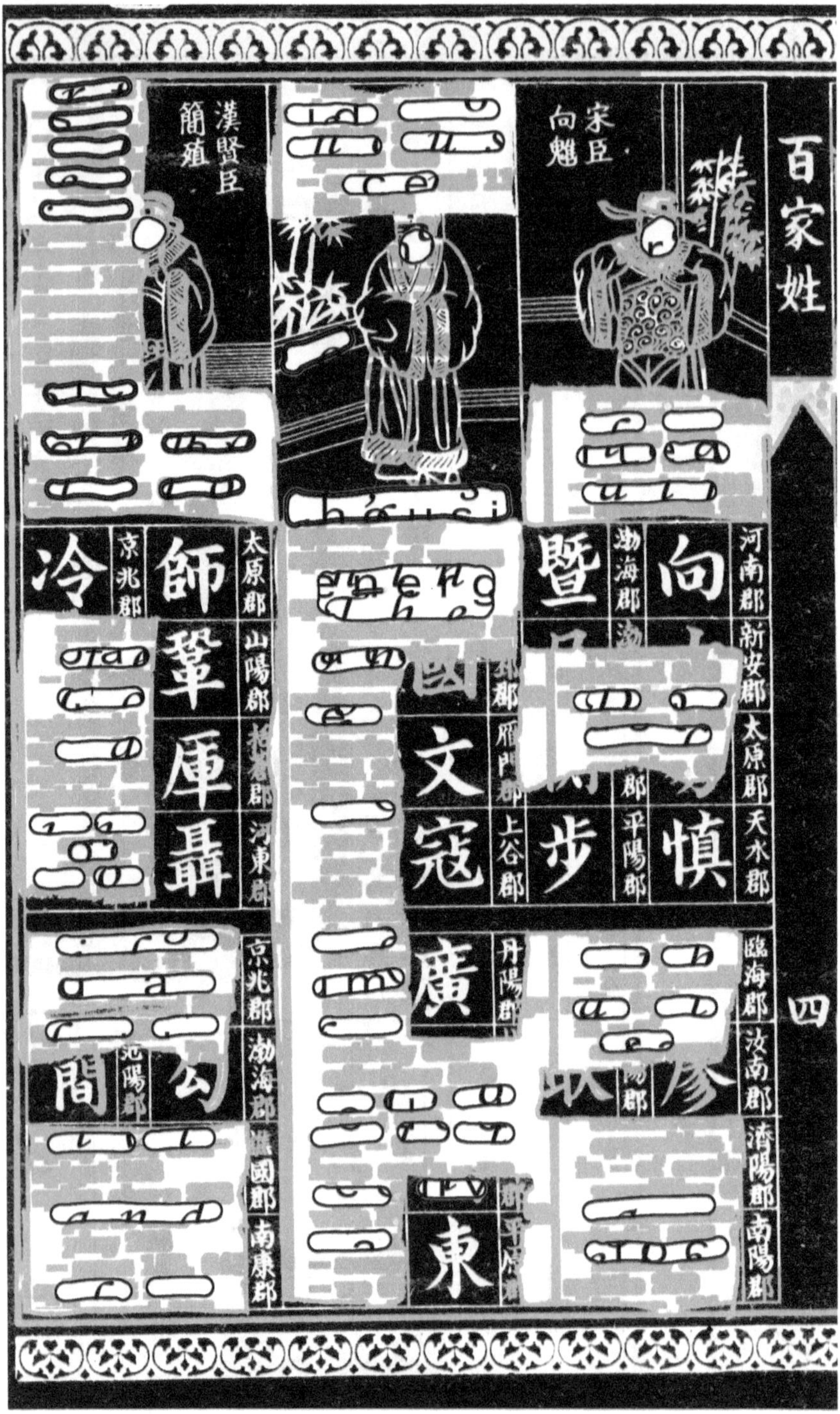
百家姓
宋臣
向魋
漢賢臣
簡殖
向
河南郡
暨
渤海郡
師
太原郡
冷
京兆郡
新安郡
太原郡
輦
山陽郡
厙
聶
河東郡
文
寇
上谷郡
慎
天水郡
步
平陽郡
廣
丹陽郡
東
臨海郡
汝南郡
濟陽郡
南陽郡
四
京兆郡
渤海郡
南康郡
閻

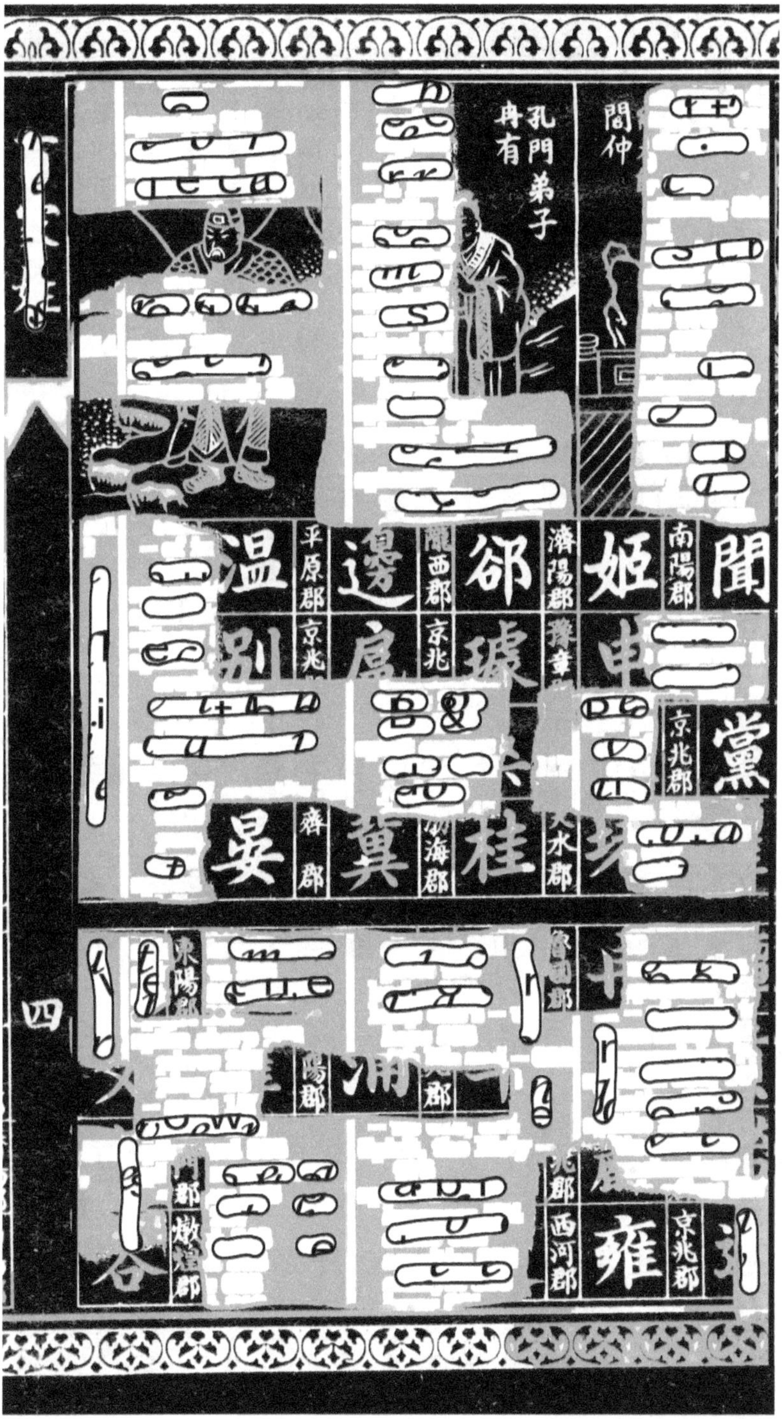

孔門弟子
冉有
閭仲
閭
南陽郡
姬
濟陽郡
郤
隴西郡
邊
温
平原郡
京兆
黨
京兆郡
晏
齊郡
冀
渤海郡
桂
天水郡
東陽郡
四
雍
京兆郡
西河郡
敦煌郡

(If upper and lower re
, between could be call
level contains common a
g and eating. There a
ets of stairs often
upward to a bedroom an
a basement. The baseme
off, and often features
main level (downward c
ally a crawl space
unfinished. A des spli
level is visible from th
ing is added, it is e
causing violent laught
aphically erroneous
version of poem 3—2 A ho
close to art of th
a prized possession ho
me banking, homebase
home builder, home-buyer
home farm, home free h
home front, home-girl
home loan, home-loving,
home movie, Home Office
home port, home room,
home school, Home Sec
home site, home-spun, h
Home-style, home theat
wreckers, homer. 3 poem

referred to teeth
lled a tongue.) he a
areas for sitting. Goo
are typically
n carpeted, one runnin
nd one descending to a
ment is usually finishe
s a garage. Beneath h
om the basement) is u
e, which is frequentl
it, where the spl
the front elevation. whe
tremely amusing. of te
ext
ter. either a typo
home, or a dyslecti
home is generally a plac
the owner, and can becom
home usage. home baking
e, home-boy, home-brew
er, home cinema, home ec
home fires, home fries
home help, home keys
home-made, home-maker
home help, home plate
home-made
home rule, home run
ce, away home shopper
home stretch, home study
tre, home video, home-
e: a typographically er
n accessory fruit com

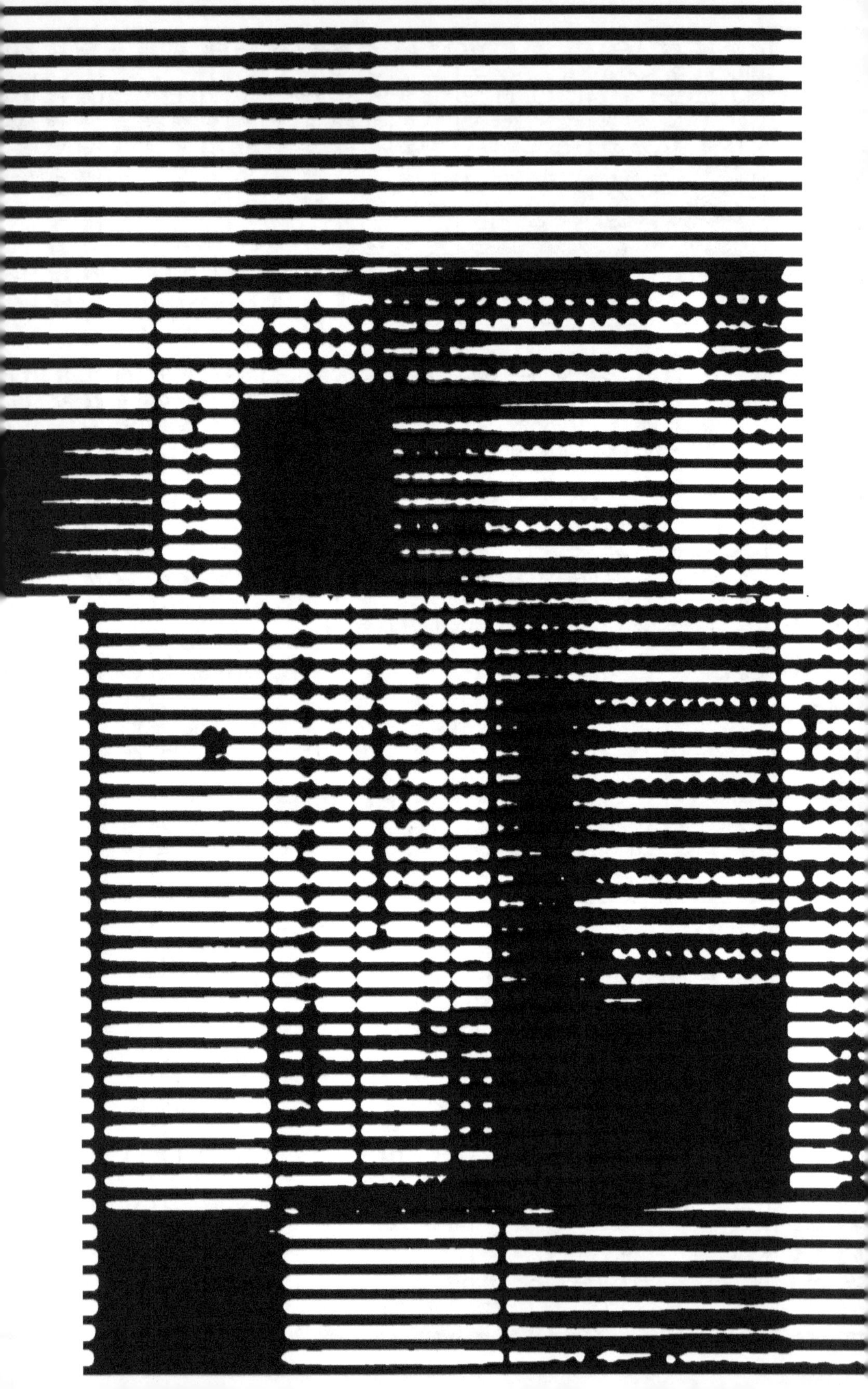

Between the level of words and the level of images – who goes there and by what means?

جسم السيارة

يختلف تصميم أجسام السيارات باختلاف الغرض من استخدامها . فمنها مايصمم ليناسب سيارات الركّاب (كالسيارات الخاصة أو الأوتوبيسات بأنواعها) ، ومنها مايناسب نقل البضائع العامة ، أو الأحجار والصخور وسواد البناء ، أو النفايات ، ومنها مايصمم خاصة للاستخدامات العسكرية ، وهكذا . قد يركب الجسم على إطار السيارة المعدنى ، أو قد يكون الجسم عديم الاطار ، كما هى الحال فى بعض سيارات الركاب .

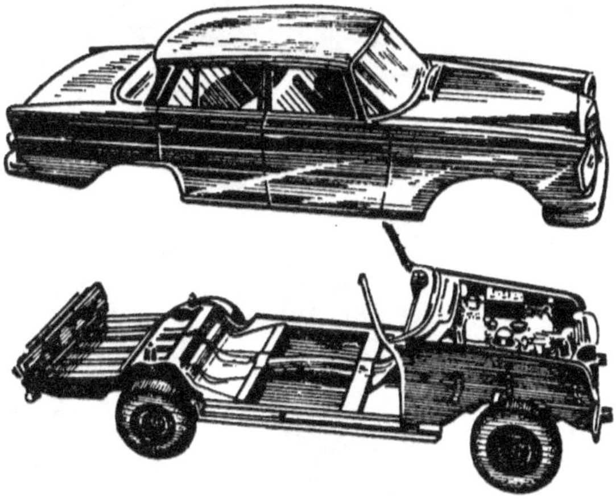

الشكل ٤٦ — جسم عديم الاطار يركب على أرضية مسطحة

e furniture' – primitive milking
and cricket tables"

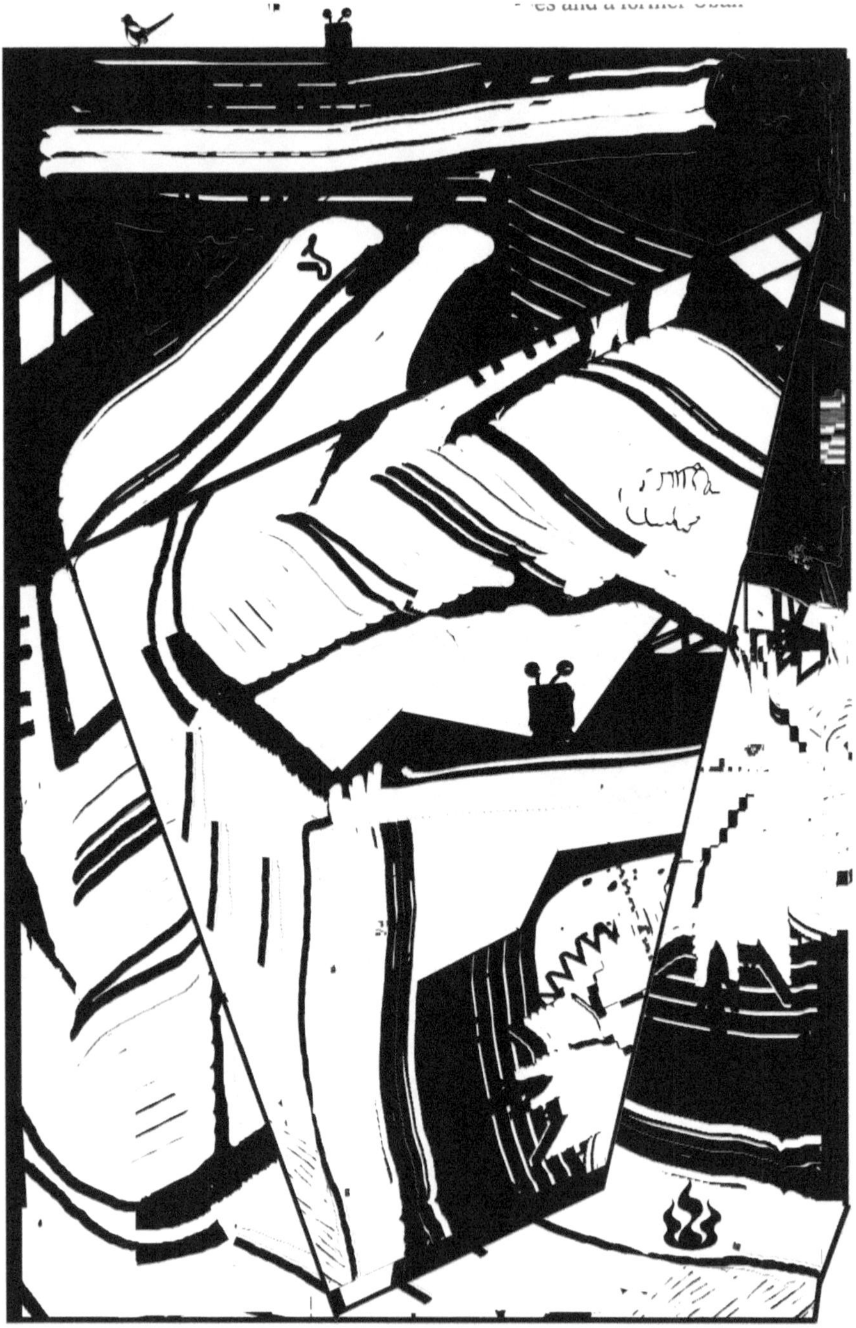

century—had been
ersonal control.
2009 Raúl made
e changes, minor

rved in his yearly
land. His visit to a
ooperative reveals
ing this transition.

d to the reforms for
obs.
at Cuba has already
versible change of
ent toward discard-
et-style system and

mers, public bath
trimmers of palm
duates—doctors, t
ts—can drive a cal
ely practice the pro
and, still

rcels. They also incl
sell most of their ha
hich fixes the price
y face the specter

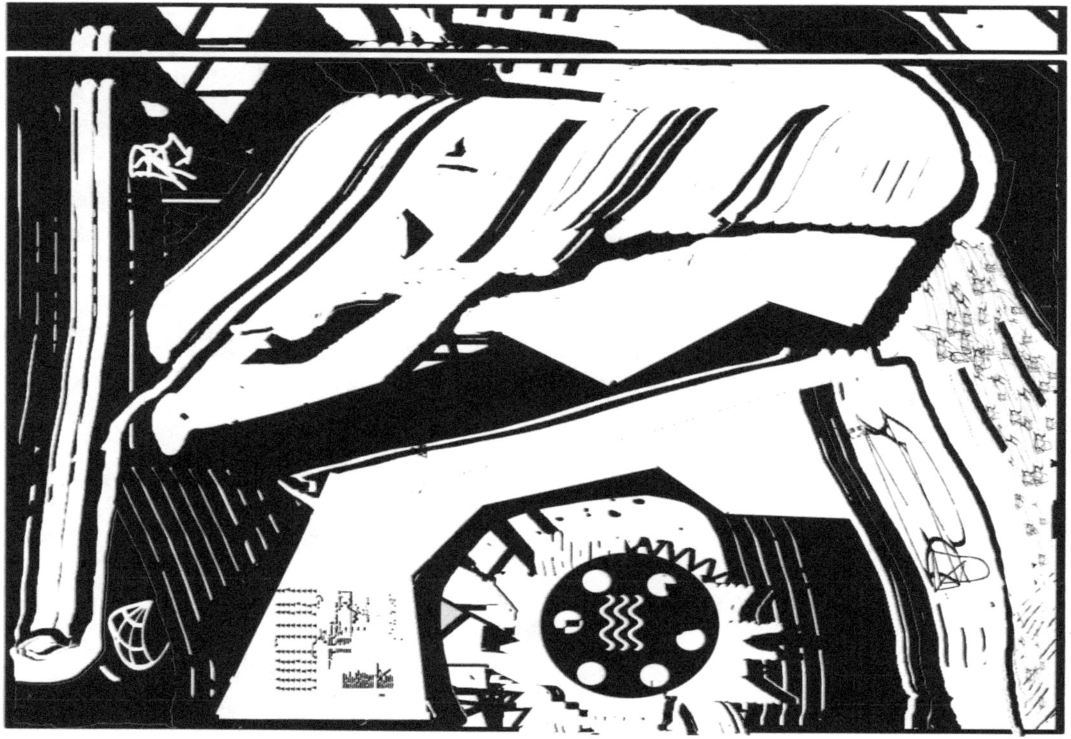

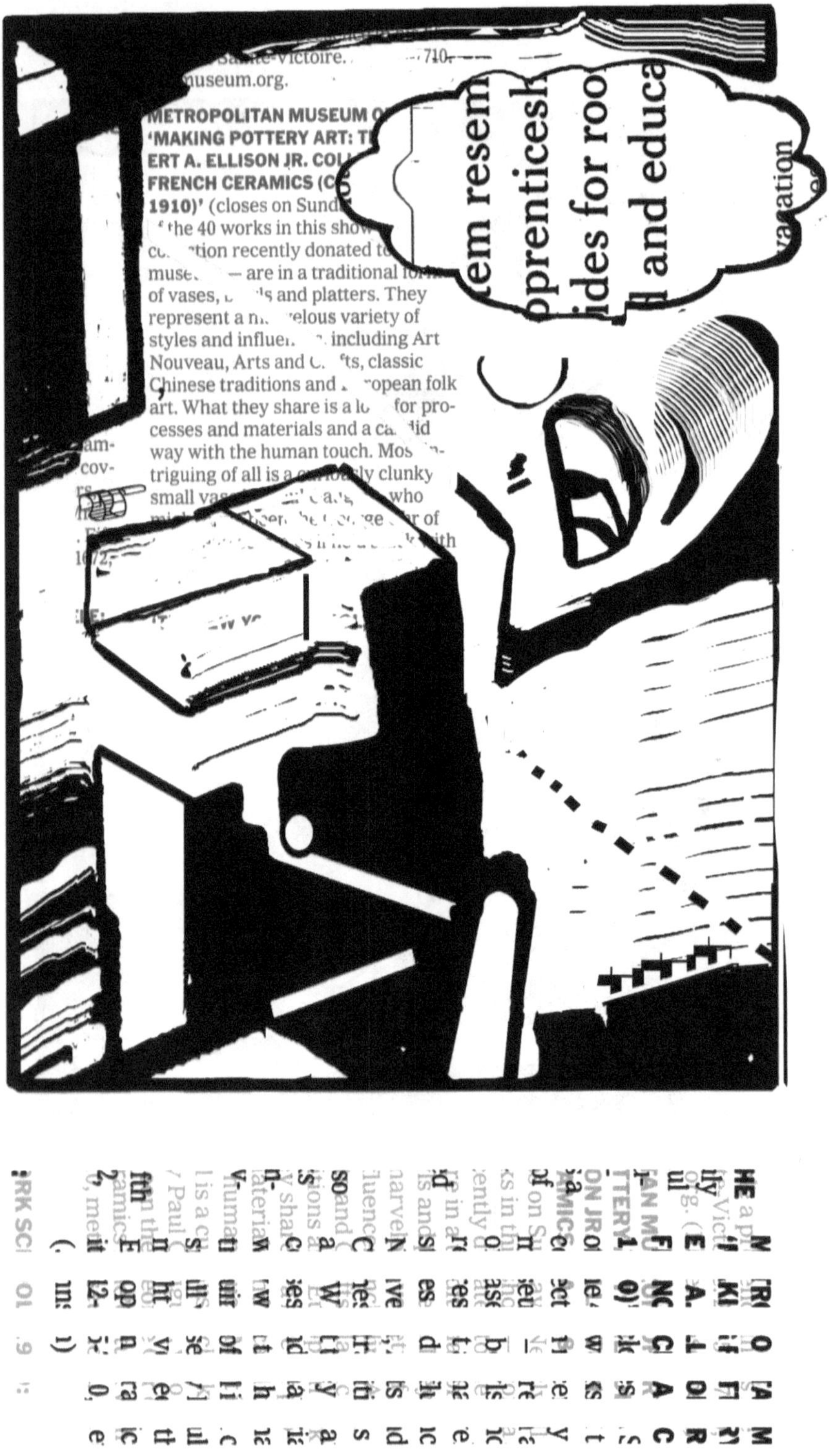
museum.org.
METROPOLITAN MUSEUM O
'MAKING POTTERY ART: T
ERT A. ELLISON JR. COL
FRENCH CERAMICS (C
1910)' (closes on Sund
the 40 works in this show
tion recently donated t
are in a traditional fo
of vases, ls and platters. They
represent a elous variety of
styles and influe including Art
Nouveau, Arts and C fts, classic
Chinese traditions and ropean folk
art. What they share is a l for pro-
cesses and materials and a c did
way with the human touch. Mos
triguing of all is a ly clunky
small va who
em resem
pprenticesh
ides for roo
and educa
vacation

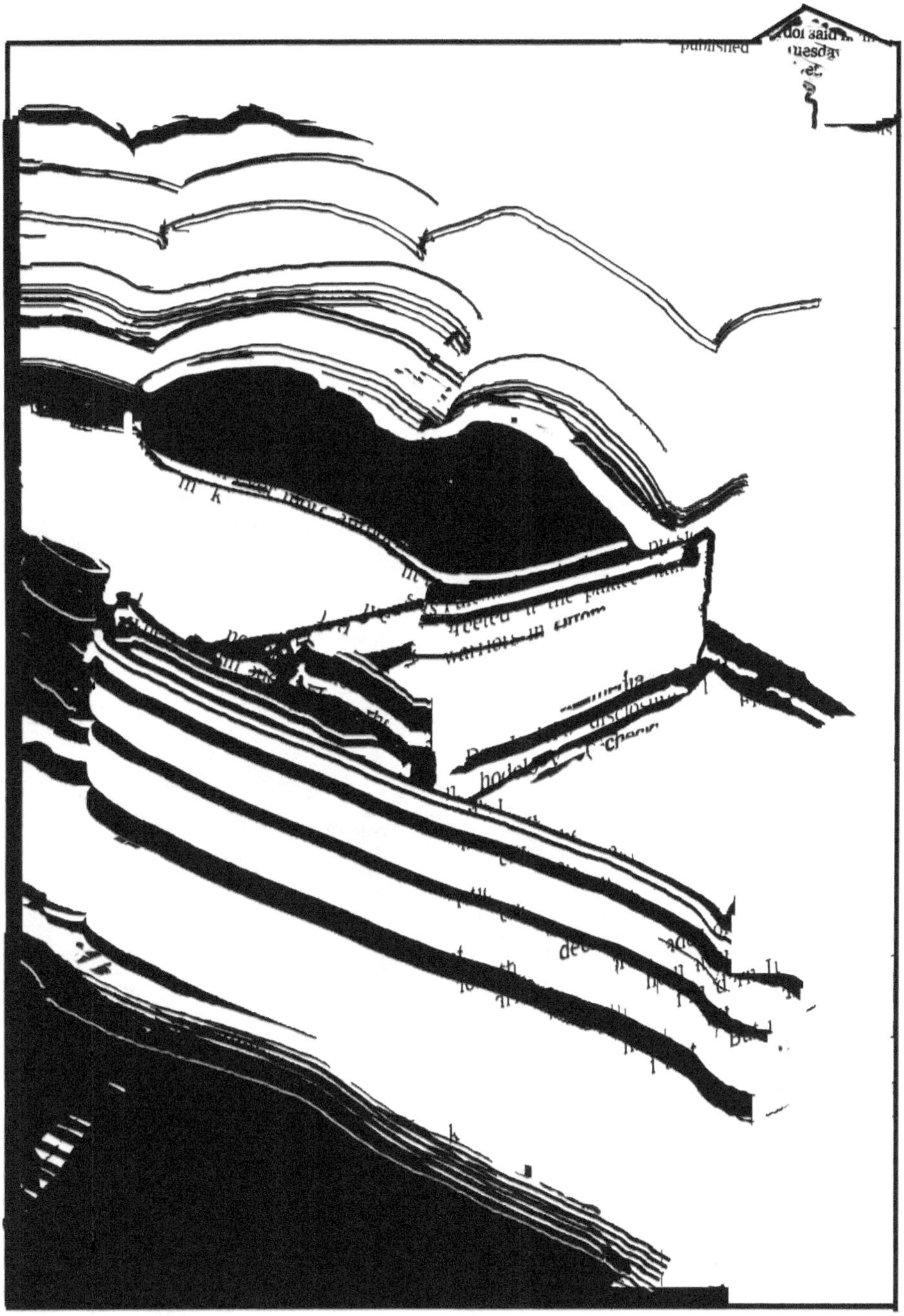

was steadily softened burgeoning agricultur from the luxurious hall homes. "Three things within the sound rem the village where I ren in his Essex village i The first was the fore village rooftops; the s that replaced straw pa greeted with equal jo took the place of woo

Pewter continue decline was caused by Tea, coffee and drinki pewter tankards made unwary fingers. "This

by the country's ter began to spread bles to more modest altered in England nen yet dwelling in n William Harrison isting the changes. eys sprouting above n beds and pillows rests; and the third, was the pewter that

l, in the 1740s, its l vogue: hot drinks. ne the rage and the e suddenly scalding habits favoured the

and transforme l wealth and so pe s of knights and no to be marvellously embrance of old r iain," wrote a certa 1576-77, before of cottage chimn econd was the dow llets and log head- and amazement, en platters.

to flourish unti a potent and nove ng chocolate becai to hold cool ale we hange in drinking

leasing lack ieen. There ed some mi ich more p an ardent f Pewter Soc erent sort splay, where iving to imp of pewter c a widower, ection gave friends," h esire that h m where hi nell wanted ectors woul

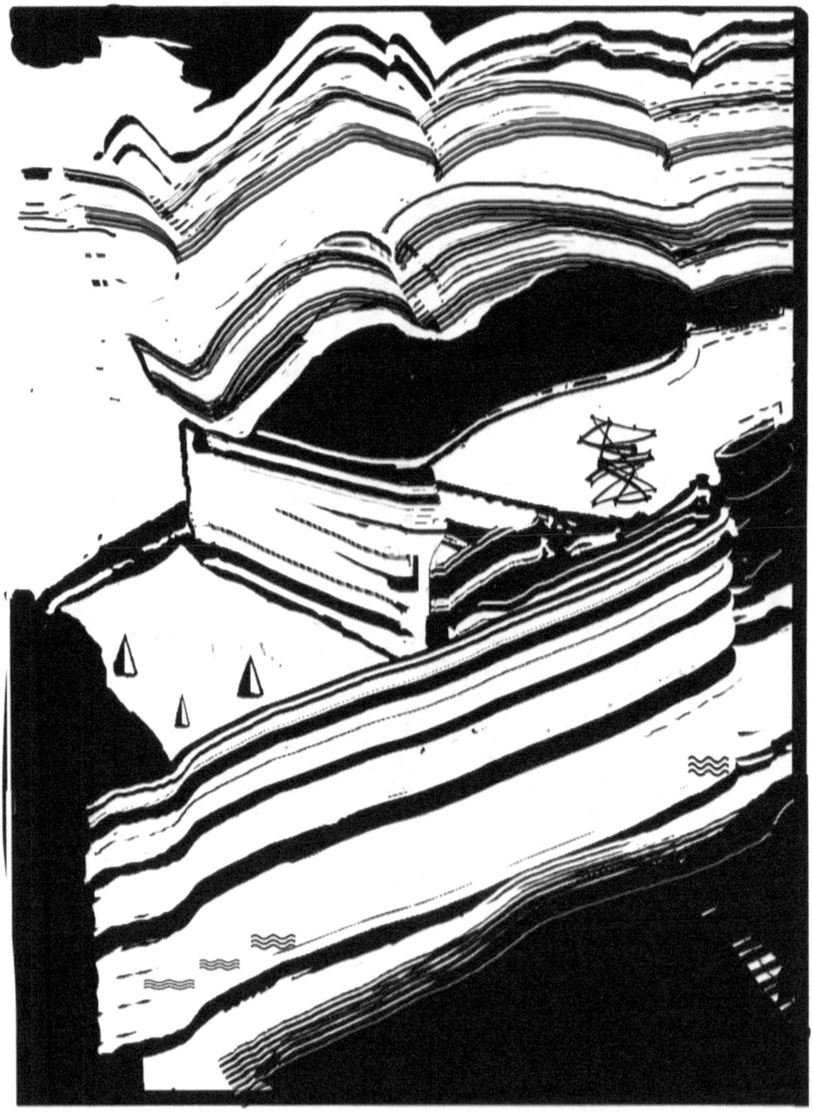

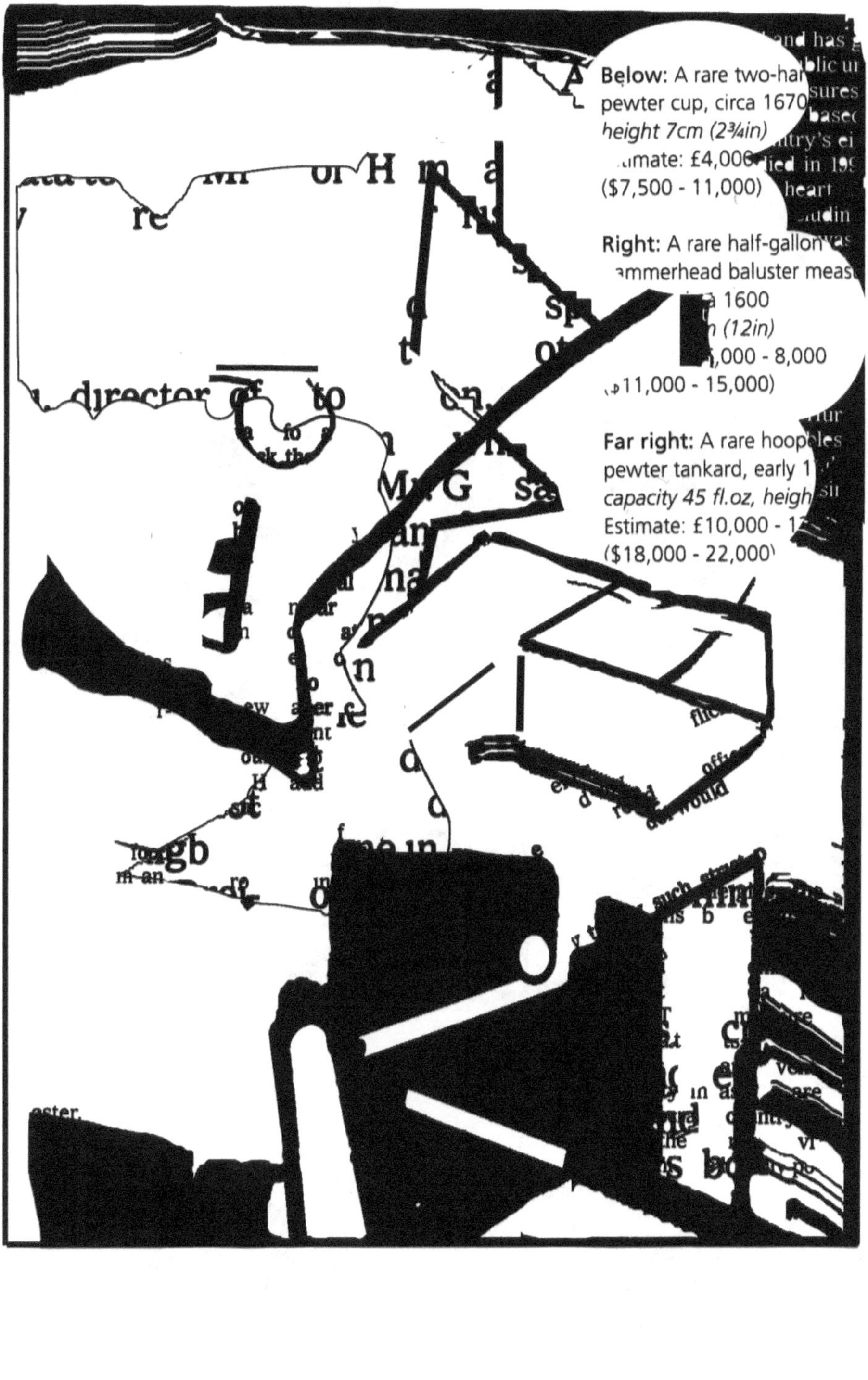

Below: A rare two-ha
pewter cup, circa 1670
height 7cm (2¾in)
($7,500 - 11,000)
Right: A rare half-gallon
ammerhead baluster meas
a 1600
(12in)
,000 - 8,000
11,000 - 15,000)
Far right: A rare hoop
pewter tankard, early 1
capacity 45 fl.oz, heigh
Estimate: £10,000 - 1
($18,000 - 22,000
director of to
Mr G

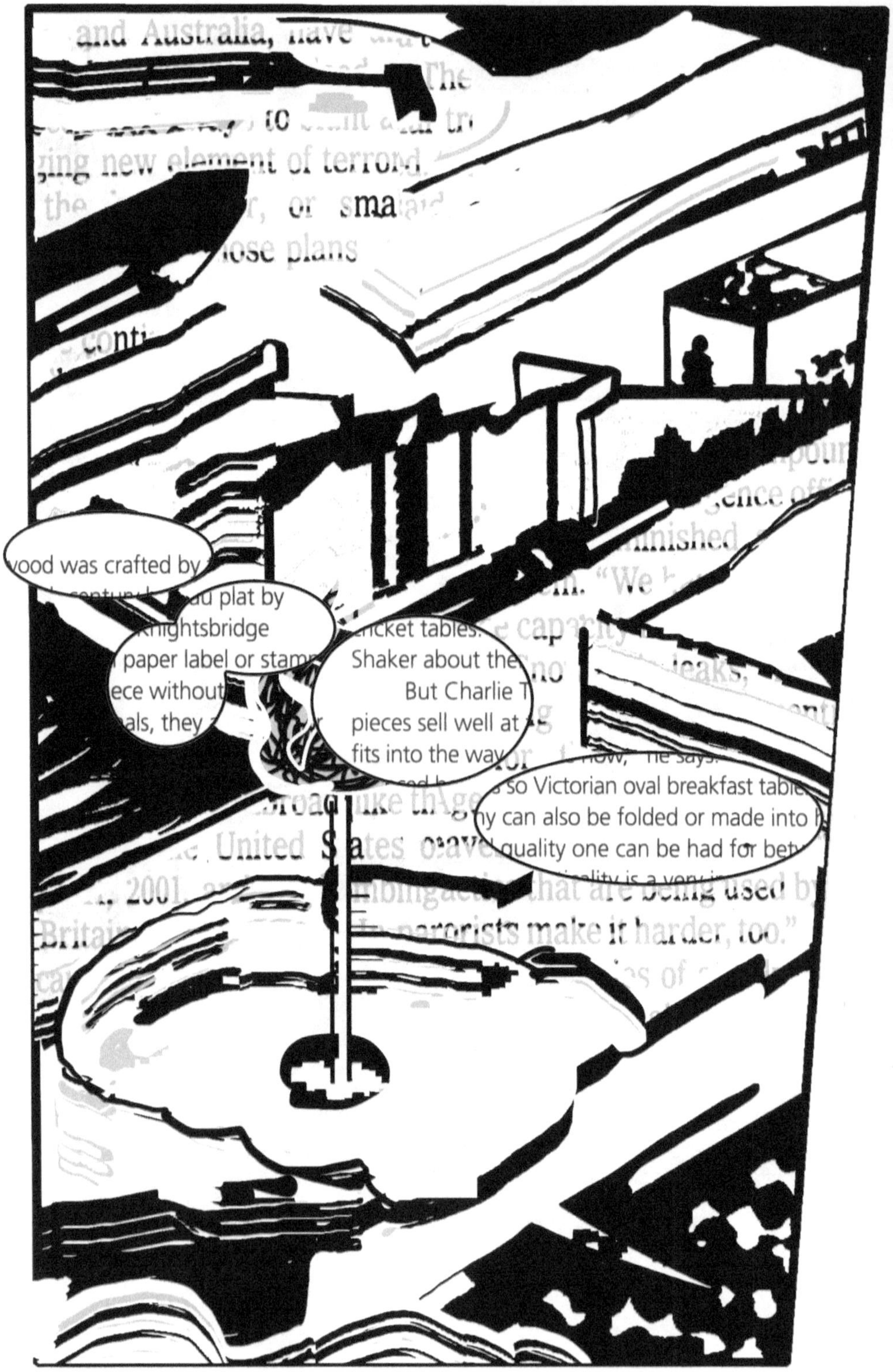
and Australia, have
ging new element of terrorist
or sma
ose plans
ence
nished
"We
capacity
leaks,
United States
Britain
terrorists make it harder, too."
vood was crafted by
u plat by
Knightsbridge
paper label or stamp
ece without
als, they
cricket tables.
Shaker about the
But Charlie T
pieces sell well at
fits into the way
so Victorian oval breakfast table
ly can also be folded or made into
quality one can be had for betw

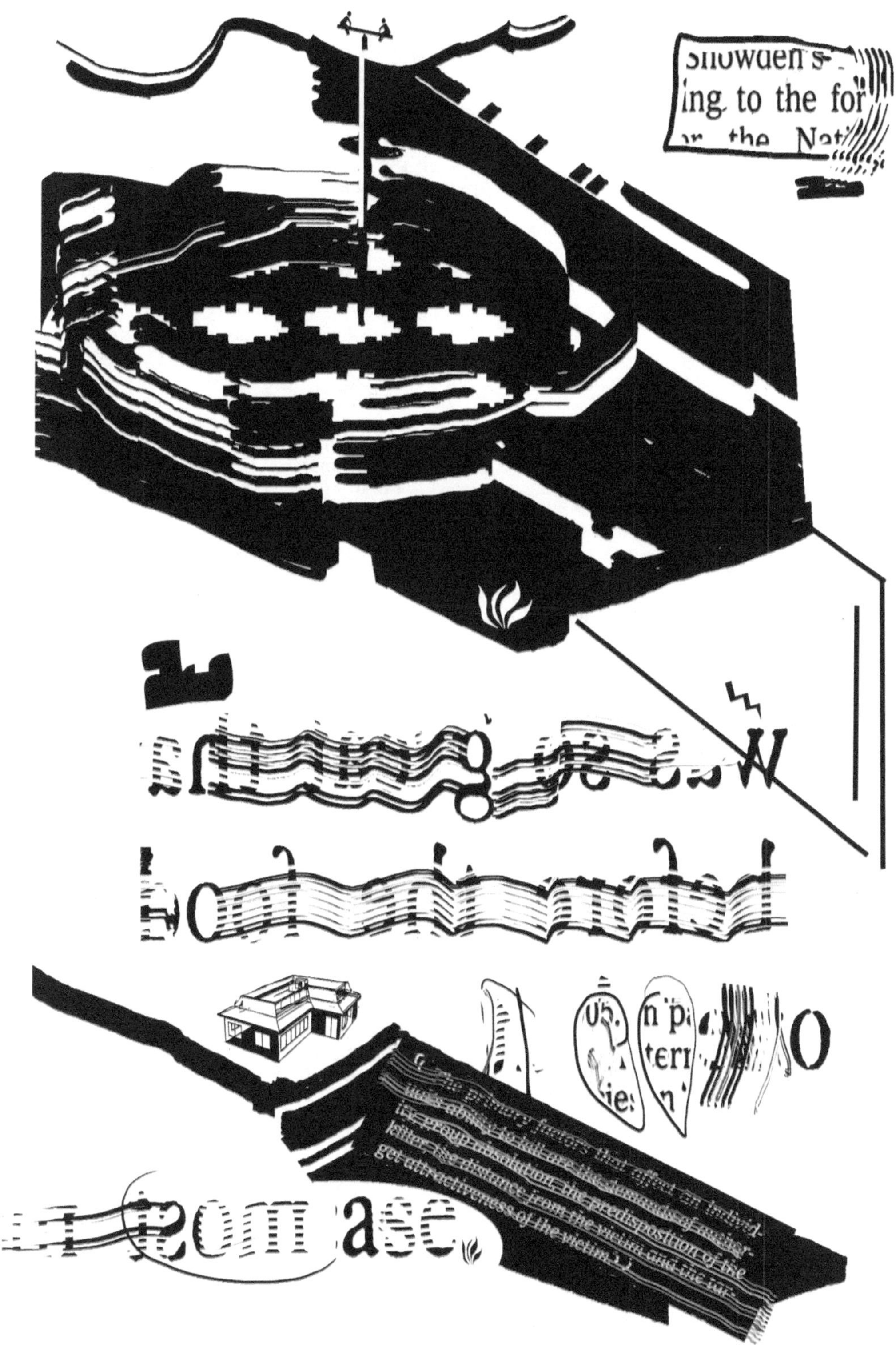
Snowden's
ing to the for
the Nat
The primary factors that affect an individ-
ual's ability to kill are the demands of author-
ity, group absolution, the predisposition of the
killer, the distance from the victim and the target attractiveness of the victim.

stress between two adjacent members or between the separate, adjacent parts of the same member. In general, a splice consists of splice material and **fastenings,** each of which must be strong enough to carry the stress. Structural steel is spliced by plates or angles which are fastened by means of **rivets, bolts** or **welding.** A **gusset plate** is not ordinarily considered a splice plate unless it is used in conjunction with other splice material to transfer stress between adjacent **chord** members at a **joint.** Structural timber is spliced by steel plates and bolts or by additional splice timbers which are connected by bolts or by timber connectors. The reinforcing rods of **reinforced concrete** are spliced by welding or by overlapping them far enough to assume that bond (see **Bond Stress**) will produce the stress transfer.

Splices are made for two reasons. First, there is a limiting length to all manufactured material. When the length of the member exceeds the limiting length of any of its parts, it is necessary to use two or more pieces for each of these parts. Splices are used to form one continuous piece. Secondly, transportation conditions and erection equipment limit the length of structural members or parts of structures which can be completed at a fabricating plant. This necessitates a field connection. A splice which is made at a fabricating plant is a shop splice while one made in the field is a field splice.

SPLIT ANODE MAGNETRON. A **magnetron** with a cylindrical anode divided into two segments, usually by slots parallel to its axis.

SPLIT SWITCH. Railway Track.

SPLIT-TAIL. Pisces, Teleostei. A small silvery **minnow,** *Pogonichthys macrolepidotus,* of central California.

SPODUMENE. The mineral spodumene is a **lithium aluminum silicate** corresponding to the formula $LiAl\,(SiO_3)_2$ and occurs in **monoclinic** prismatic crystals, occasionally of very large size. It also occurs massive. Spodumene has a perfect prismatic **cleavage** often very noticeable; uneven to splintery fracture; brittle; hardness, 6.5–7; specific gravity, 3.13–3.20; luster, vitreous to pearly; color, grayish- to greenish-white, green, yellow and purple. Its streak is white; it is transparent to translucent. Spodumene is characteristically a mineral of the **pegmatites,** and it is found in Sweden, Ireland, Madagascar and Brazil. In the United States it is for the queens of France to receive at the hour of their levée—*i.e.*, while making their toilet—the visits of certain noblemen. This custom was afterwards demanded as a right by the court physicians, messengers from the king, the queen's secretary, and some few other gentlemen, so that ten or more persons were often in the dressing-room while the queen was making her toilet and sipping her coffee. The word is now used to express that concourse of gentlemen who wait on the Queen on mornings appointed. No ladies except those attached to the court are present on these occasions.

Lev'ellers. Radicals in the time of Charles I. and the Commonwealth, who wanted all men to be placed on a level with respect to their eligibility to office. (*See* LILBURN: WHITE BOYS.)

Levelling-up. Raising the lower to the higher level. The expression was first employed by lord Mayo when opposing Mr. Gladstone's proposition to abolish the Church Establishment of Ireland. Lord Mayo meant by it that the tory government wished to endow the Roman Catholics and Dissenters as the Church of England was endowed, and not to disendow the Church of England, and lower it to the condition of other religious communities in Ireland. (1868.)

Lev'eret. The duke d'Epernon always swooned at the sight of a *leveret*, though he was not affected if he saw a hare. (*See* FOX.)

Levi'athan. The crocodile, or some extinct sea-monster, described in the Book of Job (chap. xli.). It sometimes in Scripture designates Pharaoh, king of Egypt, as in Psa. lxxiv. 14; Isa. xxvii. 1; and Ezek. xxix. 3, &c., where the word is translated "dragon."

The Leviathan of literature. Dr. Johnson. (1709-1784.)

Levit'ical. Belonging to the Levites or priestly tribe of Levi; pertaining to the Jewish priesthood, as the *Levitical law, Levitical rites.*

Lewd (Saxon, *leóde*) simply means the laity. This word carries with it a comment on the old ecclesiastical notion of the virtue of celibacy. The clergy were bound to celibacy, not so the laity, hence the clergy were the "chaste men," and the laity the "lewd or wanton ones."

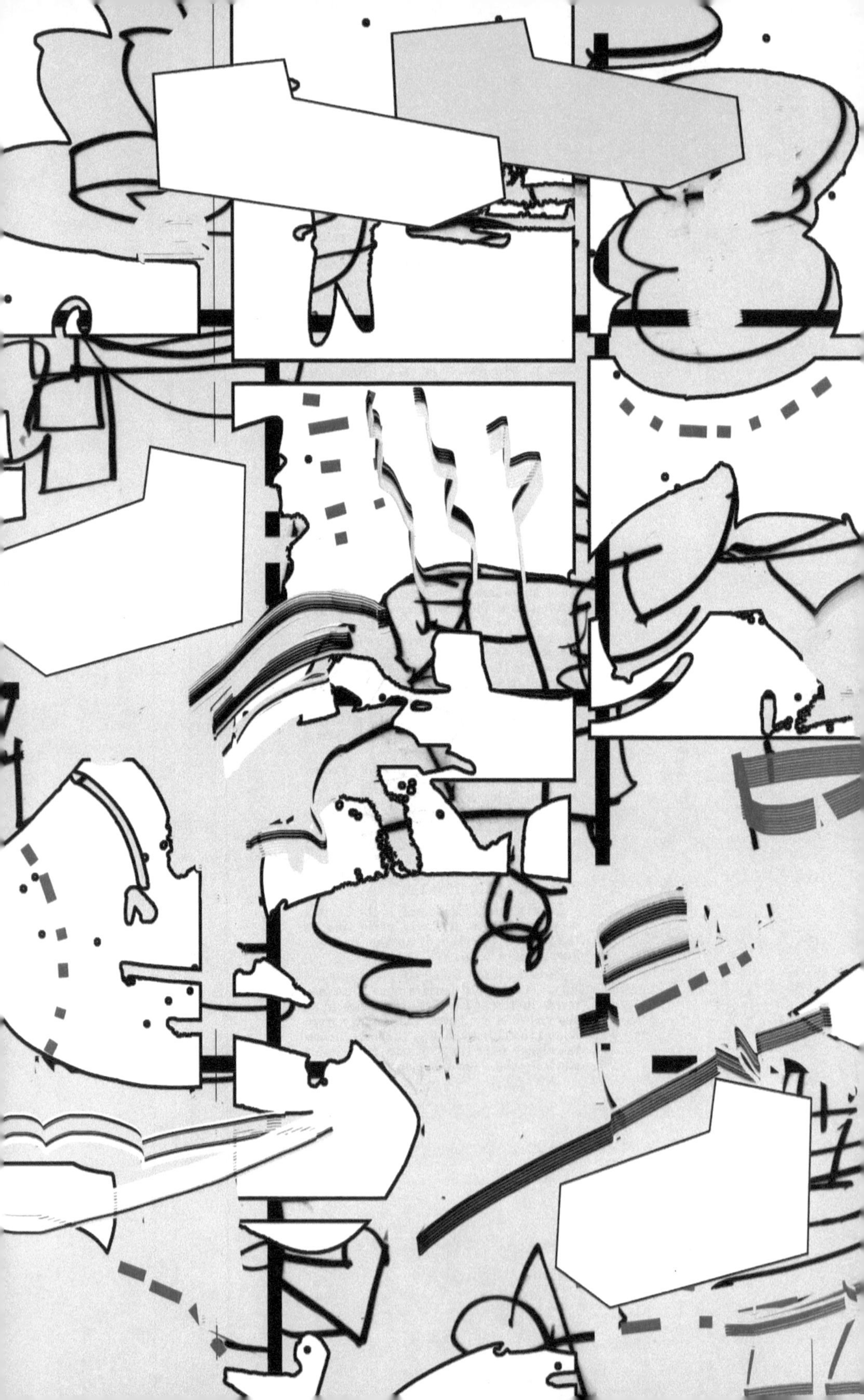

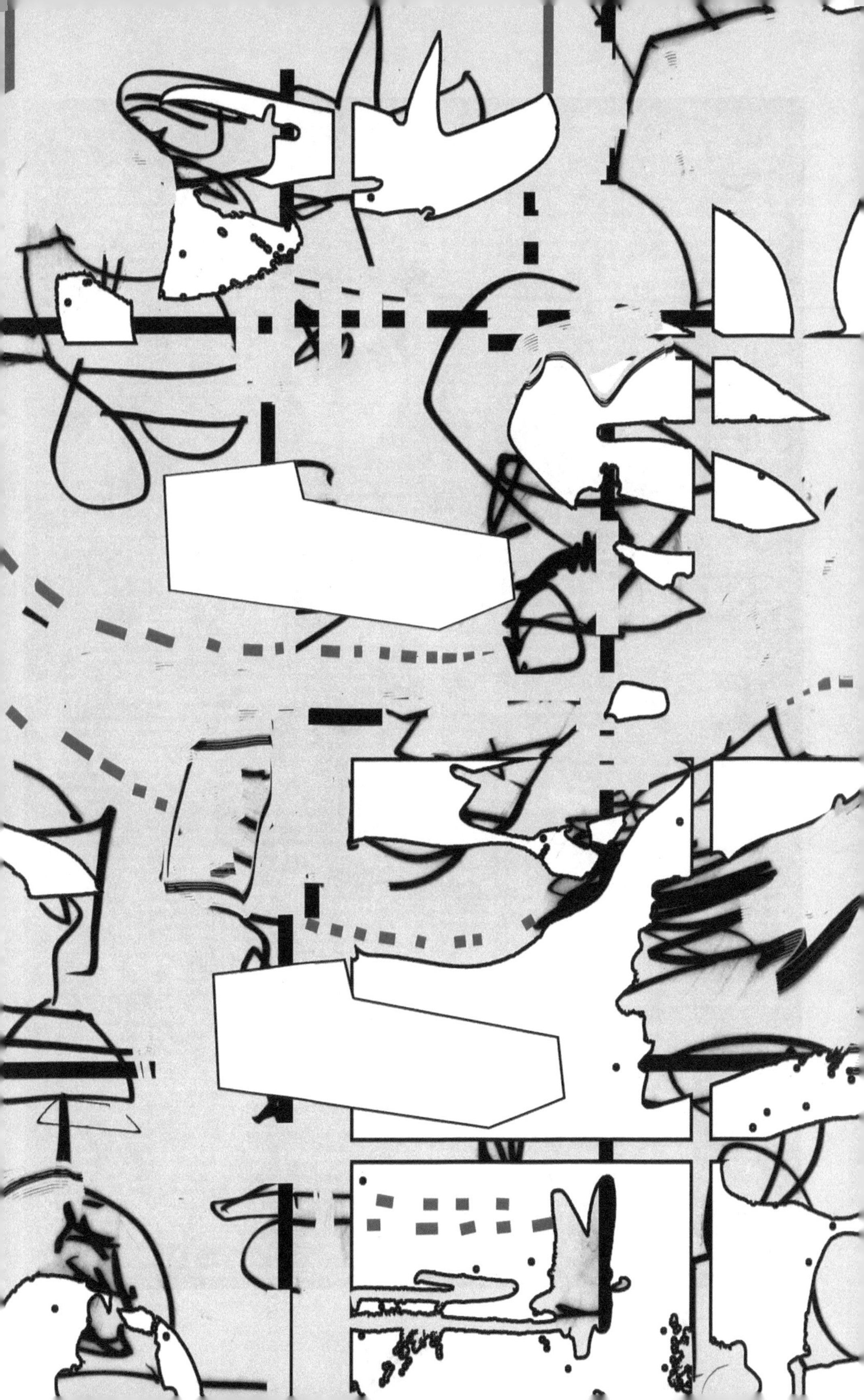

serving this purpose; also, one of a number of overlapping plates or strips of metal in armor, for protecting certain parts of the body, esp. one of the pieces of this kind for protecting the arm at the elbow (as, "The knees and feet were defended by *splints*, or thin plates of steel, ingeniously jointed upon each other": Scott's "Ivanhoe," ii.); also, an exostosis or bony enlargement of a splint-bone of a horse or an allied animal; sometimes, a splint-bone; also, splint-coal.—**splint,** *v. t.* To secure, hold in position, or support by means of a splint or splints, as a fractured bone; hence, to support as if with splints.—**splint′=ar″mor,** *n.* Armor made of splints, or overlapping plates or strips of metal.—**splint′=bone,** *n.* One of the rudimentary, splint-like metacarpal or metatarsal bones of the horse or some allied animal, closely applied one on each side of the back of each cannon-bone.—**splint′=coal,** *n.* A splintery variety of cannel-coal; also, a hard bituminous coal with a slaty structure, producing a hot fire.

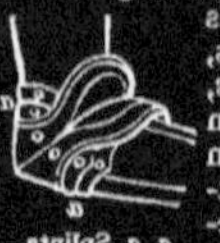
a, a, Splints.

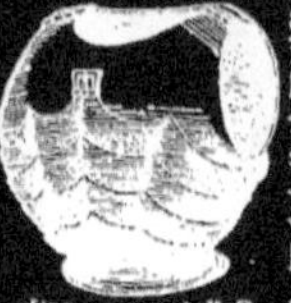
Splint-armor, 15th century.

splin-ter (splin′tėr), *n.* [ME. *splynter* = MD. D. *splinter*; related to E. *splint*.] A rough piece of wood, bone, etc., usually comparatively long, thin, and sharp, split or broken off from a main body, esp. by a violent blow (as, to get a *splinter* of wood into one's hand; "Into fiery *splinters* leapt the lance," Tennyson's "Princess," v. 483; "looking-glasses . . . shivered into ten thousand *splinters*," Steele, in "Spectator," 32); sometimes, a thin strip or piece of wood prepared or used for a special purpose; a splint.—**splin′ter,** *v.* **I.** *tr.* To split or break into splinters (as, "The postern gate shakes . . . it crashes — it is *splintered* by his blows": Scott's "Ivanhoe," xxix.); break off in splinters; also, to secure or support by a splint or splints, as a broken limb† (as, "I bound and *splintered* up its [a goat's] leg, which was broke": Defoe's "Robinson Crusoe," i. 5). **II.** *intr.* To be split or broken into splinters (as, "a lance that *splinter'd* like an icicle": Tennyson's "Geraint and Enid," 89); break off in splinters.—**splin′ter=proof,** *a.* Proof against the splinters of bursting shells.—**splin′ter-y,** *a.* Apt to splinter (as, *splintery* wood); characterized by the production of small splinters, as a kind of fracture in minerals; rough and jagged as from splintering (as, "The ridgy precipices . . . showed their *splintery* and rugged edges": Scott's "Anne of Geierstein," i.); also, full of splinters; also, of the nature of or resembling a splinter.

split (split), *v. t.*; *split* (also *splitted*), *splitting*. [D. *splitten*, akin to *splijten*, MLG. *splîten*, G. *spleissen*, split: cf. *splice*.] To rend or cleave lengthwise; separate or part from end to end or between layers, often forcibly or by cutting; also, to separate off by rending or cleaving lengthwise (as, to *split* a piece from a block); also, less definitely, to tear or break asunder, rend, or burst (as, "Our helpful ship was *splitted* in the midst": Shakspere's "Comedy of Errors," i. 1. 104); hence, to divide into distinct parts or portions (as, "the practice of *splitting* freeholds for the purpose of multiplying votes": Macaulay's "Hist. of Eng.," ii.); separate (a part) by such division; divide (persons) into different groups, factions, parties, etc., as by discord; separate off (a group, etc.) by such division; divide between two or more persons, etc. (as, to *split* a bottle of wine with a friend; to *split* one's votes or vote, see phrase below); separate into parts by interposing something (as, to *split* an infinitive: see *split infinitive*, under *split*, *p. a.*); also, to disclose or reveal (something secret: slang).—**to split hairs,** to make excessively fine distinctions, as in reasoning.—**to split one's votes, vote, or ticket,** to vote for different candidates for an office or for candidates of different parties, as when one has more than one vote or is voting for candidates for a number of offices; in the U. S., commonly, to vote otherwise than for a straight party ticket.—**to split the difference,** to divide equally the difference between the claims of two parties, each party yielding half, in order to effect an agreement; compromise on the basis of a concession by each side of half of something claimed.—**split,** *v. i.* To break or part lengthwise, or suffer longitudinal division; also, to become separated off by such division, as a piece or part from a whole; also, less definitely, to break asunder; part by striking on a rock, by the violence of a storm, etc., as a ship; hence, to part, divide, or separate in any way (as, "Presently they *split* into couples, drifting a little apart": Galsworthy's "Patrician," ii. 10); break up or separate through disagreement, etc. (as, a body *splits* into factions; "Seeing that the Democrats have *split*, this is more than an invitation to candidature," Drinkwater's "Abraham Lincoln," i.; a group *splits* from a party); also, to divide something with another or others (collog.); also, to split one's votes, vote, or ticket (as, "I'll plump or I'll *split* for them as treat me the handsomest": George Eliot's "Felix Holt," xi.); also, to betray confidence, or turn informer (slang: as, "Lord strike you dead on the spot, if ever you *split*," Dickens's "Great Expectations," xl.); also, to go with great speed (collog.).—**split,** *n.* The act or an act of splitting; also, a crack, rent, or fissure caused by splitting; also, a piece or part separated by or as by splitting; a strip split from an osier, used in basket-making; one of the parallel strips forming the reed of a loom; one of the thicknesses of leather into which a skin is sometimes split or cut; often, a breach or rupture in a party, etc., or between persons (as, "The *split* among the Hussites was largely due to the drift of the extremer section towards a primitive communism": H. G. Wells's "Outline of History," xxxv. § 3); a schism; a faction, party, etc., formed by a rupture or schism; also, something split, as a fish; a split vote (collog.); something combining different elements, as a drink composed of two liquors (collog.); also, a drink containing only half the usual quantity (collog.); a bottle, as of aërated water, half the usual size (collog.); also, *sing.* or *pl.*, the feat of separating the legs while sinking to the floor, until they extend at right angles to the body, as in stage performances.—**at full split,** or **full split,** or **like split,** at full speed. [Collog.]—**split,** *p. a.* That has undergone splitting; parted lengthwise; cleft; divided (as, a *split* vote or ticket: see phrase under *split*, *v. t.*); in *bot.*, deeply divided into segments; cleft.—**split infinitive,** in *gram.*, a simple infinitive with a modifier between the *to* and the verb, as 'to readily understand': a usage not grammatically incorrect, but commonly avoided by careful writers.

split=saw (split′så), *n.* A kind of rip-saw.

split-tail (split′tāl), *n.* A cyprinoid fish, *Pogonichthys macrolepidotus*, of California rivers: named from the form of the caudal fin.

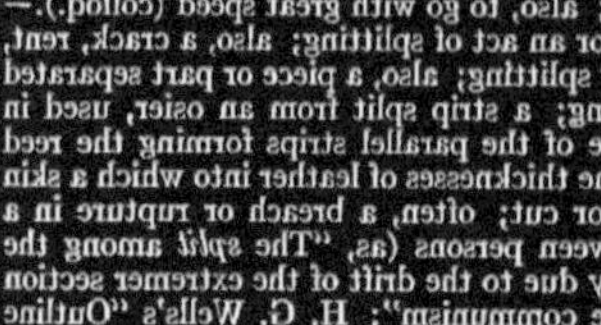
Splittail.

split-ter (split′ėr), *n.* One who or that which splits.

split-ting (split′ing), *p. a.* That splits; overpoweringly noisy, as if to split the ears; violent or severe, as a headache; very fast or rapid (collog.: as, "a *splitting* pace," Dickens's "Our Mutual Friend," iii. 15).

splodge (sploj), *n.* [Var. of *splotch*.] A splotch, or irregular spot; a splash; a blot: as, "that great *splodge* of ink" (W. De Morgan's "Joseph Vance," x.).—**splodg′y,** *a.*

splore (splōr), *n.* [Origin obscure.] A frolic; an escapade; also, a disturbance; a quarrel or fight. [Sc. and north. Eng.]

splotch (sploch), *n.* [Origin uncertain.] A large, irregular spot; a splash; a blot; a stain.—**splotch,** *v. t.* To mark with splotches.—**splotch′y,** *a.* Marked with splotches.

splurge (splėrj), *n.* [Appar. a made word, vaguely imit.] An ostentatious display; any pretentious proceeding or affair: as, to make a *splurge* in politics or in society; there was a big *splurge* at Mrs. Blank's last night. [Collog.]—**splurge,** *v. i.*; *splurged*, *splurging*. To make a splurge. [Collog.]—**splur-gy** (splėr′ji), *a.* Splurging; ostentatious. [Collog.]

splut-ter (splut′ėr), *v.* [Appar. a var. of *sputter*.] **I.** *intr.* To talk hastily and confusedly or incoherently, as in excitement or embarrassment (as, "I wish . . . I could talk to her without *spluttering*!" Arnold Bennett's "Clayhanger," ii. 1); sputter; also, to make a sputtering sound, or emit particles of something explosively, as an apple in roasting or

(variable) ḑ as d or j, ș as s or sh, ț as t or ch, ẕ as z or zh; o, F. cloche; ü, F. menu; ch, Sc. loch; ṅ, F. bonbon; ′, primary accent; ″, secondary accent; †, obsolete; <, from; +, and; =, equals. See also lists at beginning of book.

serving this purpose; also, one of a number of overlapping plates or strips of metal in armor, for protecting certain parts of the body, esp. one of the pieces of this kind for protecting the arm at the elbow (as, "The knees and feet were defended by *splints*, or thin plates of steel, ingeniously jointed upon each other": Scott's "Ivanhoe," ii.); also, an exostosis or bony enlargement of a splint-bone of a horse or an allied animal; sometimes, a splint-bone; also, splint-coal.—**splint,** *v. t.* To secure, hold in position, or support by means of a splint or splints, as a fractured bone; hence, to support as if with splints.—**splint′=ar″mor,** *n.* Armor made of splints, or overlapping plates or strips of metal.—**splint′=bone,** *n.* One of the rudimentary, splint-like metacarpal or metatarsal bones of the horse or some allied animal, closely applied one on each side of the back of each cannon-bone.—**splint′=coal,** *n.* A splintery variety of cannel-coal; also, a hard bituminous coal with a slaty structure, producing a hot fire.

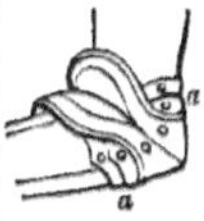

a, a, Splints.

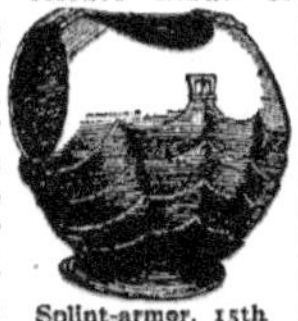
Splint-armor, 15th century.

splin-ter (splin′tėr), *n.* [ME. *splynter* = MD. D. *splinter*; related to E. *splint.*] A rough piece of wood, bone, etc., usually comparatively long, thin, and sharp, split or broken off from a main body, esp. by a violent blow (as, to get a *splinter* of wood into one's hand; "Into fiery *splinters* leapt the lance," Tennyson's "Princess," v. 483; "looking-glasses . . . shivered into ten thousand *splinters*," Steele, in "Spectator," 32); sometimes, a thin strip or piece of wood prepared or used for a special purpose; a splint.—**splin′ter,** *v.* **I.** *tr.* To split or break into splinters (as, "The postern gate shakes . . . it crashes — it is *splintered* by his blows": Scott's "Ivanhoe," xxix.); break off in splinters; also, to secure or support by a splint or splints, as a broken limb† (as, "I bound and *splintered* up its [a goat's] leg, which was broke": Defoe's "Robinson Crusoe," i. 5). **II.** *intr.* To be split or broken into splinters (as, "a lance that *splinter'd* like an icicle": Tennyson's "Geraint and Enid," 89); break off in splinters.—**splin′ter=proof,** *a.* Proof against the splinters of bursting shells.—**splin′ter-y,** *a.* Apt to splinter (as, *splintery* wood); characterized by the production of small splinters, as a kind of fracture in minerals; rough and jagged as from splintering (as, "The ridgy precipices . . . showed their *splintery* and rugged edges": Scott's "Anne of Geierstein," i.); also, full of splinters; also, of the nature of or resembling a splinter.

split (split), *v. t.*; *split* (also *splitted*), *splitting.* [D. *splitten*, akin to *splijten*, MLG. *spliten*, G. *spleissen*, split: cf. *splice.*] To rend or cleave lengthwise; separate or part from end to end or between layers, often forcibly or by cutting; also, to separate off by rending or cleaving lengthwise (as, to *split* a piece from a block); also, less definitely, to tear or break asunder, rend, or burst (as, "Our helpful ship was *splitted* in the midst": Shakspere's "Comedy of Errors," i. 1. 104); hence, to divide into distinct parts or portions (as, "the practice of *splitting* freeholds for the purpose of multiplying votes": Macaulay's "Hist. of Eng.," ii.); separate (a part) by such division; divide (persons) into different groups, factions, parties, etc., as by discord; separate off (a group, etc.) by such division; divide between two or more persons, etc. (as, to *split* a bottle of wine with a friend; to *split* one's votes or vote, see phrase below); separate into parts by interposing something (as, to *split* an infinitive: see *split infinitive*, under *split, p. a.*); also, to disclose or reveal (something secret: slang).—**to split hairs,** to make excessively fine distinctions, as in reasoning.—**to split one's votes, vote,** or **ticket,** to vote for different candidates for an office or for candidates of different parties, as when one has more than one vote or is voting for candidates for a number of offices; in the U. S., commonly, to vote otherwise than for a straight party ticket.—**to split the difference,** to divide equally the difference between the claims of two parties, each party yielding half, in order to effect an agreement; compromise on the basis of a concession by each side of half of something claimed.—**split,** *v. i.* To break or part lengthwise, or suffer longitudinal division; also, to become separated off by such division, as a piece or part from a whole; also, less definitely, to break asunder; part by striking on a rock, by the violence of a storm, etc., as a ship; hence, to part, divide, or separate in any way (as, "Presently they *split* into couples, drifting a little apart": Galsworthy's "Patrician," ii. 10); break up or separate through disagreement, etc. (as, a body *splits* into factions; "Seeing that the Democrats have *split*, this is more than an invitation to candidature," Drinkwater's "Abraham Lincoln," i.; a group *splits* from a party); also, to divide something with another or others (colloq.); also, to split one's votes, vote, or ticket (as, "I'll plump or I'll *split* for them as treat me the handsomest": George Eliot's "Felix Holt," xi.); also, to betray confidence, or turn informer (slang: as, "Lord strike you dead on the spot, if ever you *split*," Dickens's "Great Expectations," xl.); also, to go with great speed (colloq.).—**split,** *n.* The act or an act of splitting; also, a crack, rent, or fissure caused by splitting; also, a piece or part separated by or as by splitting; a strip split from an osier, used in basket-making; one of the parallel strips forming the reed of a loom; one of the thicknesses of leather into which a skin is sometimes split or cut; often, a breach or rupture in a party, etc., or between persons (as, "The *split* among the Hussites was largely due to the drift of the extremer section towards a primitive communism": H. G. Wells's "Outline of History," xxxv. § 3); a schism; a faction, party, etc., formed by a rupture or schism; also, something split, as a fish; a split vote (colloq.); something combining different elements, as a drink composed of two liquors (colloq.); also, a drink containing only half the usual quantity (colloq.); a bottle, as of aërated water, half the usual size (colloq.); also, *sing.* or *pl.*, the feat of separating the legs while sinking to the floor, until they extend at right angles to the body, as in stage performances.—**at full split,** or **full split,** or **like split,** at full speed. [Colloq.]—**split,** *p. a.* That has undergone splitting; parted lengthwise; cleft; divided (as, a *split* vote or ticket: see phrase under *split, v. t.*); in *bot.*, deeply divided into segments; cleft.—**split infinitive,** in *gram.*, a simple infinitive with a modifier between the *to* and the verb, as 'to readily understand': a usage not grammatically incorrect, but commonly avoided by careful writers.

split=saw (split′sâ), *n.* A kind of rip-saw.

split-tail (split′tāl), *n.* A cyprinoid fish, *Pogonichthys macrolepidotus*, of California rivers: named from the form of the caudal fin.

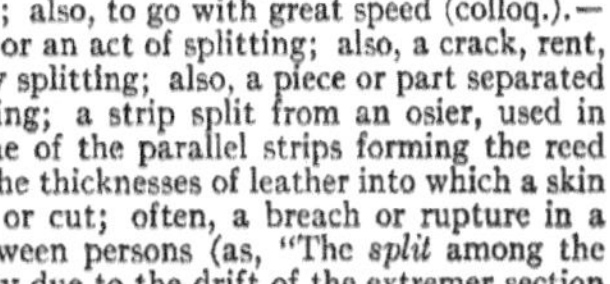
Splittail.

split-ter (split′ėr), *n.* One who or that which splits.

split-ting (split′-ing), *p. a.* That splits; overpoweringly noisy, as if to split the ears; violent or severe, as a headache; very fast or rapid (colloq.: as, "a *splitting* pace," Dickens's "Our Mutual Friend," iii. 15).

splodge (sploj), *n.* [Var. of *splotch.*] A splotch, or irregular spot; a splash; a blot: as, "that great *splodge* of ink" (W. De Morgan's "Joseph Vance," x.).—**splodg′y,** *a.*

splore (splōr), *n.* [Origin obscure.] A frolic; an escapade; also, a disturbance; a quarrel or fight. [Sc. and north. Eng.]

splotch (sploch), *n.* [Origin uncertain.] A large, irregular spot; a splash; a blot; a stain.—**splotch,** *v. t.* To mark with splotches.—**splotch′y,** *a.* Marked with splotches.

splurge (splėrj), *n.* [Appar. a made word, vaguely imit.] An ostentatious display; any pretentious proceeding or affair: as, to make a *splurge* in politics or in society; there was a big *splurge* at Mrs. Blank's last night. [Colloq.]—**splurge,** *v. i.*; *splurged, splurging.* To make a splurge. [Colloq.]—**splur-gy** (splėr′ji), *a.* Splurging; ostentatious. [Colloq.]

splut-ter (splut′ėr), *v.* [Appar. a var. of *sputter.*] **I.** *intr.* To talk hastily and confusedly or incoherently, as in excitement or embarrassment (as, "I wish . . . I could talk to her without *spluttering!*" Arnold Bennett's "Clayhanger," ii. 1); sputter; also, to make a sputtering sound, or emit particles of something explosively, as an apple in roasting or

(variable) ḏ as d or j, ş as s or sh, ţ as t or ch, ẓ as z or zh; o, F. cloche; ü, F. menu; ċh, Sc. loch; ṅ, F. bonbon; ′, primary accent; ″, secondary accent; †, obsolete; <, from; +, and; =, equals. See also lists at beginning of book.

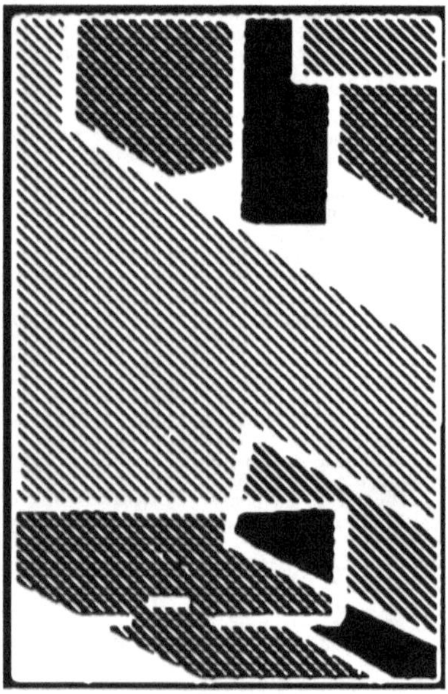

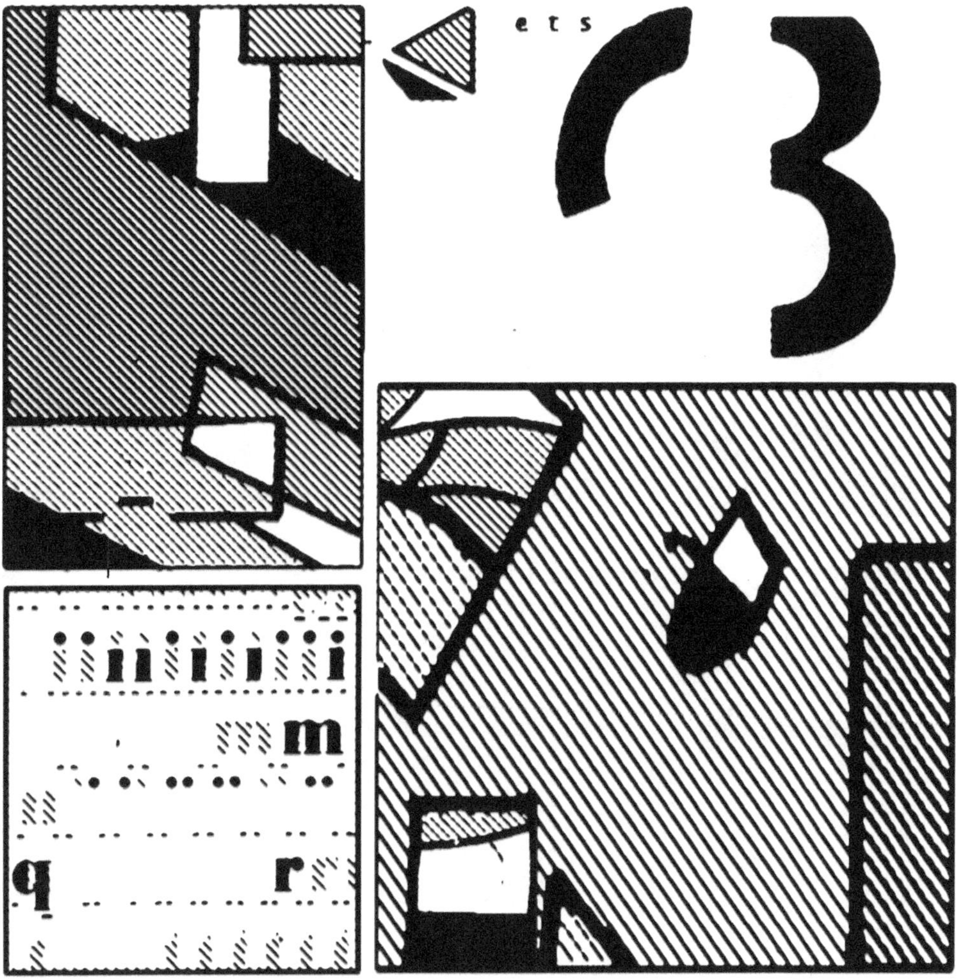
e t s

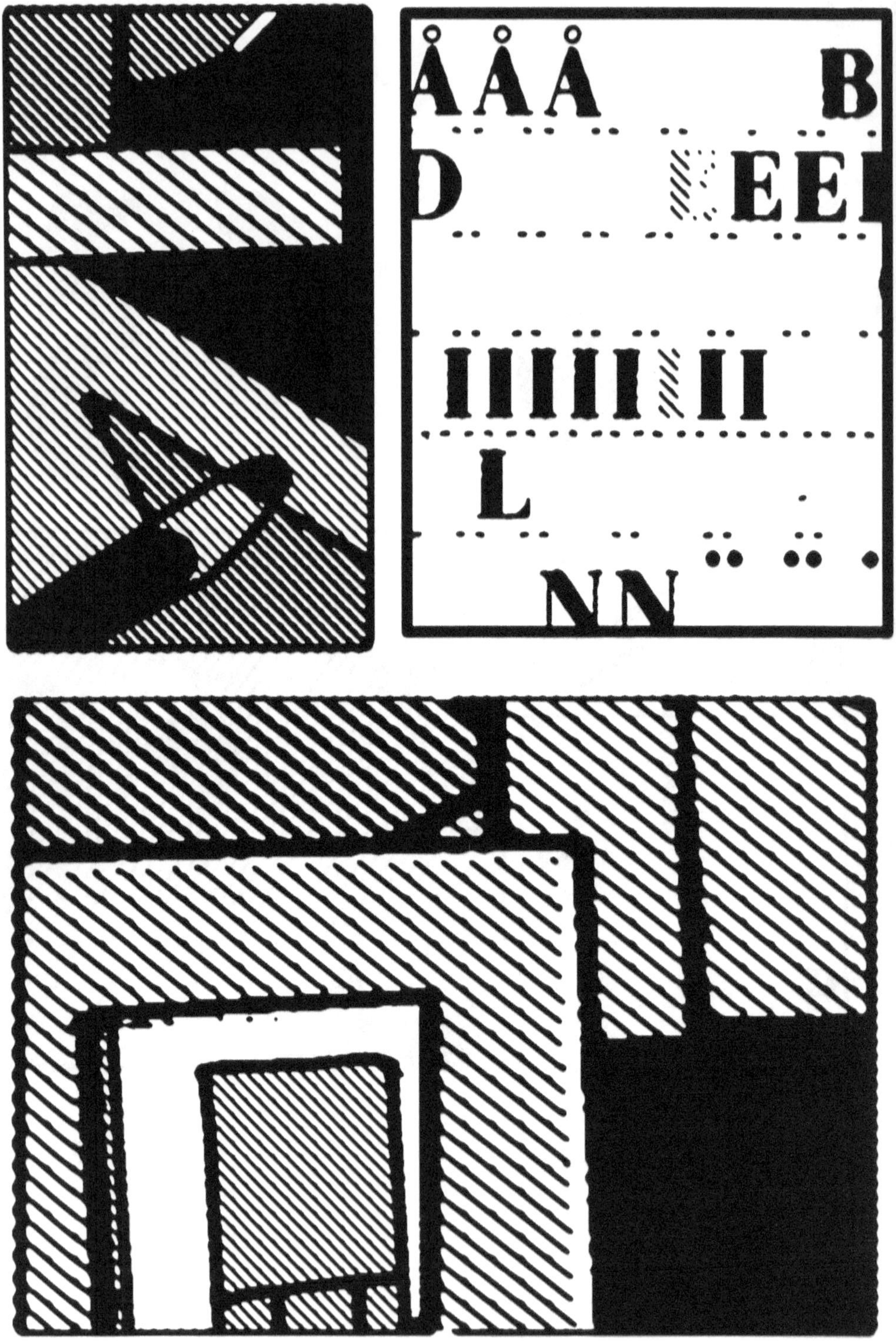
ÅÅÅ B
D EE
IIIII II
L
NN

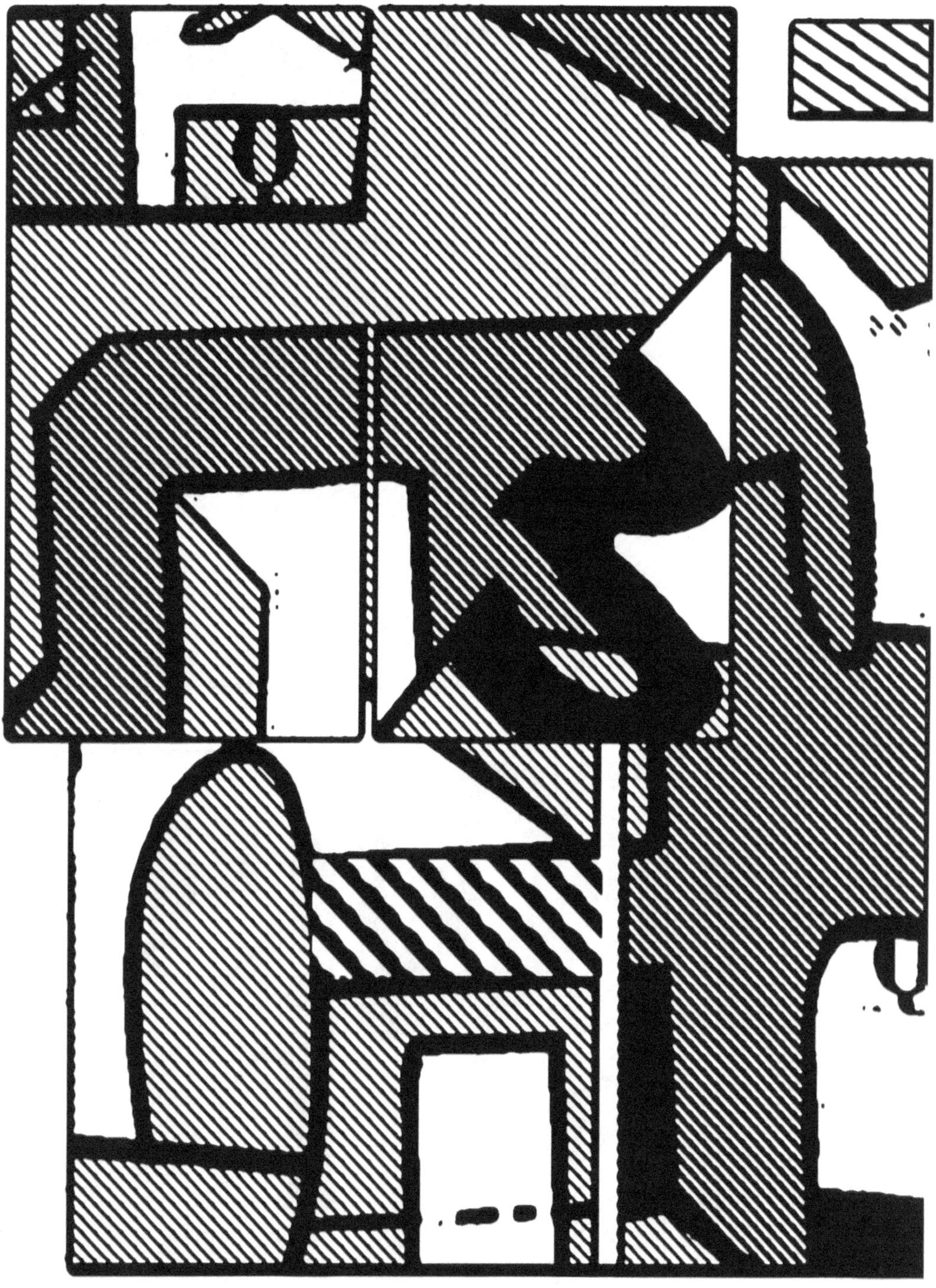

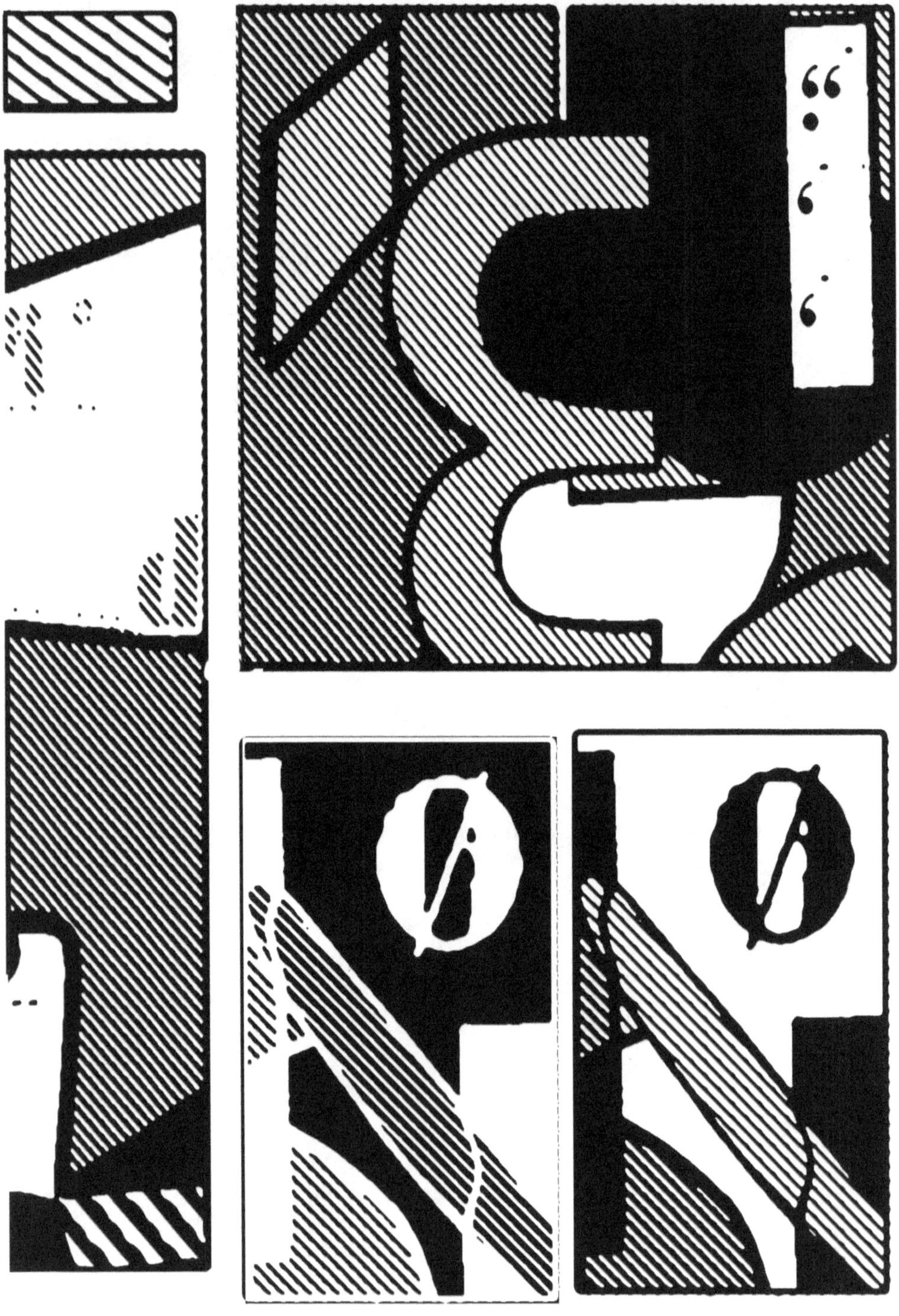

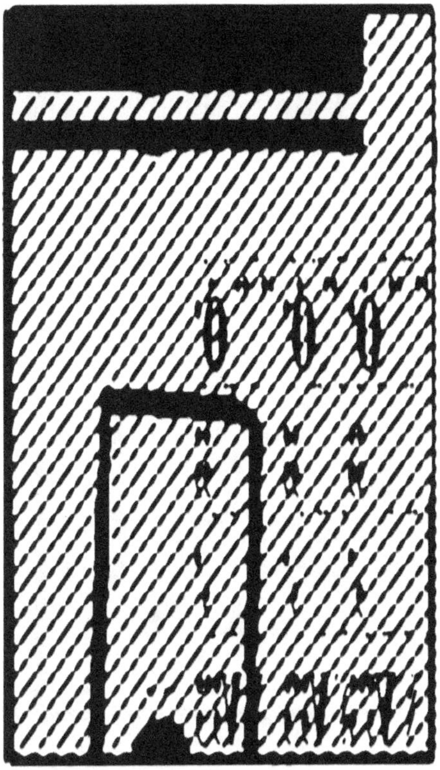

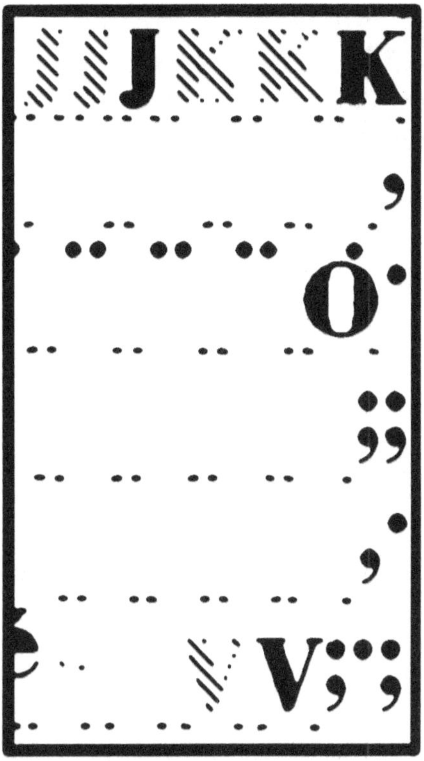
J K
Ö
V

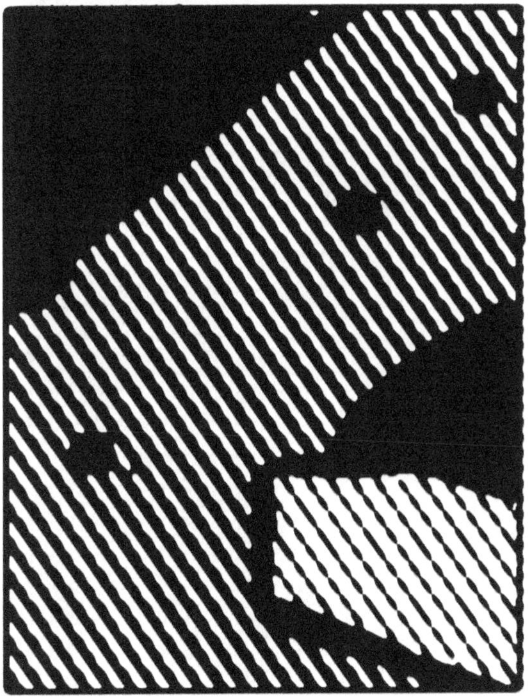

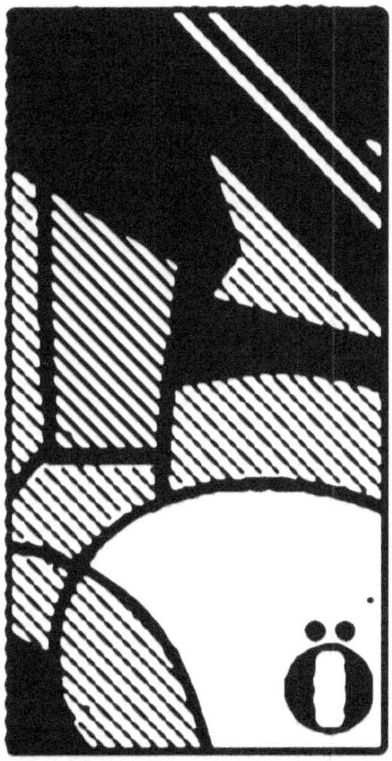
Ö

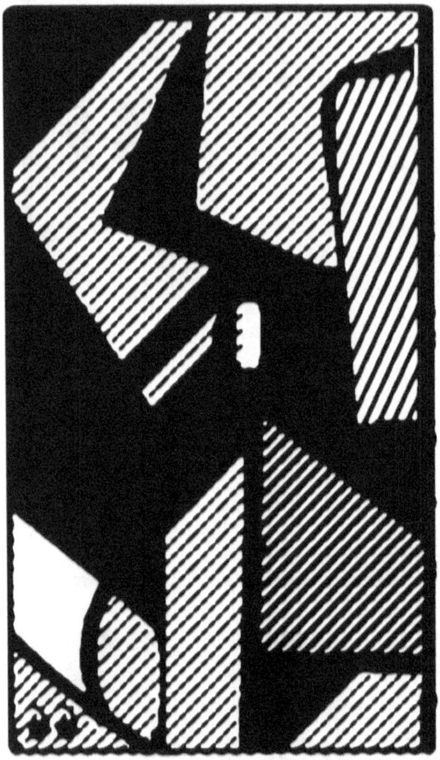

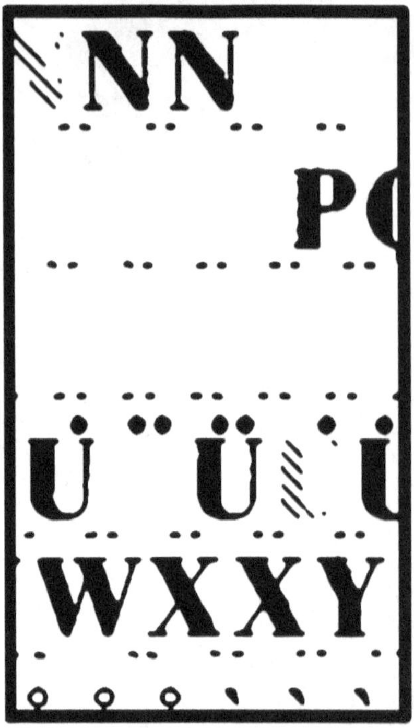
NN
WXXY

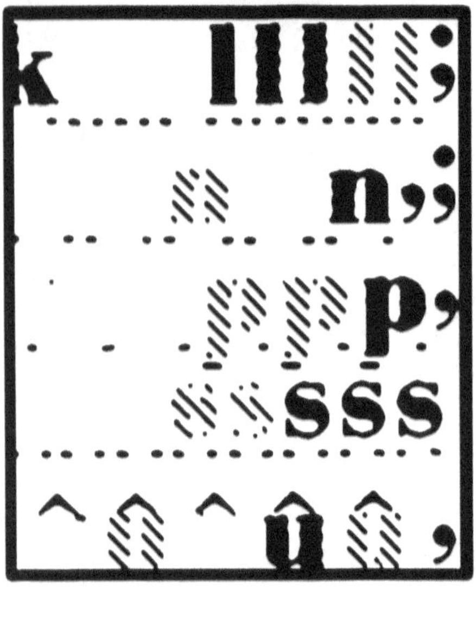
k lll;
n,;
p,
sss

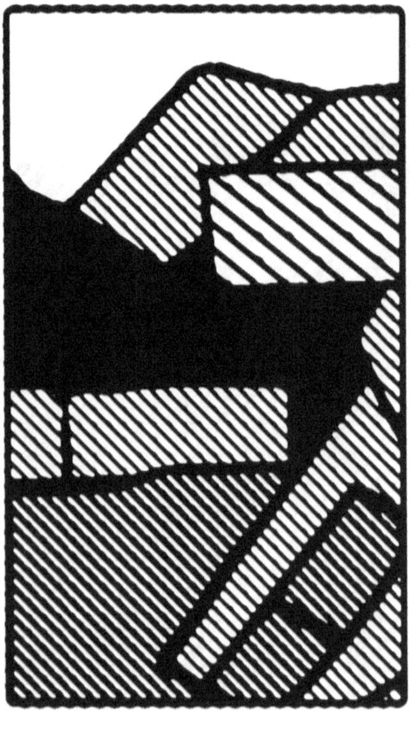

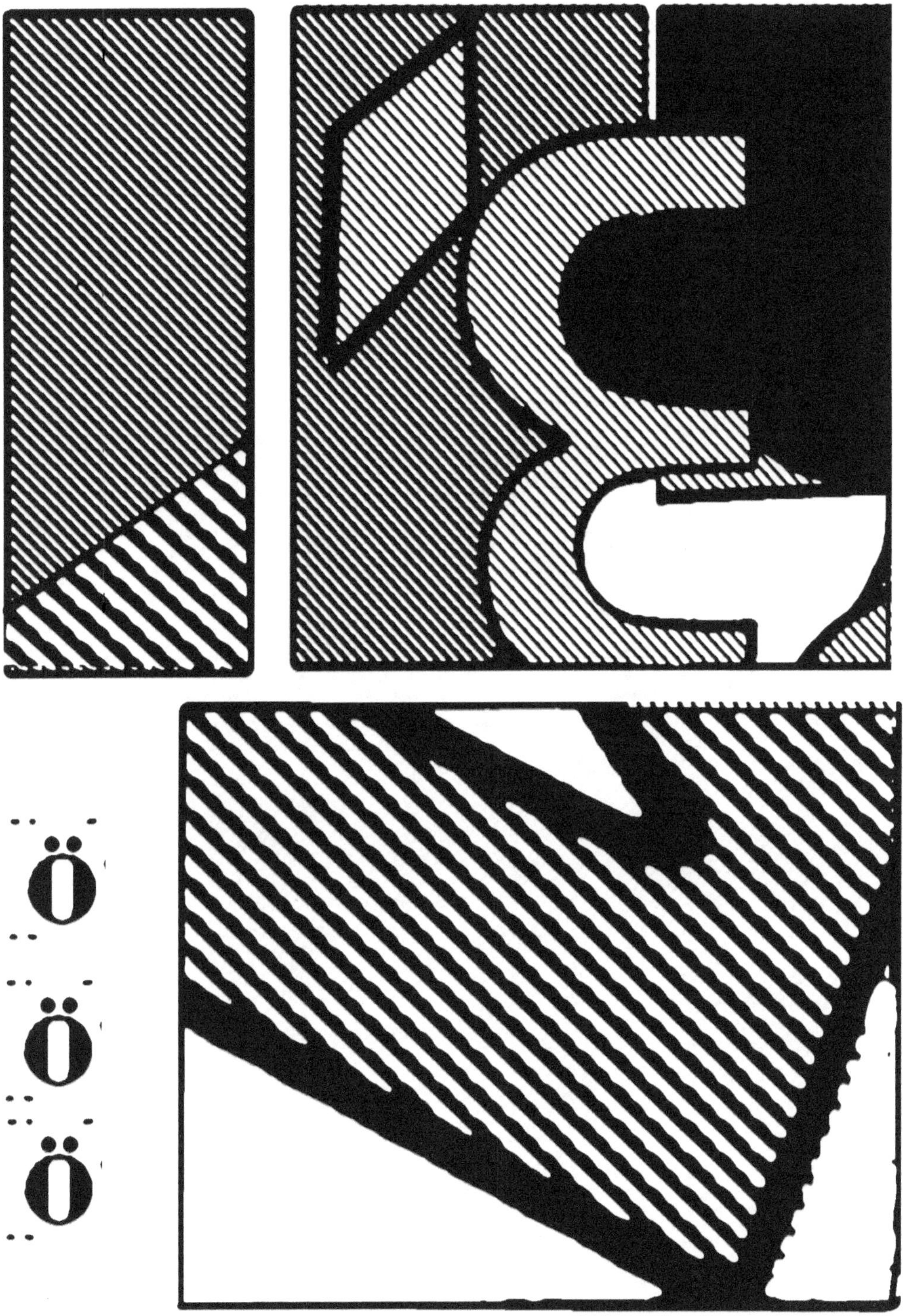

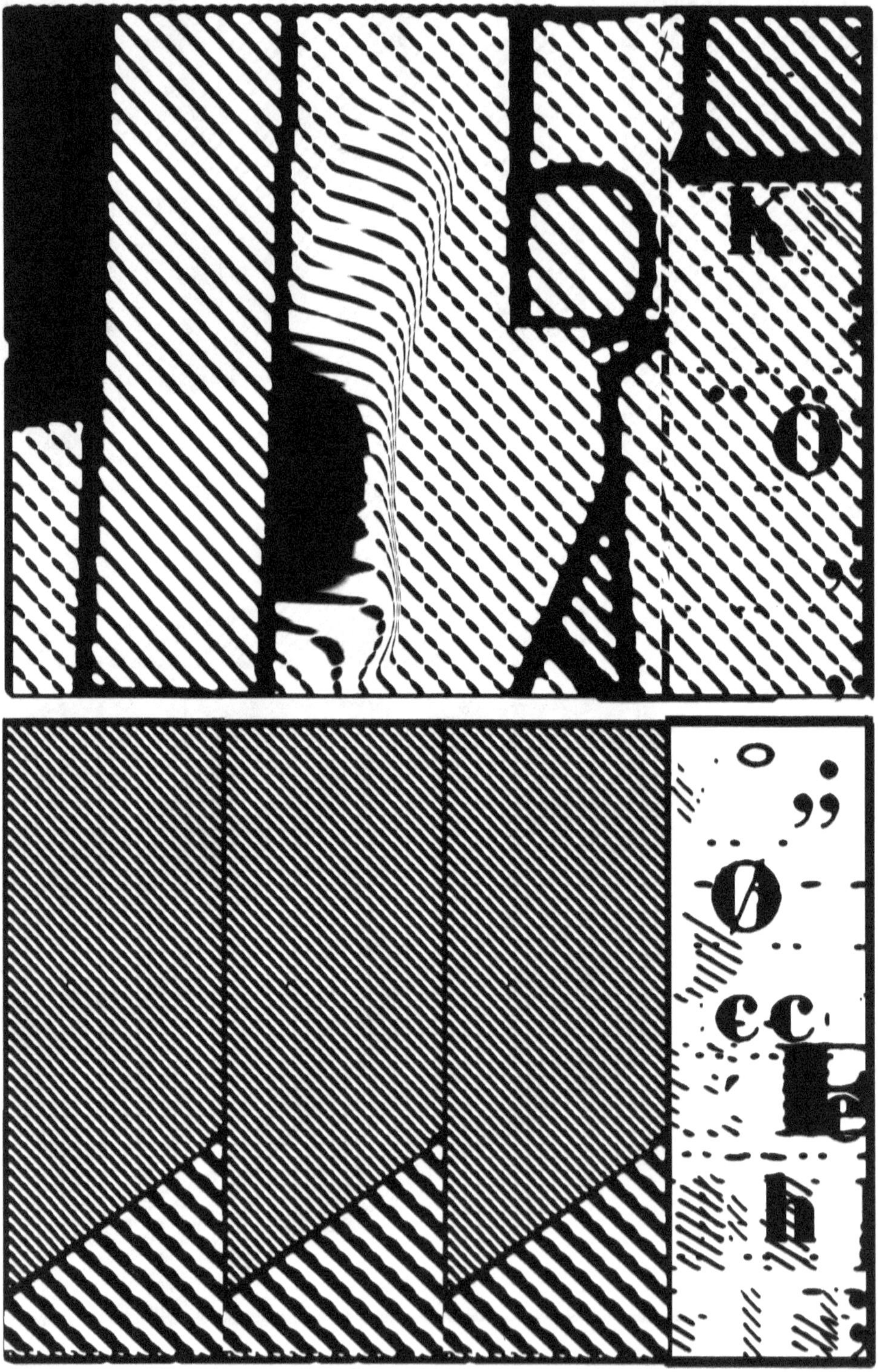

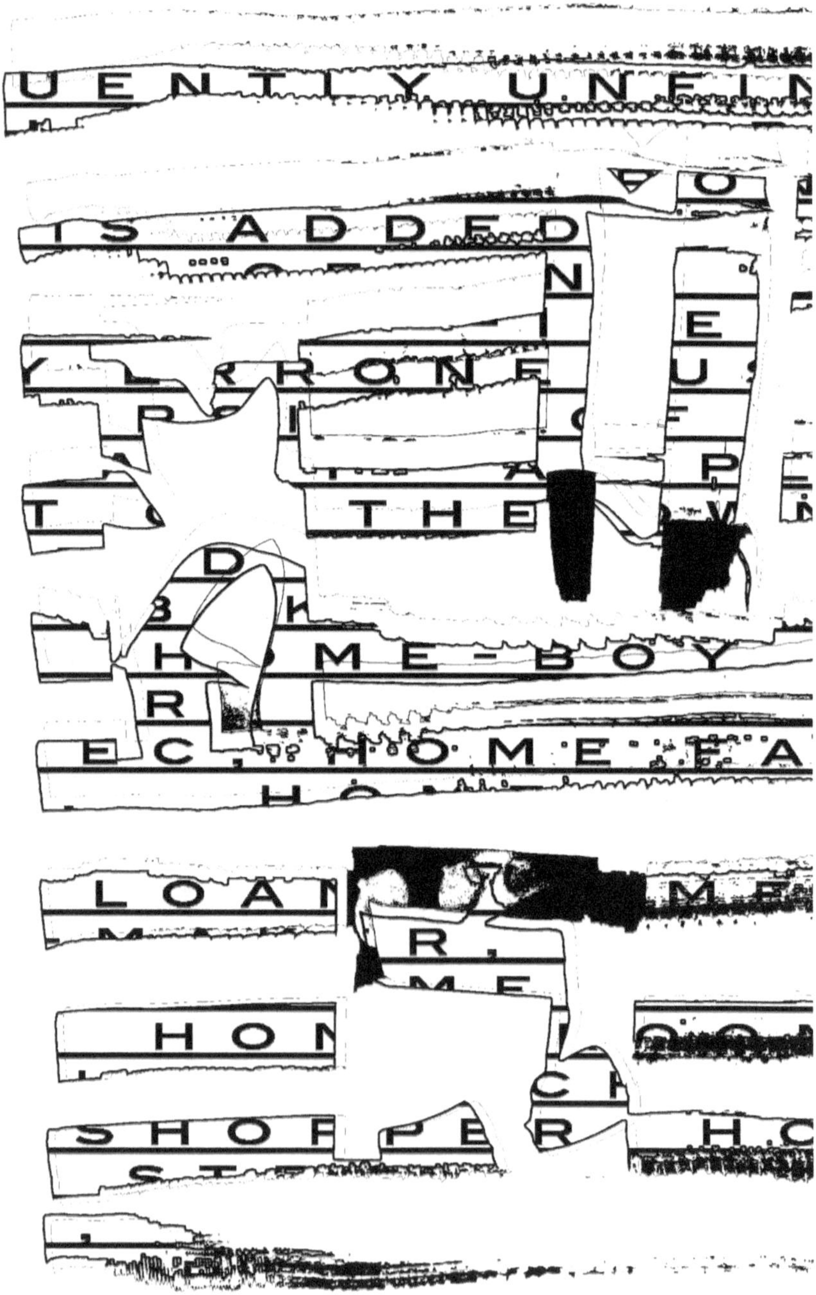
UENTLY UNFIN
IS ADDED
YERRONE
THE
HOME-BOY
EC,HOME FA
LOAN
HON
SHOPPER H.C

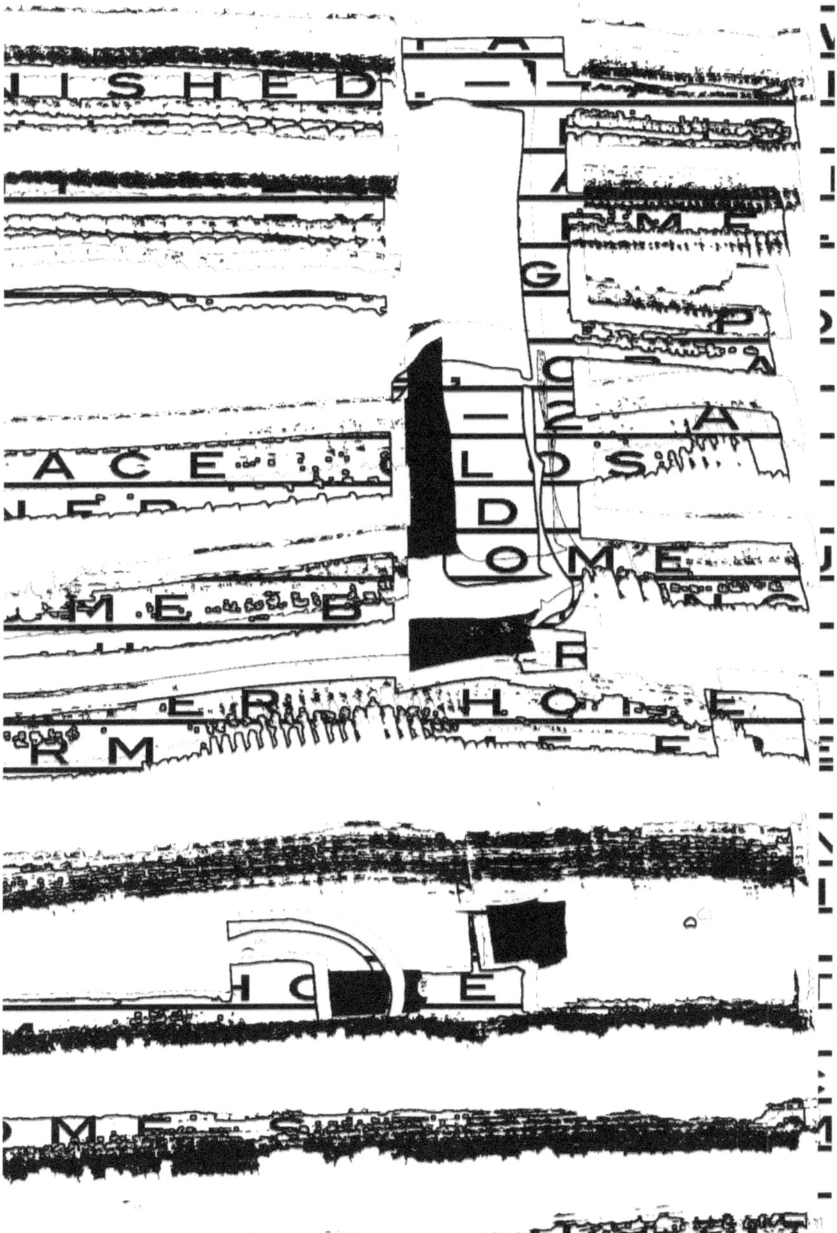
NISHED
ACE
LOS
D
OME
ME B
R
ER HOME
RM
HOME

3. b. Perusing a hymn-book by the light of a pine s. 1862.

attrib. and *Comb.*: **s. net, -netting** *Naut.*, a net or netting of small rope spread on board a warship during action to protect the men from falling splinters; **-new** *a.* (*dial.*) quite new.

Splinter (spli·ntəɹ), *v.* 1582. [f. the sb.] 1. *trans.* To break or split into splinters or long narrow pieces, or in such a way as to leave a rough jagged end or projections. †2. = SPLINT *v.* 2. Also with *up.* –1720. 3. *intr.* To split 1625. b. *poet.* To pierce *through* in the form of, or after the manner of, splinters 1821.

1. A strong bull..splintered with his horns the upper post 1806. *fig.* The Courtier, Scholler, Souldier, all in him; All dasht and splinterd thence SHAKS. 3. b. The moon..Splinters through the broken glass CLARE. Hence **Spli·nterless** *a.* that will not s.

Splinter-bar. Also **splinter bar.** 1765. [SPLINTER *sb.*] 1. A swingle-tree or whipple-tree. 2. A cross-bar in a carriage, coach, etc., which is fixed across the head of the shafts, and to which the traces are attached 1794.

Spli·nter-proof, *sb.* and *a.* 1805. [See PROOF *a.*] *Mil.* A. *sb.* A structure serving for protection from the splinters of bursting shells. B. *adj.* Of sufficient strength to ward off the splinters of bursting shells 1834.

Splintery (spli·ntəri), *a.* 1796. [f. SPLINTER *sb.* and *v.* + -Y [1].] 1. *Min.* Of fracture: Characterized by the production of small splinters. 2. Of stone, minerals, etc.: Liable to split into splinters; breaking or separating easily into splinters; *spec.* having a splintery fracture 1807. b. Of rocks, etc.: Marked by splintering; rough or jagged 1829. 3. Of the nature of a splinter; resembling a splinter in shape or form 1839. 4. Full of splinters 1857.

Split (split), *sb.* 1597. [f. SPLIT *v.* and *ppl. a.*] 1. A narrow break or opening made by splitting; a cleft, crack, rent, or chink; a fissure. b. *techn.* An angular groove cut on glass vessels 1850. 2. A piece of wood separated or formed by splitting. Now *U.S.* 1617. b. *techn.* In the leather trade, a section of a skin obtained by splitting it into several thicknesses 1858. 3. A rupture, division, or dissension in a party or sect, or between friends 1729. 4. *Mining.* A division of a ventilating air-current 1883. 5. *slang.* An informer; a detective 1812. 6. *colloq.* a. A split soda; a bottle of mineral water half the usual size 1884. b. A split roll or bun 1905. c. A split vote 1894.

The splits: the acrobatic feat of lowering oneself to the floor with the legs in a straight line 1861.

Split (split), *v.* Pa. t. and pa. pple. **split** (also †**splitted,** †**splitten**). 1590. [ad. MDu. *splitten* (Du. *splitten*, WFris. *splitte*).] I. *trans.* 1. Of storms, rocks, etc.: To break up (a ship); to cause to part asunder. Chiefly in *pass.* b. Of persons: In *pass.*, to suffer shipwreck. Also *fig.* 1602. 2. To divide longitudinally by a sharp stroke or blow; to cause to burst or give way along the grain or length; to cleave or rend 1593. b. *Naut.* Of wind: To rend or tear (a sail). Also of persons or a vessel: To have (a sail) rent or torn by the wind. 1625. 3. *fig.* a. Of violent grief or pain 1594. b. Of loud noise 1602. c. Of excessive laughter 1687. 4. a. To divide or apportion to, or between, two or more persons 1670. b. To divide or break up into separate parts or portions 1706. c. To divide or separate (persons) into parties, factions, groups, etc. 1712. d. To divide or separate by the interposition of something 1824. 5. *slang.* To disclose, reveal, let out 1850.

1. Our helpefull ship was splitted in the midst SHAKS. 2. At Cajeta, in Italy, a mountain was split in this manner by an earthquake GOLDSM. *fig.* Blow, and s. thyself SHAKS. b. We split our maintop-sail 1748. 3. a. Let sorrow s. my heart, if euer I Did hate thee SHAKS. b. The air was split with shrill outcries 1865. c. He laughed ready to s. his sides 1809. 4. a. Not worth splitting a guinea;..toss who shall pay for both DICKENS. b. He..falls to splitting his Text most methodically 1706. c. They are easily split into parties by intrigue 1861. d. Mrs. Williamson splits her infinitives 1895.

Phrases. *S. me* (or *my windpipe*), used as an imprecation. *To s. a hair* or *hairs, straws, words*, to make fine or subtle distinctions, to be over-subtle or captious. *To s. the difference*, to halve an amount in dispute between two parties; to take the mean between two sums or quantities; to compromise on this basis.

II. *intr.* †1. As predicate to *all*: To go to pieces –1611. 2. Of a ship: To part or break by striking on a rock or shoal, or by the violence of a storm 1593. b. Of persons: To suffer shipwreck in this manner. Freq. *fig.* 1610. 3. To part asunder, to burst, to form a fissure or fissures, esp. in a longitudinal direction 1625. b. Used hyperbolically to denote the effect of excessive laughter, pain, or repletion 1677. c. To admit of being cleft 1846. 4. To part, divide, or separate in some way 1712. b. To break up into separate groups or parties 1824. 5. To break up *into* factions, sects, etc.; to separate through disagreement or difference of opinion; to fall out or disagree 1730. b. *slang.* To break or quarrel *with* a person 1835. 6. *slang.* To turn evidence or informer; to peach; to betray confidence 1795.

1. *Mids. N.* I. ii. 32. 2. This is the most dangerous Rock to s. upon, in all the Archipelago 1718. b. Mercy on vs. We s., we s. SHAKS. 3. b. I laugh'd till I thought I should s. SWIFT. My head was like to s. 1756. c. The wood splits clean and easy 1846. 4. At the point where Hermon splits into its two parallel ranges 1856. 5. 'Don't let us s. on a small point of detail,' he began 1890. 6. If anybody is to s., I had better be the person DICKENS.

Split-, the verbal stem in combs., as **s.-farthing** *a.*, mean, miserly.

Split (split), *ppl. a.* 1648. [f. SPLIT *v.*] 1. That has undergone the process of splitting; divided in this manner; riven, cleft. b. Of a surface: Exposed by splitting 1715. c. *Bot.* Cleft or divided very deeply 1832. 2. Separated, divided, parted, or apportioned in some way 1839.

Special collocations: **s. brilliant,** a brilliant the foundation squares of which are divided horizontally into two triangular facets; **s. infinitive** (see INFINITIVE); **s. peas,** peas shelled, dried, and split for making pease-puddings, soup, etc.; **-pin,** a pin or cotter split at one end; **-ring,** a metal ring split spirally, on which keys, etc. may be hung; **s. second**(**s,** applied to chronographs having two independent centre second hands, one under the other; **-shot, -stroke,** in various games, a shot or stroke which sends in divergent directions two or more balls placed in contact; **-tail,** (*a*) a Californian fish of the carp family; (*b*) the pintail duck.

Splitter (spli·təɹ). 1623. [f. SPLIT *v.* + -ER [1].] One who, or that which, splits or cleaves, in various senses 1648. b. *spec.* One employed in splitting fish 1623.

Splodge (splǫdʒ). 1854. [Imitative.] A thick, heavy, or clumsy splotch. Hence **Splo·dgy** *a.*

Splosh (splǫʃ), *adv.* [Contamination of *splash* and *plop.*] With a heavy fall or blow.

Splotch (splǫtʃ), *sb.* 1601. [perh. imitative.] A large irregular spot or patch of light, colour, or the like. Hence **Splotch** *v. trans.* to cover with splotches; to splash or stain in patches. **Splo·tchy** *a.* covered with or having the appearance of splotches.

Splurge (splɔ̈ɹdʒ), *sb.* *U.S.* 1834. [Imitative.] 1. An ostentatious display or effort. 2. A heavy splash or downpour 1879. So **Splurge** *v.* *U.S.* *intr.* (*a*) to make an ostentatious display, to show off; (*b*) to splash heavily.

Splutter (splʊ·təɹ), *sb.* 1677. [Imitative.] 1. A noise or fuss. b. Violent and confused declamation, discourse, or talk; an instance of this 1688. 2. A loud or violent sputter or splash 1815.

1. b. Dinner..with a confused s. of German to the neighbours on my right HUXLEY. 2. A couple of ducks..made away with a great s. 1873.

Splutter (splʊ·təɹ), *v.* 1728. [f. prec.] 1. *trans.* To utter hastily and indistinctly 1729. 2. a. To scatter in small splashes 1835. b. To bespatter (a person) 1869. 3. *intr.* To talk or speak hastily and confusedly 1728. 4. To make a sputtering sound or sounds 1818. 5. Of a pen: To scatter ink in writing 1837. 6. To fly in small splashes or pieces 1849.

1. King James spluttered out his alarm at Jesuit plots in clumsy Latin 1870. 4. Waning candles s. in the sockets 1860.

Spode (spōᵘd). 1893. The surname of a maker of china, Josiah *Spode* (1754–1827), used *attrib.* to designate ware made by him. Also *ellipt.*, = Spode-ware.

‖**Spodium** (spōᵘ·diɒ̈m). Now *rare.* late ME. [L., ad. Gr. σπόδιον, = σποδός ashes.]

P.
[f. LEUCO-
, identical
) 1844.
mod.L., a.
f. λευκός.]
1887. [f.
Chem. An
s a decom-
[f. late Gr.
φαίνεσθαι
eflexions.]
d sodium.
Gr. λευκο-
φλεγματ-
lency, de-
ody -1732.
. [f. Gr.
A mucous
gans; the
a. Gr., f.
nism. b.
the body.
Gr. λευκός
albino.
pl. form
leudes, a.
kish king-
VANT a.;
ouchancy:
F. levant,
the point
essed le'-
es of the
e Mediter-
ntries ad-
ng up the
23. 3. =
= 'east-,
sense 1 b,
feathers,
. a. Forth
P.L. x. 704.
nsf. use of
nt, to bee
(Cotgr.).]
ake a bet
is lost.
F. levant,
.] Law.
t. 'rising
ANT sb.²]
esp. of a
2. trans.
. me l, a
va·nter²,
LEVANT
. 1 (rare).
. 2. A
Mediter-
1649. [f.
pertain-
n. Also,
s of the
the Le-
ve of the
very rich
ionem, f.
on of the
evied; a
L., f. as
†2. Surg.
atory (in
. masc.;
LIEVE v.]

†Leve, *v.*¹ [OE. (Anglian) *léfan*, (WS.) *lýfan*, f. OTeut. **lauƀ*- LEAVE *sb.*] To allow, permit. Also (esp. of God or Christ), to grant. -1513.

And leue me nevere swich a cas be-falle CHAUCER.

†Leve, *v.*² [OE. (Anglian) *léfan*, (WS.) *líefan*, short f. *gélefan*, *gelíefan*; see BELIEVE.] 1. *intr.* = BELIEVE I. 1. -1535. 2. *trans.* = BELIEVE II. 1-3. -1570.

Leve, obs. f. LEAF, LIEF, LIVE *v.*

Levee (lɪ̆vī·, le·vi), *sb.*¹ *U.S.* Also **levy**. 1718. [a. F. *levée*, fem. of *levé*, pa. pple. of *lever* to raise.] 1. An embankment to prevent the overflow of a river. 2. A landing-place, pier, quay 1842.

Levee (le·vi), *sb.*² Also **†levy, levée**. 1672. [ad. F. *levé*, var. of *lever* rising (subst. use of *lever* inf.); cf. COUCHEE. The pronunc. (lɪ̆vī·) or (levī·) is preferred in the U.S.] †1. The action of rising, *spec.* from one's bed -1827. 2. A reception of visitors on rising from bed; a morning assembly held by a prince, etc. 1672. b. In Great Britain and Ireland, an assembly held (in the early afternoon) by the sovereign or his representative, at which men only are received 1760. c. A miscellaneous assemblage of visitors, irrespective of the time of day; applied (*U.S.*) to the President's receptions 1766. †3. The company assembled at a levee -1771.

2. b. He goes to the Levée once a year THACKERAY. c. The evening l. of the Minister of the Home Department 1831.

Levee (lɪ̆vī·), *v.*¹ *U.S.* 1858. [f. LEVEE *sb.*¹] *trans.* To raise levees or embankments along (a river) or in (a district).

†Le·vee, *v.*² 1725. [f. LEVEE *sb.*²] *trans.* To attend the levees of; to pursue at levees -1770.

Leveful(le, var. of LEEFUL.

Level (le·vĕl), *sb.* ME. [a. OF. *livel*, later *nivel*, mod.F. *niveau*;—pop.L. **libellum* = class.L. *libella*, dim. of *libra* balance.]

I. 1. An instrument which indicates a line parallel to the plane of the horizon, used in testing the relation to the horizontal of a surface to which it is applied. Also *fig.* †2. Level condition or position; horizontality -1726. 3. Position as marked by a horizontal line; an imaginary line or plane at right angles to the plumb-line, considered as determining the position of one or more points or surfaces 1535. 4. Position, plane, standard, in social, moral, or intellectual matters 1609. 5. A level or flat surface 1634. 6. A level tract of land; applied *spec.* (as a proper name) to *Bedford L.* or *the Great L.* in the fen district of England; *The Levels* (formerly *The L.*), the tract including Hatfield Chase in Yorkshire; etc. 1623. 7. *Mining.* a. A nearly horizontal drift, passage, or gallery in a mine. 1606. b. A 'drift' for drainage purposes.

1. *fig.* We steal by lyne and leuell, and 't like your grace *Temp.* IV. i. 239. 2. Phr. *On, upon a l.*, in a horizontal line or plane. *The l.*, the horizontal; *in l.*, on the ground (cf. L. *in plano*). 3. Phr. *On a l. with*: in the same horizontal plane as. *To find one's or its l.*: said of persons or things arriving at their proper place with respect to those around or connected with them. †*To hold its l. with*: to be on an equality with (Shaks.). 4. The calamity..had reduced all to one l. 1832. 5. He..Came on the shining levels of the lake TENNYSON. *The l.*, the earth's surface (*rare*).

II. From the vb. †1. a. The action of aiming a gun, etc., aim -1718. †b. That which is aimed at; a mark -1600. †c. *fig.* Aim, purpose, design -1605. 2. (*Surveying*) †*To make a l. of*: to ascertain the differences of elevation in (a piece of land). Also, *to take a l.* = LEVEL *v.* I. 4 (absol.). 1693.

1. As if that name shot from the dead leuell of a Gun, Did murder her *Rom. & Jul.* III. iii. 103.

Comb.: **l.-error**, 'the microscopic deviation of the axis of a transit instrument from the horizontal position' (Smyth); **-range** (in *Gunnery*), 'the same as Point-blank Shot, or the Distance that a piece of Ordinance carries a Ball in a direct Line' (Phillips); **-staff** = *levelling staff* (LEVELLING *vbl. sb.*).

Level (le·vĕl), *a.*, *adv.* 1538. [f. LEVEL *sb.*]

A. *adj.* 1. Having an even surface; 'not having one part higher than another' (J.). b. *fig.* Of quantities: Expressed in whole numbers. Of a race: Even. 1826. 2. Horizontal; at right angles to the plumb-line 1559. 3. On

a level *with* something else. Also *fig.*, on an equality *with*; readily accessible or intelligible *to*. 1559. 4. Of two or more things: Situated in the same level or plane. Also *fig.* 1601. 5. Lying, moving, or directed in a (more or less) horizontal plane; esp. *poet.*, e.g. of the rays of the sun when it is low 1667. 6. Of even quality, tone, or style; of even tenor 1655. 7. †a. 'Equipoised, steady' (Schmidt). See 2 *Hen. IV*, II. i. 123, *Twel. N.* II. iv. 32. b. Well balanced: said of the head, etc. Orig. *U.S.* 1870. 8. Plain, point-blank. KEATS. 9. *One's l. best*: one's very best; one's utmost (*colloq.* or *slang*; orig. *U.S.*) 1851.

1. Along the l. Seas they flew POPE. 2. Phr. *L. lines* (Shipbuilding), lines determining the shape of a ship's body horizontally, or square from the middle line of the ship. 3. We should..apply ourselves to that which is l. to our capacities BUTLER. *L. crossing*: a place at which a road and a railway, or two railways, cross each other at the same l. 5. The last l. rays were glittering on the stream 1832. 6. A leisured and l. life 1899. 7. b. To tell a woman her head is l. is apparently a compliment in America 1870. Hence **Le·vel-ly** *adv.*, **-ness.**

†B. *adv.* With direct aim; on a level *with* -1659.

As l. as the cannon to his blank *Haml.* IV. i. 42.

Level (le·vĕl), *v.* Inflected **levelled, levelling** (*U.S.* **leveled, leveling**). ME. [f. LEVEL *sb.*]

I. 1. *trans.* To make level or even; to remove inequalities in the surface of. †Also, to spread levelly. 1440. b. *Dyeing.* To make (colour) even 1874. 2. To place on the same level or plane. Also *fig.* 1563. 3. To bring to the level of the ground; to lay low, to raze 1614. b. To knock (a person) down 1760. c. *transf.* and *fig.* To reduce or remove (inequalities) 1642. 4. *Surveying.* To ascertain the differences of level in (a piece of land); to 'run' a section of; hence, to lay out. Also *absol.* or *intr.*, to take levels. 1598.

1. Phr. *To l. out*: to extend on a level; †*fig.* to contrive, procure (an opportunity). The road that grandeur levels for his coach EMERSON. 2. Gunpowder leveled peasant and prince W. PHILLIPS. Phr. *To l.* (a person or thing) *with* (now rare), *to*, †*unto*: to put on a level, equality, or par with. Also occas. *intr.* for *pass.* to be on a par with; With such Accomodation and besort As leuels with her breeding SHAKS. *To l. up, down*: to bring up, down to the level of something; Sir, your levellers wish to l. *down* as far as themselves; but they cannot bear levelling *up* to themselves JOHNSON. 3. Phr. *To l. to* or *with the ground, in the dust.* c. The mercantile spirit levels all distinctions LAMB.

II. 1. To aim (a missile weapon); to lay (a gun) 1530. †b. To shoot (a missile) *out* (*of* a weapon) -1664. c. To direct (one's looks); to dart (rays) 1594. d. *fig.* To aim, direct, point 1576. 2. *absol.* or *intr.* To aim with a weapon; †*occas.* said of the weapon. Also freq. *transf.* and *fig.* Somewhat *arch.* 1500. †b. To guess *at* -1596.

1. Phr. *To l. one's aim*; Each at the Head Level'd his deadly aime MILT. b. [He] leuelled a quarrel out of a cros bowe STOW. d. This fellow's writings ..are levelled at the clergy FIELDING. 2. To leuell at perfection 1626. b. *Merch. V.* I. ii. 41.

†Level-coil. 1594. [Corruptly ad. Fr. phr. (*faire*) *lever le cul* (*à quelqu'un*), to make a person rise from his seat (*lever* to raise, *cul* buttock). The Fr. name of the game is *lève-cul.*] A rough, noisy game, formerly played at Christmas, in which each player in turn is driven from his seat and supplanted by another. Hence = riotous sport, noisy riot; phr. *to keep le·vel-coil.* Also *advb.* = turn and turn about. -1684.

Leveller (le·vĕlər). Also (now *U.S.*) **leveler.** 1598. [f. LEVEL *v.* + -ER ¹.] 1. One who or that which levels. 2. One who would level all differences of position or rank among men 1607. 3. *pl.* Name of a rebel secret society in Ireland in the 18th c. 1762.

1. Sleep is equally a l. with death JOHNSON.

Levelling (le·vĕliŋ), *vbl. sb.* Also (now *U.S.*) **leveling.** 1580. [f. LEVEL *v.* + -ING ¹.] 1. Aiming, aim. 2. The action of bringing to a uniform horizontal surface, or of placing in a horizontal position by means of a level. Also *fig.* 1598. 3. *Surveying.* 'The art of determining the relative heights of points on the surface of the ground as referred to a hypothetical surface which cuts the direction of gravity

everywhere
1812.
Comb.: l.-
essentially o
in surveying
with a vane
(*Photogr.*),
plate in a ho
Le·vellin
ing. 1635.
pertaining
Leven.
ELEVENTH
Leven,
Lever (l
AF. **lever*
raise. Th
of iron or
some heav
handspike,
or rod -16
structure o
fixed at o
acted on
tending to
1648.
The force
called the *w*
pose the *pow*
second, or *th*
crum, the w
three.
3. *spec.* a.
(*b*) a starti
the barrel
c. In *Den*
1846. d.
1. *fig.* Jeal
attrib. an
longing to a
as a l., work
2. Special
capement
the connexi
made by m
with a l. e
hornbeam o
Lever (
intr. To a
To lift, p
with a leve
Lever,
Leverag
+ -AGE.]
arrangeme
concr. a sy
lever; the
use of a le
plishing a
2. Phr. *L.*
of a force fr
men the mo
Leveret
levret(t)e,
young har
transf. an
spiritless p
Japanese
leveret's fu
2. b. Arro
†Le·vese
léaf LEAF
canopy or
†Levet.
raise.] A
rouse sold
-1705.
Leviabl
+ -ABLE.]
be levied.
called upo
a thing: T
Leviath
a. Heb. *li*
(real or i
mentioned
= a ship o
vast powe
xxvii. 1.)
commonw
attrib. or
recently to
1. There i
to take his
3. The mul

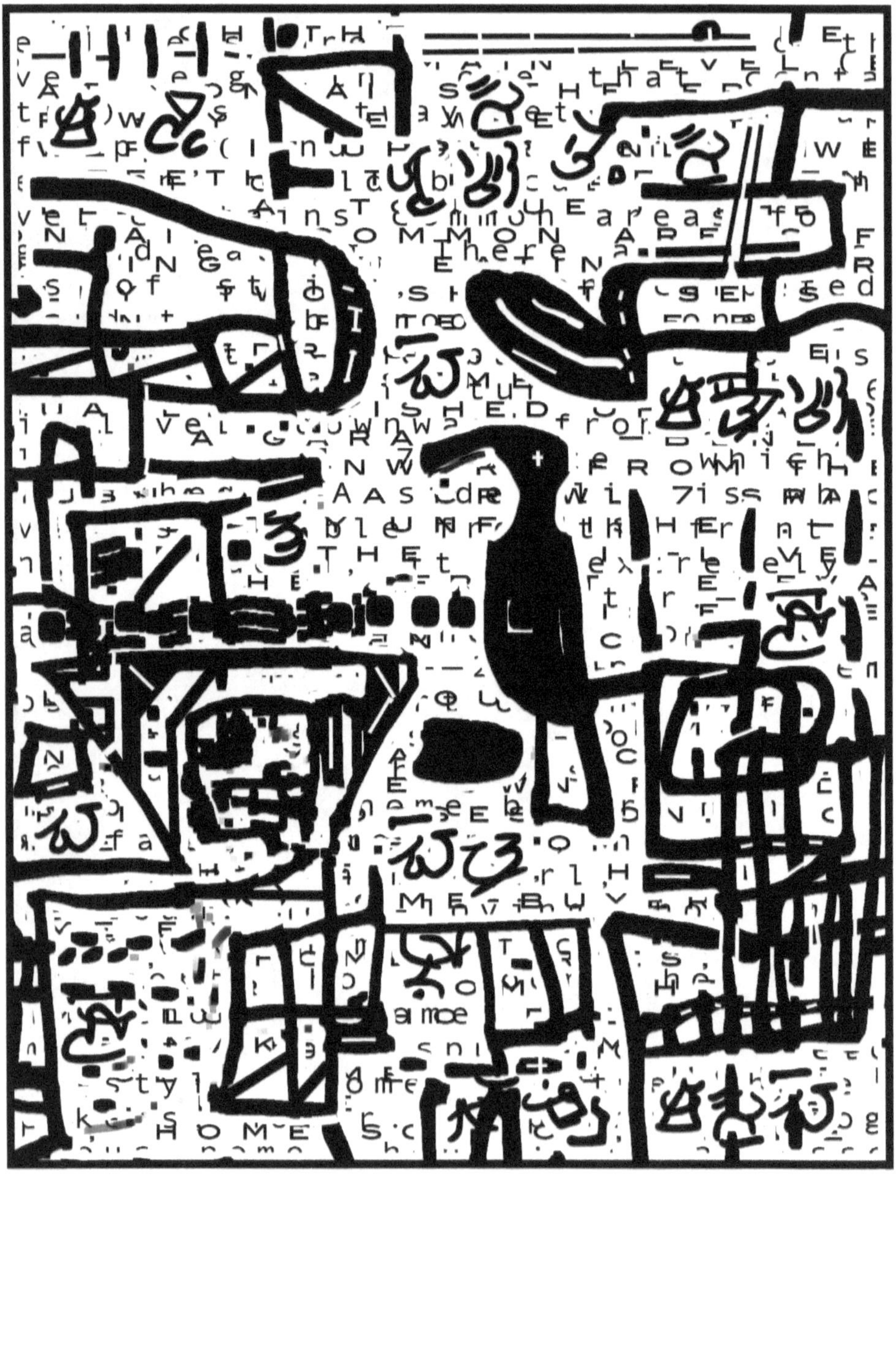
that
COMMON
areas
FROM which
HOME

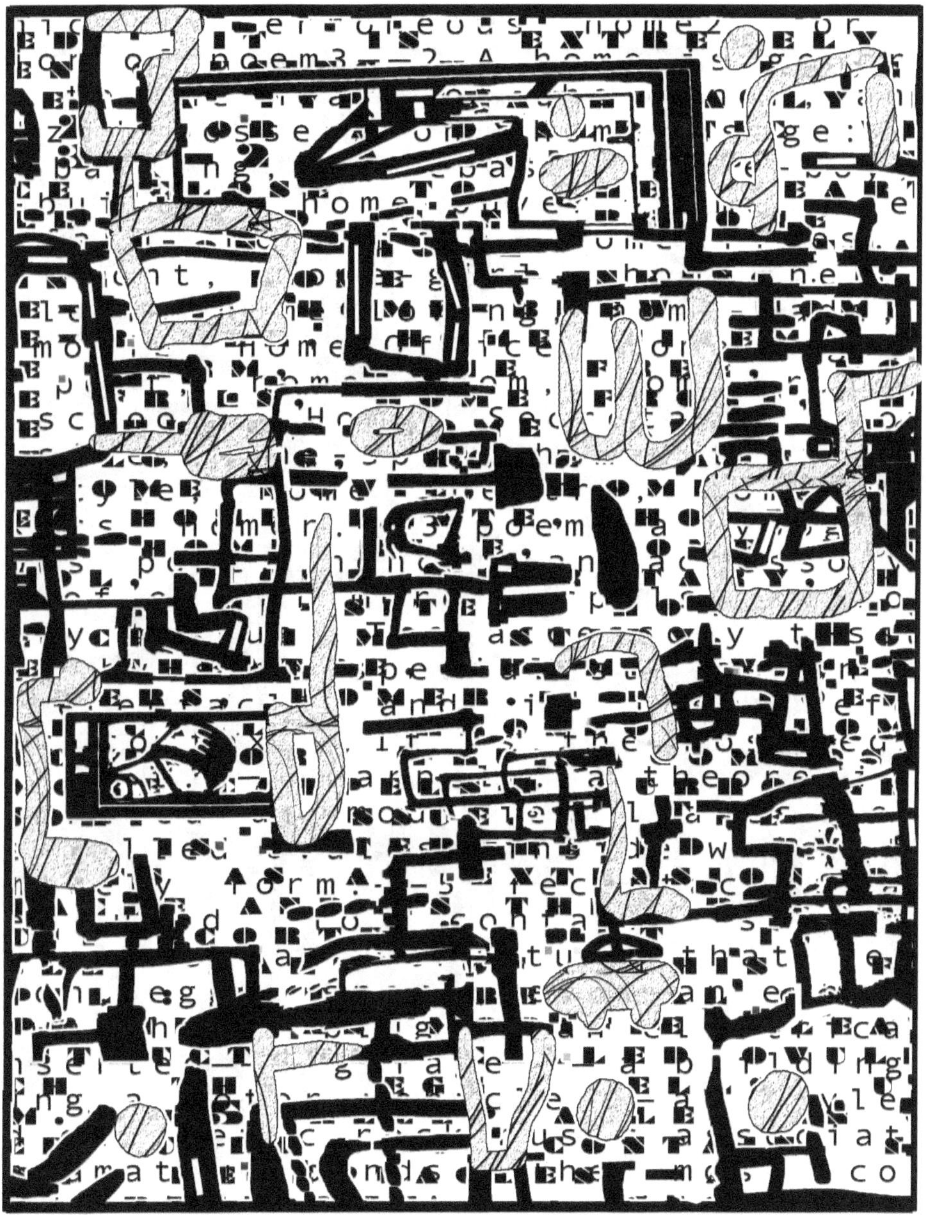

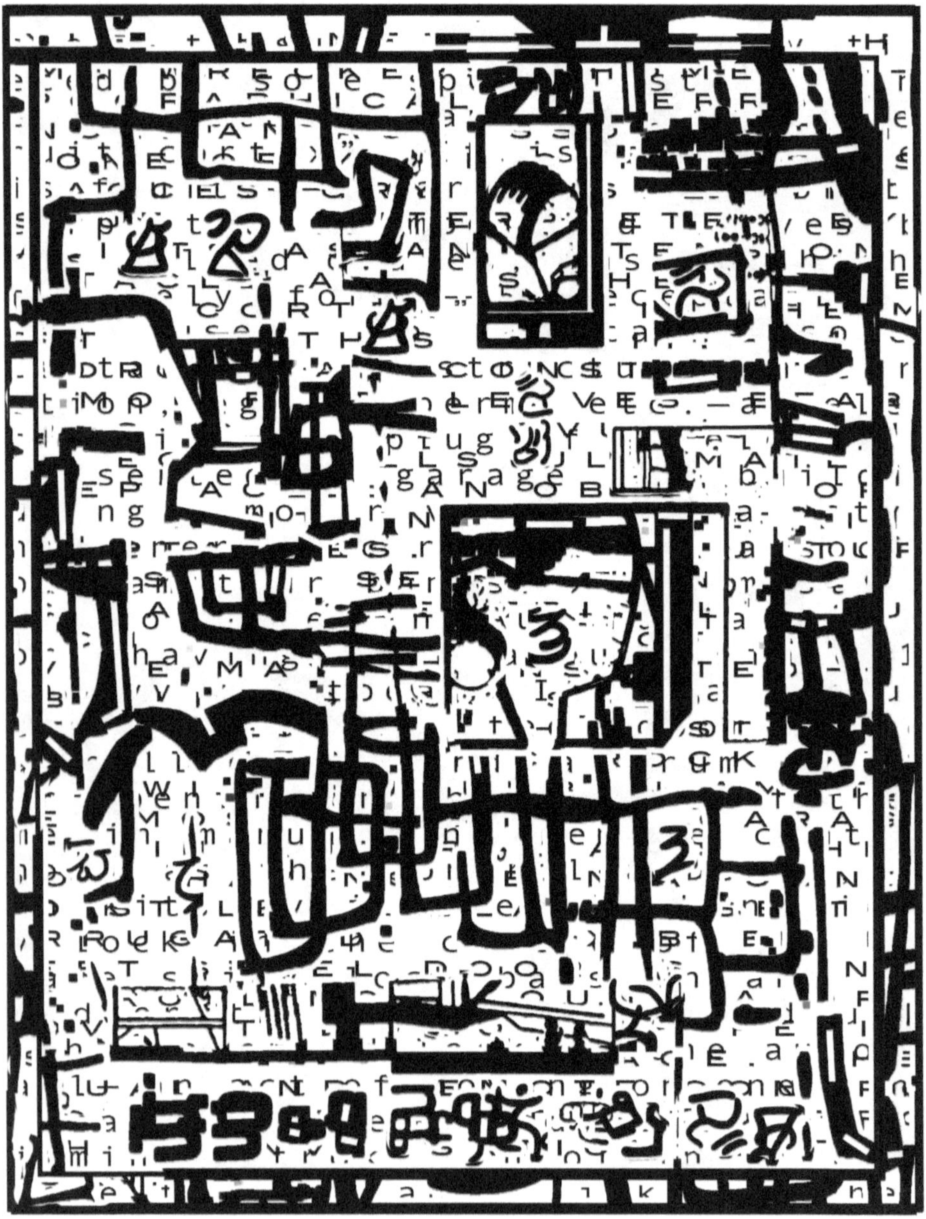

plug
garage

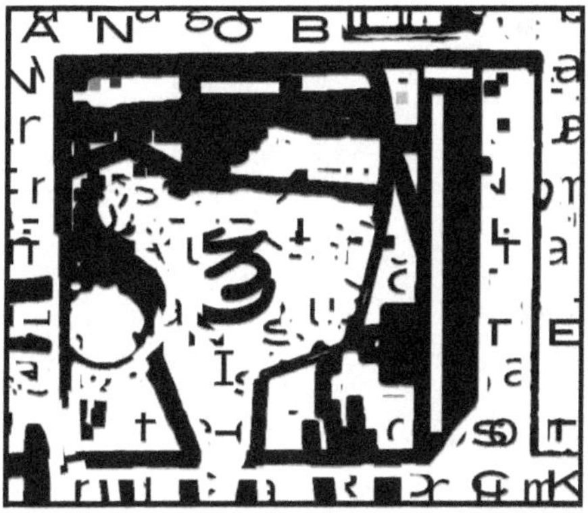

spine
Appendage, fin, spine (extending from a fish, etc.): *dala*$_4$.
Spine (of the body): *ivi laanui*.

spiny puffer
Fish sp.: spiny puffer: *daudu*.

spiny starfish
Spiny starfish: *dolo-mea*.

spirit
A spirit which is worshipped: *diinonga*.
Ghost, spirit, god: *eidu*.
Spirit, soul, name-group: *hagasaalunga*$_2$.
The spirit of a human being after his death: *samouli*.

spirit possession
Spirit possession: *hagavvale*.

spit
Spit out (esp. food): *luei*.
Spit, drool, sputum: *saavale*.

splash
Splash (once): *kobu*.
Splash (or make noise like splashing) repeatedly: *gobugobu*.
The splash of a small object (like a *dango*) hitting the water at high velocity: *kobu dango*.
To splash water on something with the hand: *dabui*.

splashed
Splashed, sprinkled: *pii*.

split
Be split open: *mahanga*.
Split in two: *hhanga lua*.
Split open, open up, or separate, all at once: *hhanga*.

spoil
Spoil (a child): *hakide gee*.
Spoil (children), bring up (children)

sponge sp.
Sponge sp. (several spp.): *galagala*.
Sponge sp.: *galavagu*.

spoon
Scoop up (liquids only), spoon: *asu*.

spoonful
Mouthful or spoonful of food: *maanga*.

spot
A spot (e.g., on the skin): *dongi*.

spotted
Spotted (covered with spots): *daubulebule*.

spouse
One's first spouse: *aduisiisi*.
Spouse: *bodu; hagaasoaso; soolonga*.
To have a spouse: *hai de ama*.

spray
Dust, gas, steam, vapor, fumes, spray (e.g., of waves): *mama*.
Spray: *sii valavala*.

spread
Spread news or rumors: *dele de longo*.
Spread one's legs (esp. a woman in the act of sexual intercourse): *hela**.
Spread one's legs: *hhanga luu vae*.
Spread one's legs wide apart at one time: *hhela**.
Spread venereal disease: *hilo saele*.

spread out
Laid out or spread out all over: *holadage*.
To be spread out: *madoha*.
To spread out (something): *doha*.
To spread out, or lay out flat, something which is folded, piled up, or bent, etc.: *hola*.

sprinkled
Splashed, sprinkled: *pii*.

lesser

Smaller, lesser (in rank, importance, strength, development, etc.): *kii iho.*

lesson

Lesson, make learn, cause to teach: *hagaagoago*$_1$.

lest

Lest: *kana.*

let go

Let go, throw away, lose something: *dili.*

let out

Let out (something), disburse (money): *hagasao*$_2$.

let's

Let's (later): *aha naa.*
Let's (now): *aha nei.*
Let's —: *daa de —.*
Let's — right away!: *deengaa.*

letter

A letter (of the alphabet): *siianga*$_1$.

level

Level (an area): *ulu*$_1$.
Level (not bumpy): *baba*$_1$.
Level: *soe.*
Not level (esp. a person when sleeping): *ulalo.*
Not level: *uba.*
Not level, tipped to one side: *diba*$_1$.
Somewhat level or straight: *soesoe.*
Straight or level all over (as a playing field): *soesoe.*
To level off (ground, etc.): *hagasoesoe.*

lever

A log used as a lever or fulcrum: *hala a buadaia.*

lice

Abounding in lice: *gudua; guduaanga.*
Lice (immature): *manu-ligi.*
Lice eggs: *lie.*
Pick head lice: *ageli; agule.*

lick

Lick: *ssamu.*

lie

A lie (an untruth): *moele.*
Falsehood, lie: *me hhadu.*
Lie (falsehood): *muna hhadu.*
Lie (tell a falsehood): *hadu muna; ngudu lagolago.*

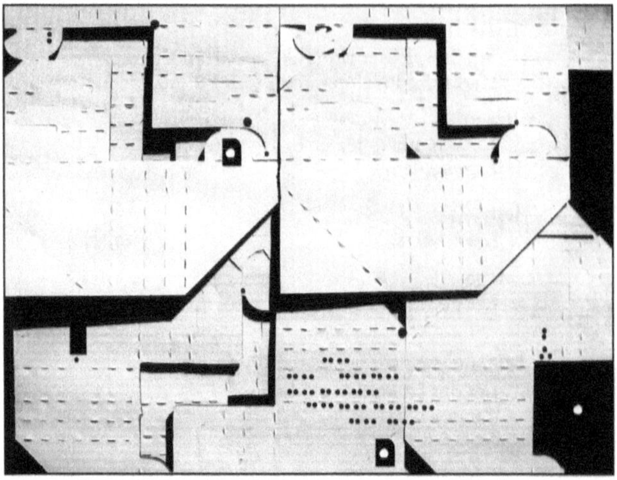

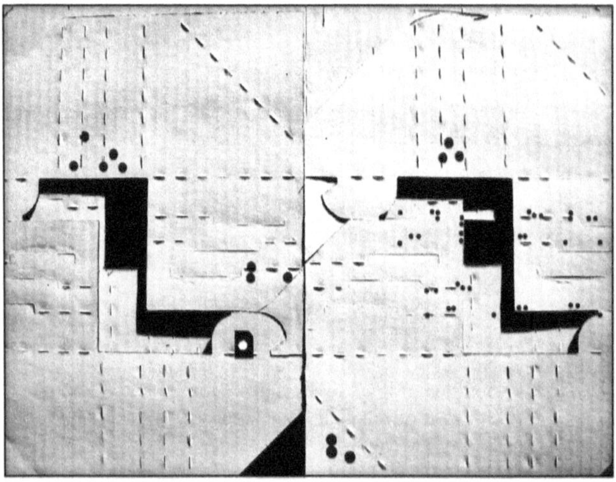

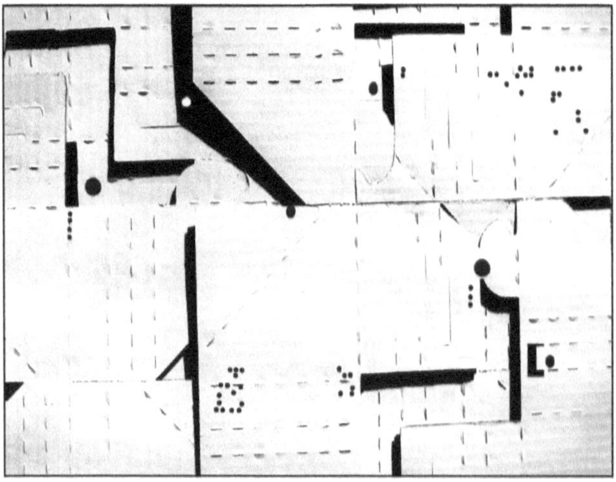

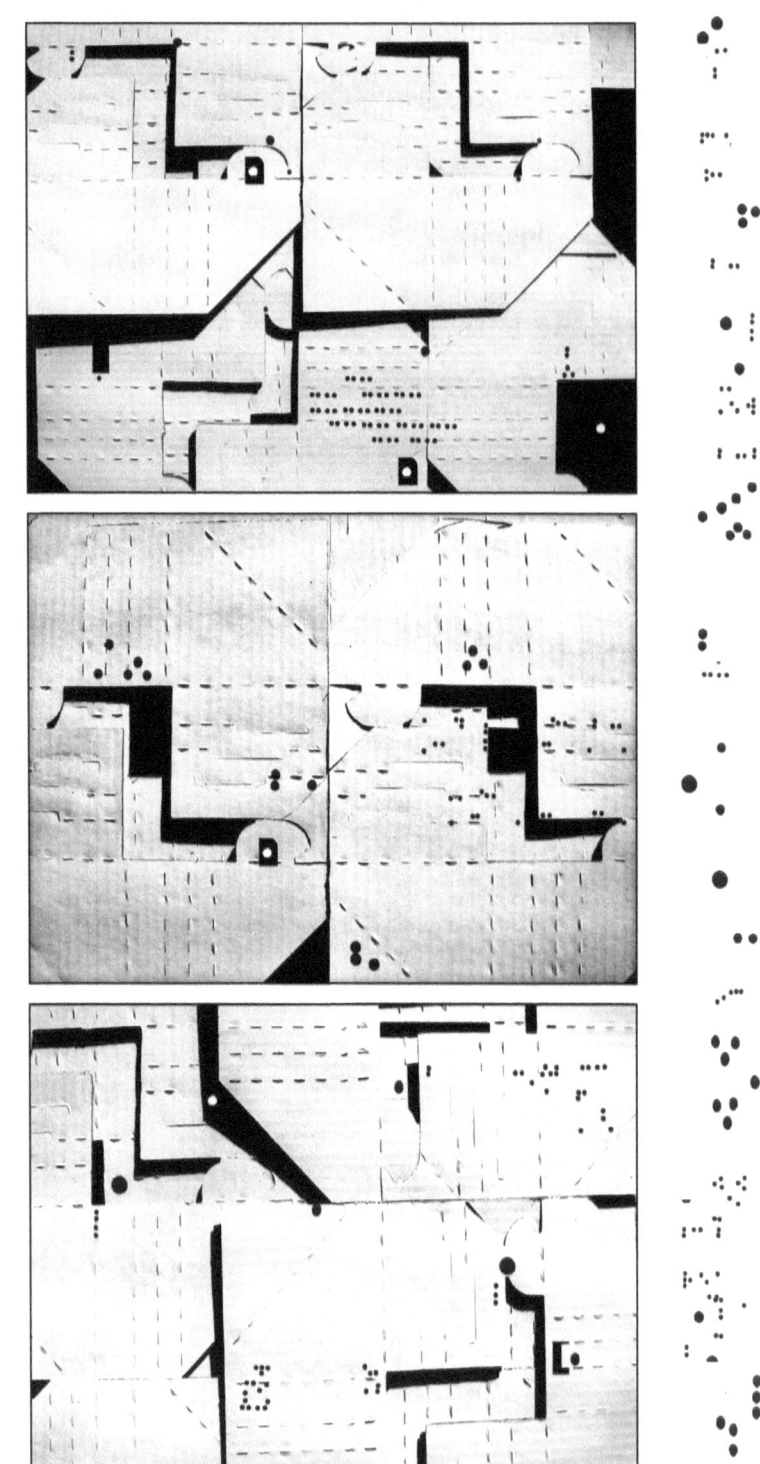

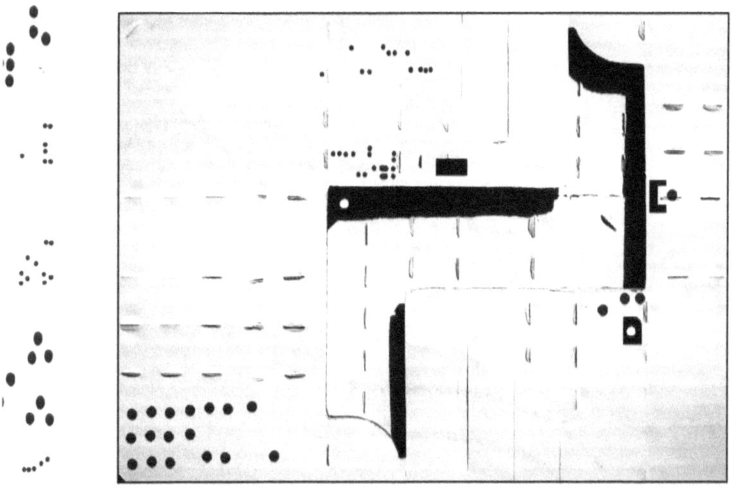

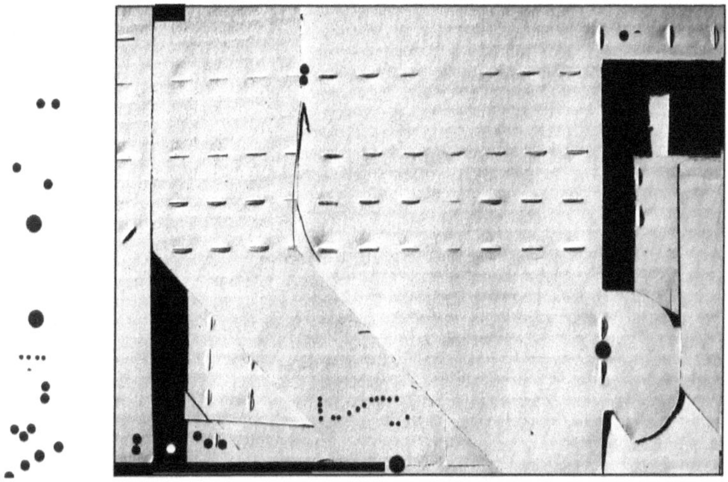

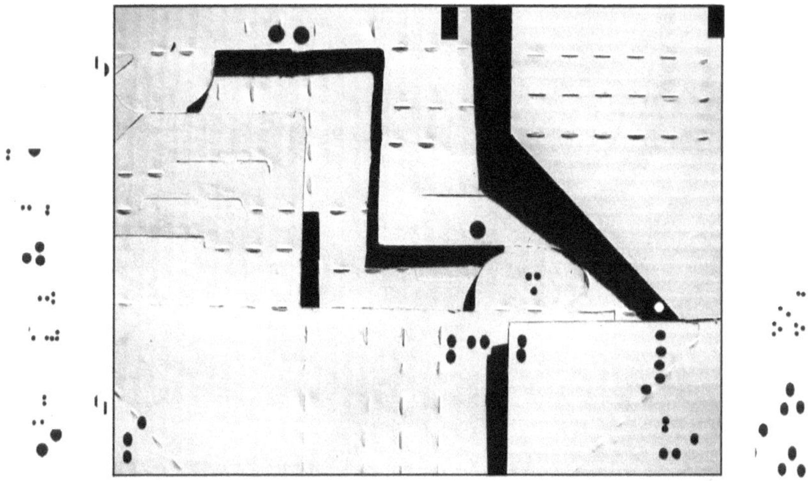

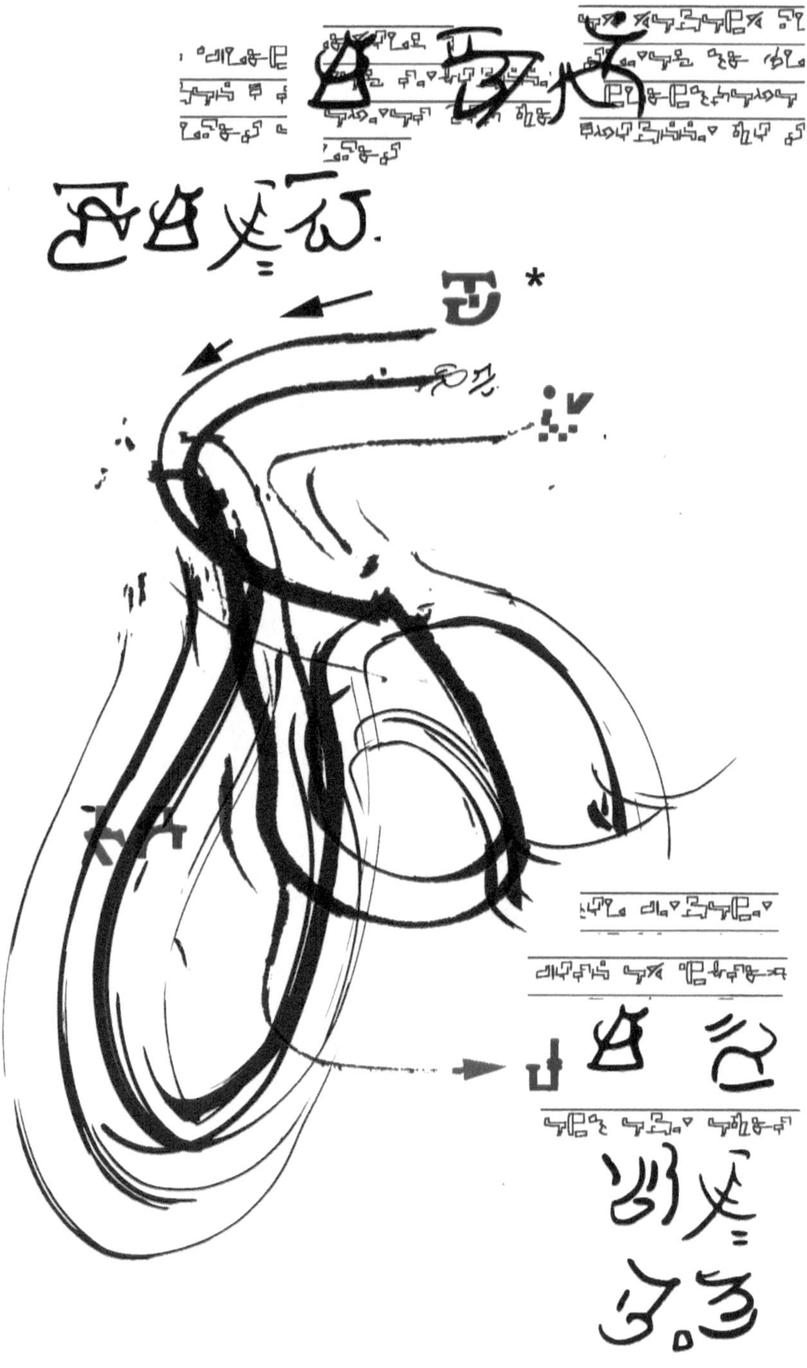

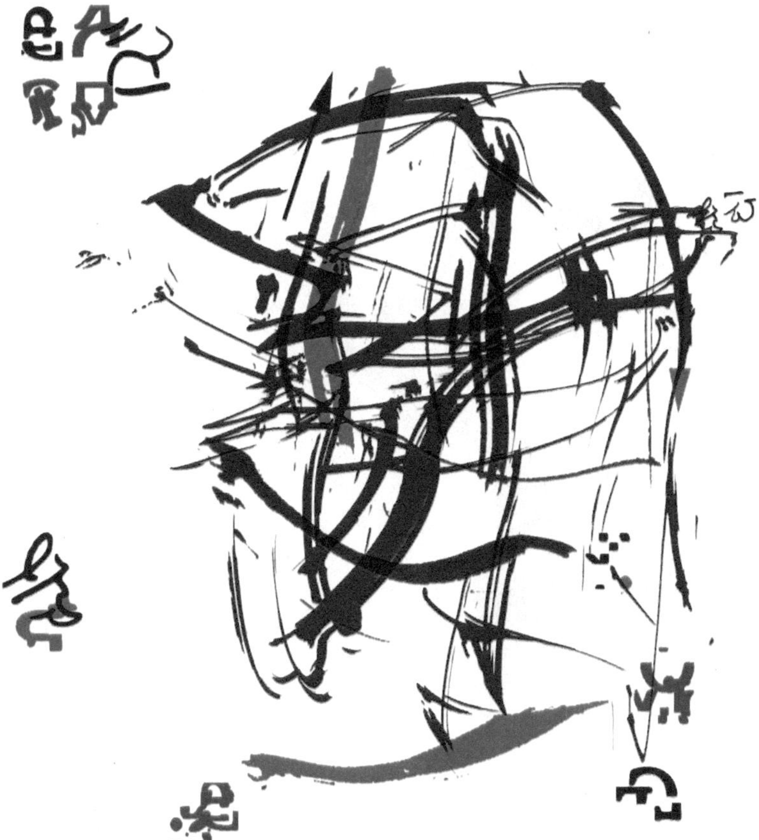

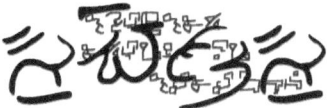

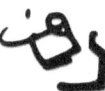

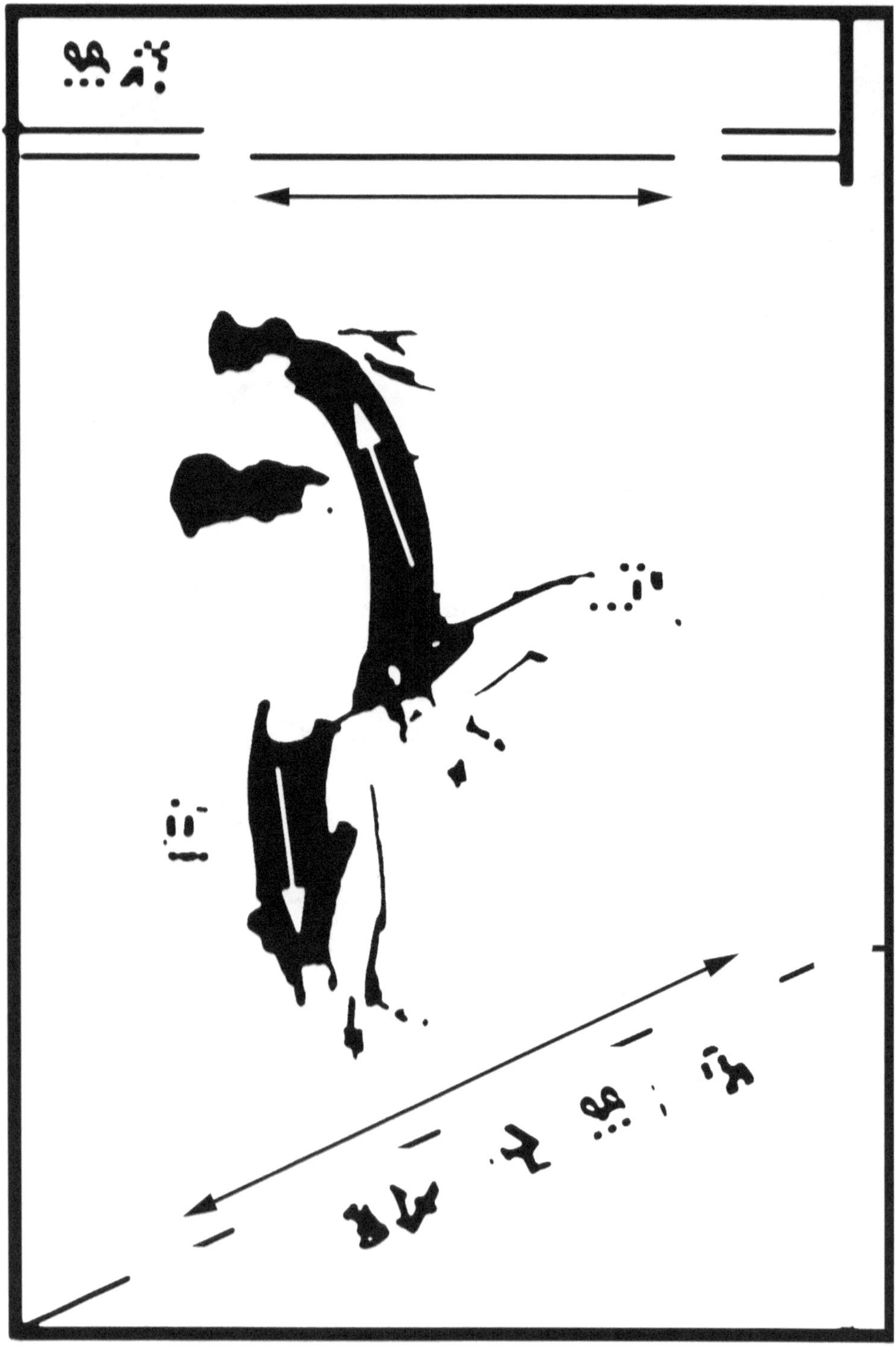

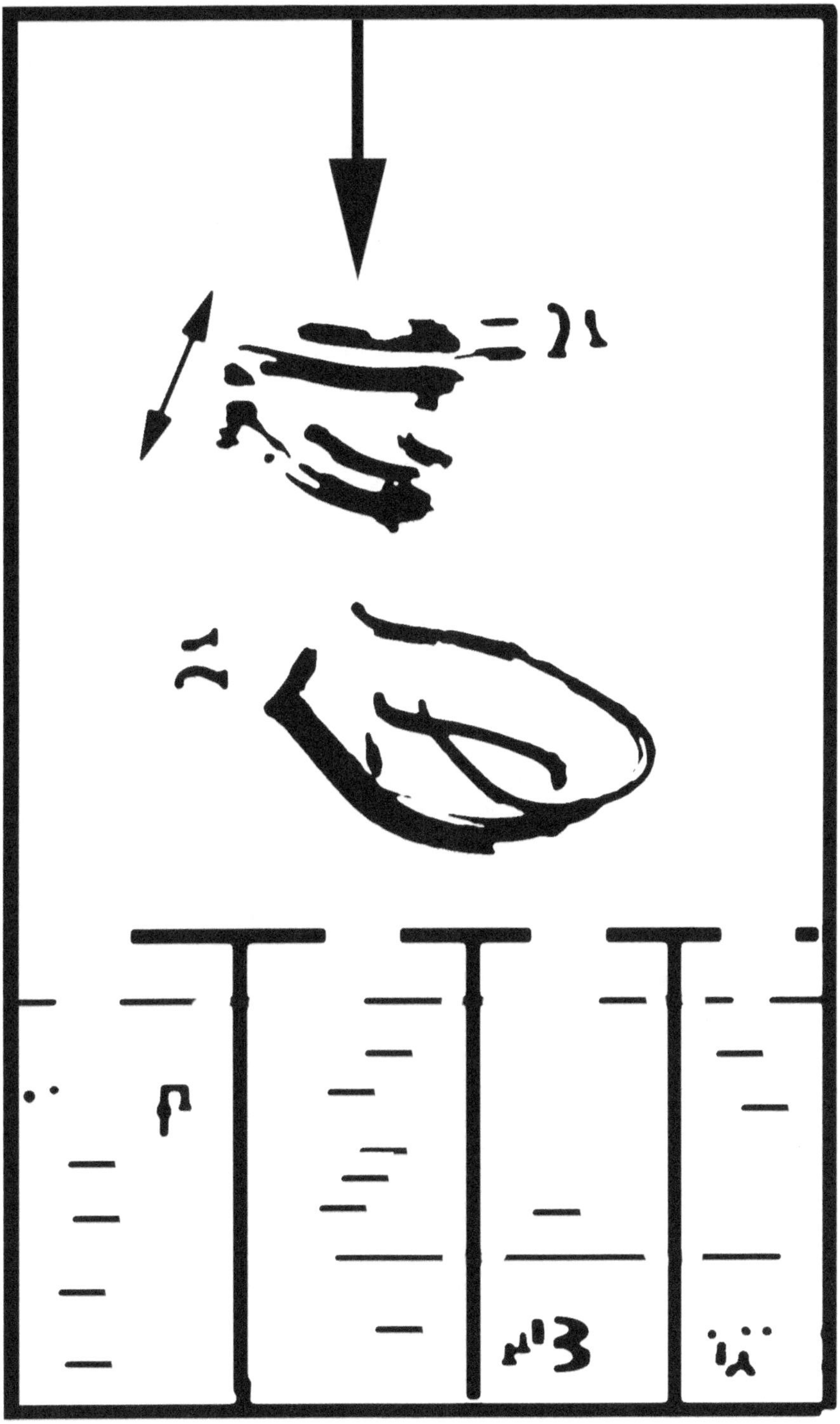

display 882
–board 666
splay 291
–footed 243
spleen
melancholy 837
hatred 898
anger 900
sullen 901*a*
harbour – 907
spleenless 906
splendour
bright 420
beautiful 845
glorious 873
display 882
splenetic 837, 901*a*
splice *join* 43
cross 219
interjacent 228
repair 660
– the main brace
tipsy 959
spliced, be –
marriage 903
splint 215
splinter
small piece 32
divide 44
filament 205
brittle 328
split *divide* 44
discontinuity 70
bisect 91
brittle 328
divulge 529
quarrel 713
fail 732
portion 786
laugh 838
– the difference 29, 774
– the ears 404
– the head 410
– hairs
discriminate 465
sophistry 477
fastidiousness 868
– upon a rock 732
– one's sides 838
splutter *energy* 171
spit 297
stammer 583
haste 684
spoil *vitiate* 659
hinder 706
lenity 740
plunder 791
booty 793
deface 846
satiate 869
– sport 706
– trade 708
spoiled child 869, 899
– of fortune 734
spoiler 792
spoke *radius* 200
tooth 253
obstruct 706
put a – in one's wheel *render powerless* 158
hinder 706
spokesman 524, 582
spolia opima 793
spoliate 791
spoliative 793
spondee 597
spondulics 800
sponge *moisten* 339
dry 340
pulp 354
clean 652
despoil 791
hanger on 886
drunkard 959
apply the –
obliterate 552
non-payment 808
– out 552
sponging-house 752
spongy *porous* 252
soft 324
marshy 345
sponsion 771
sponsor
witness 467
security 771
be – for
promise 768
obligation 926
sponsorship 771
spontaneous
voluntary 600
willing 602
impulsive 612
spontoon 727
spoof 545
spook 980
spool 312
spoon
receptacle 191
ladle 272
bill and coo 902
born with a silver – in one's mouth 734
Spoonerism 218, 853
spoonful 25, 32

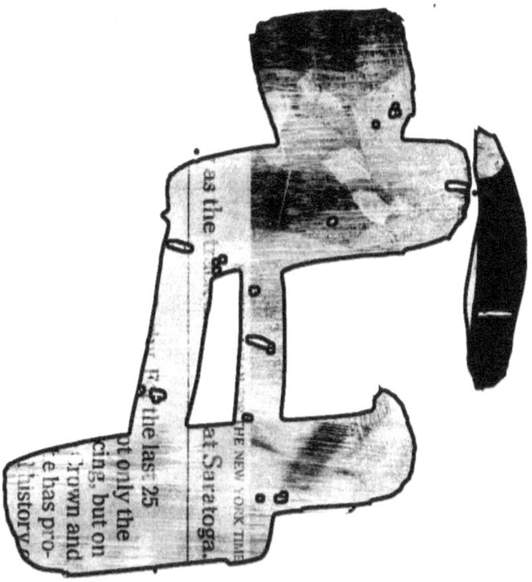
as the
at Saratoga.
the las 25
ot only the
cing, but on
rown and
e has pro-

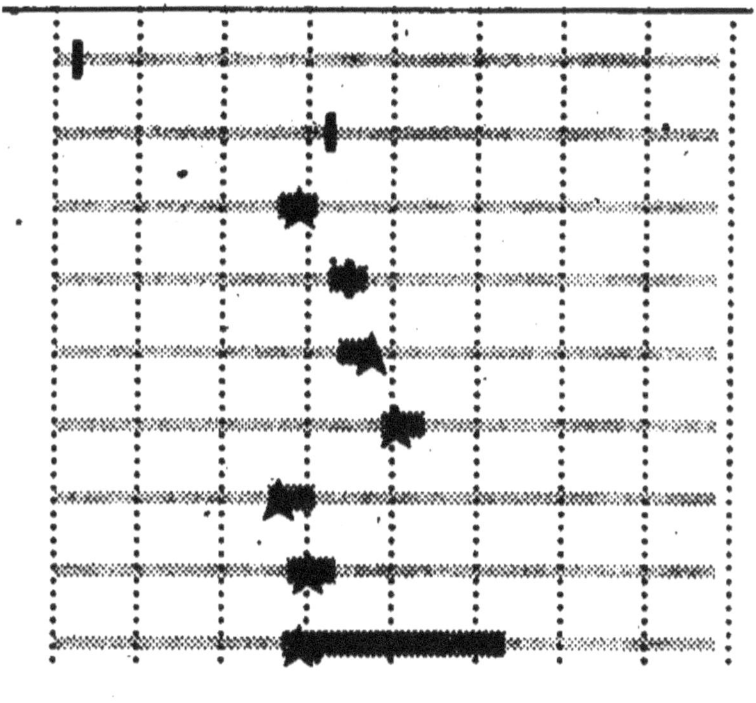

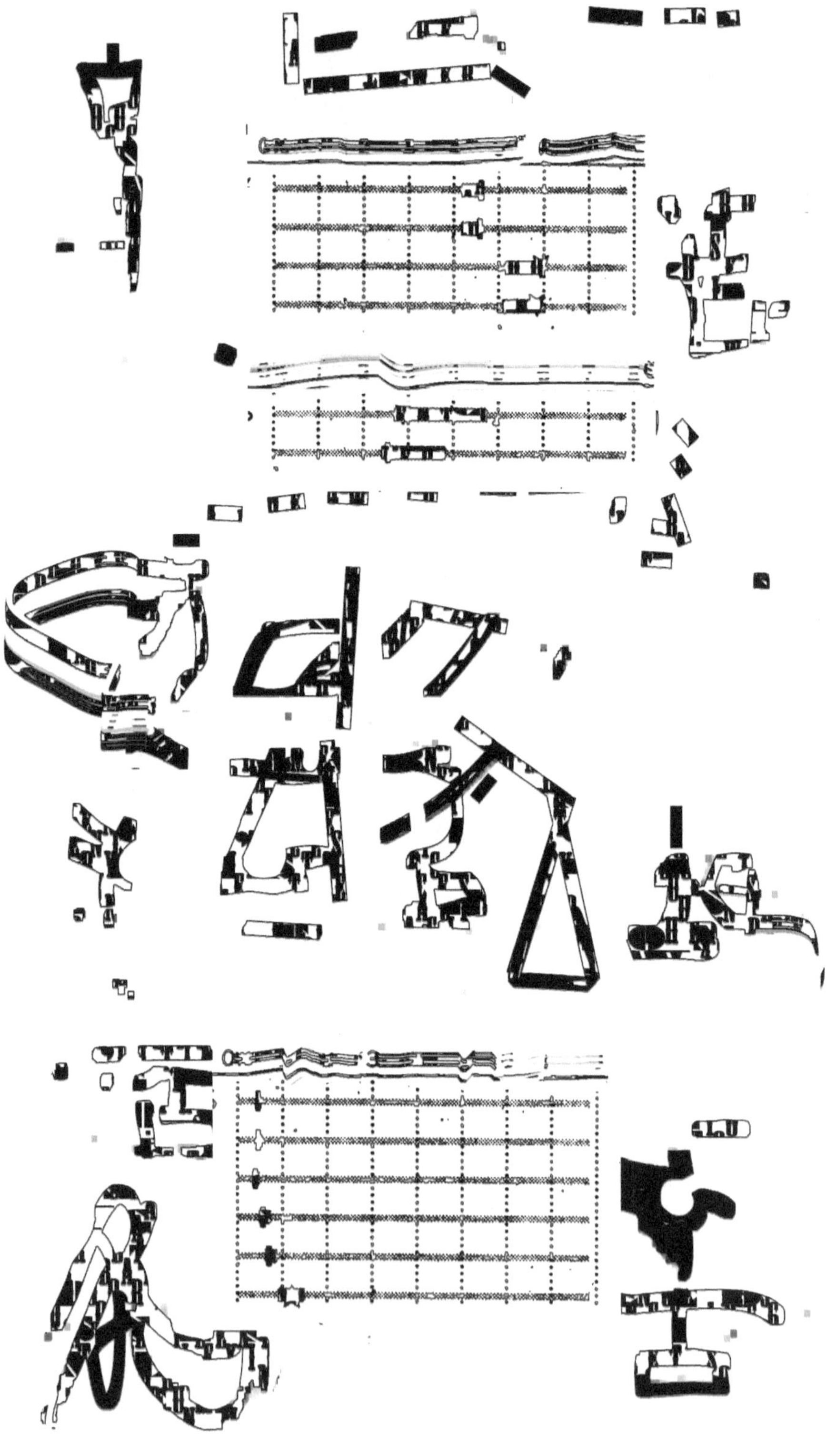

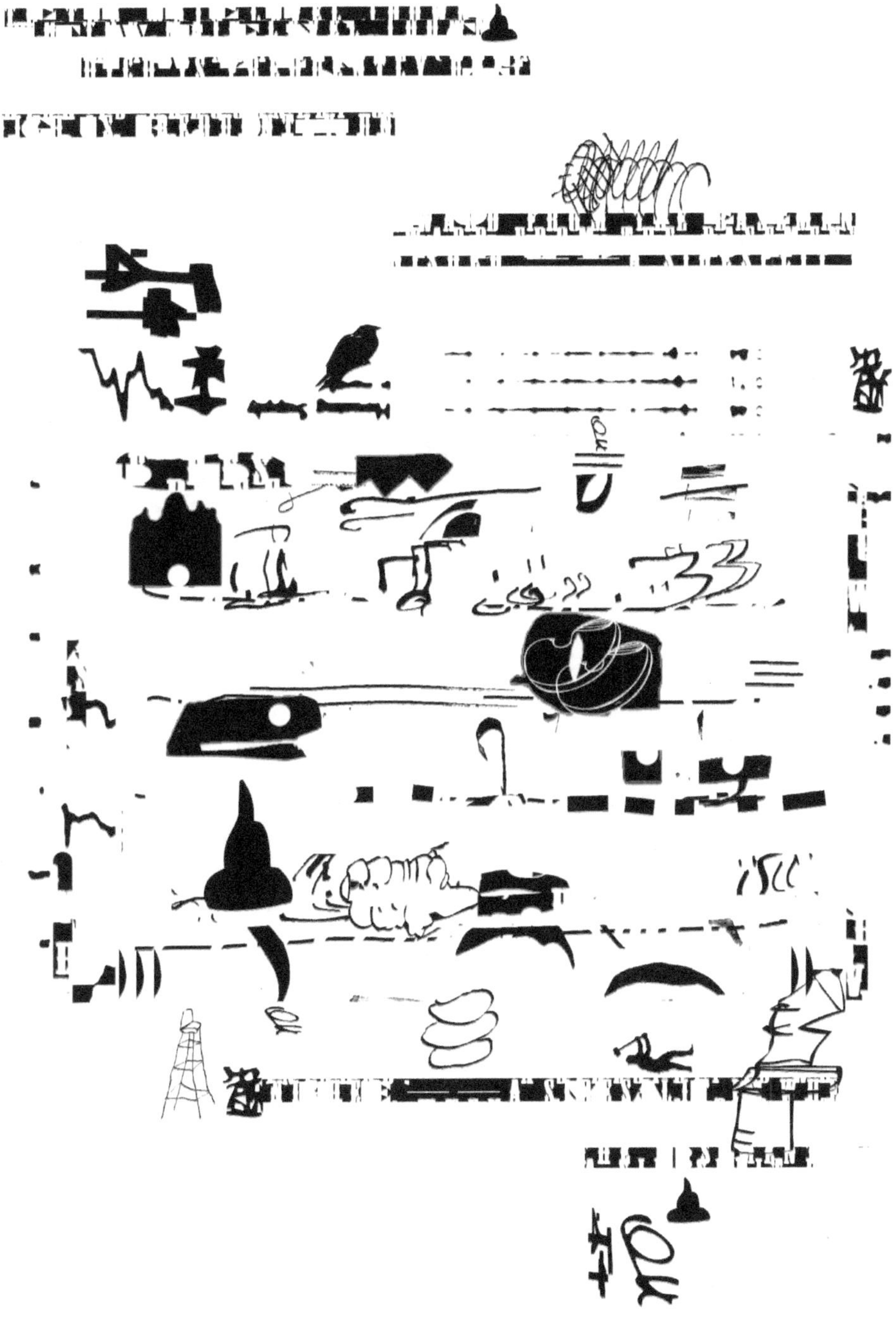

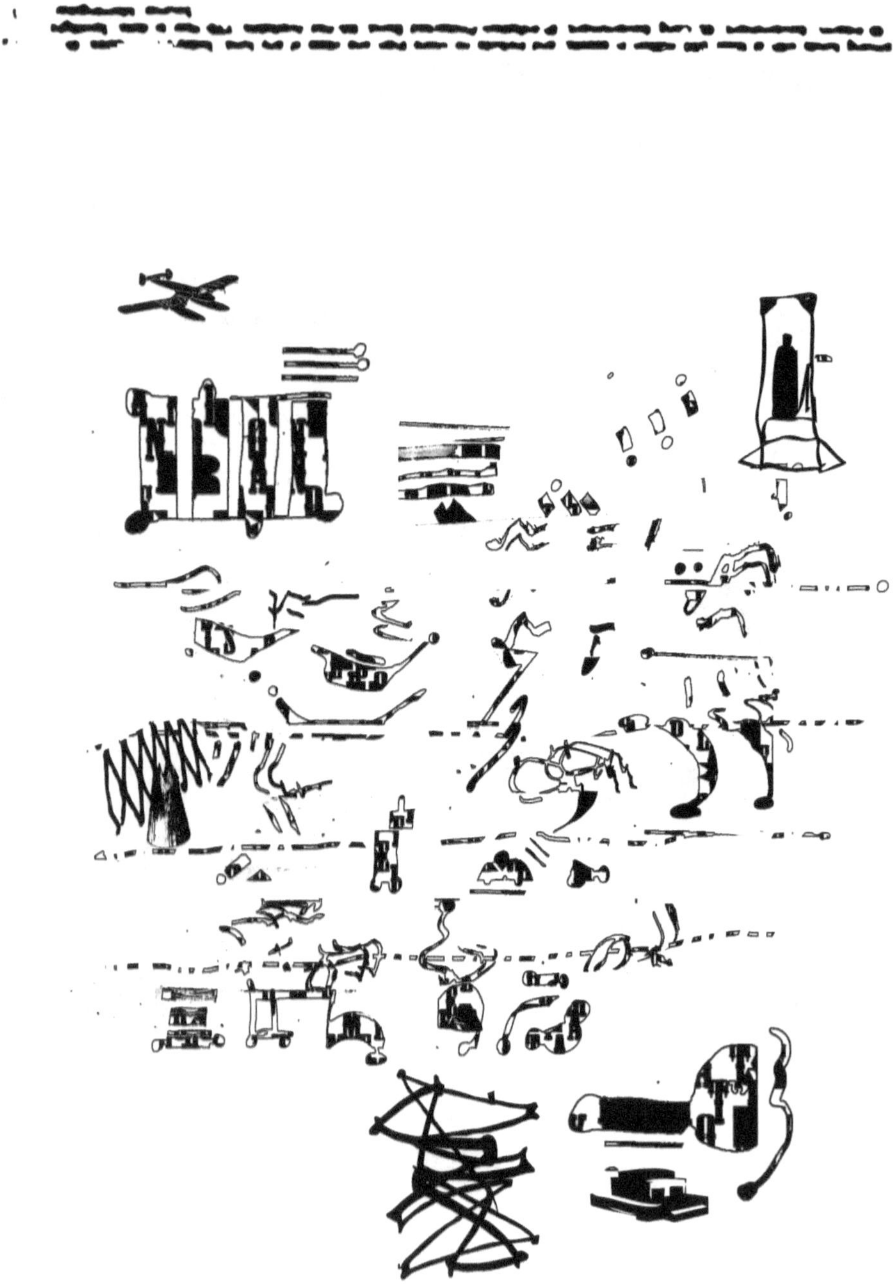

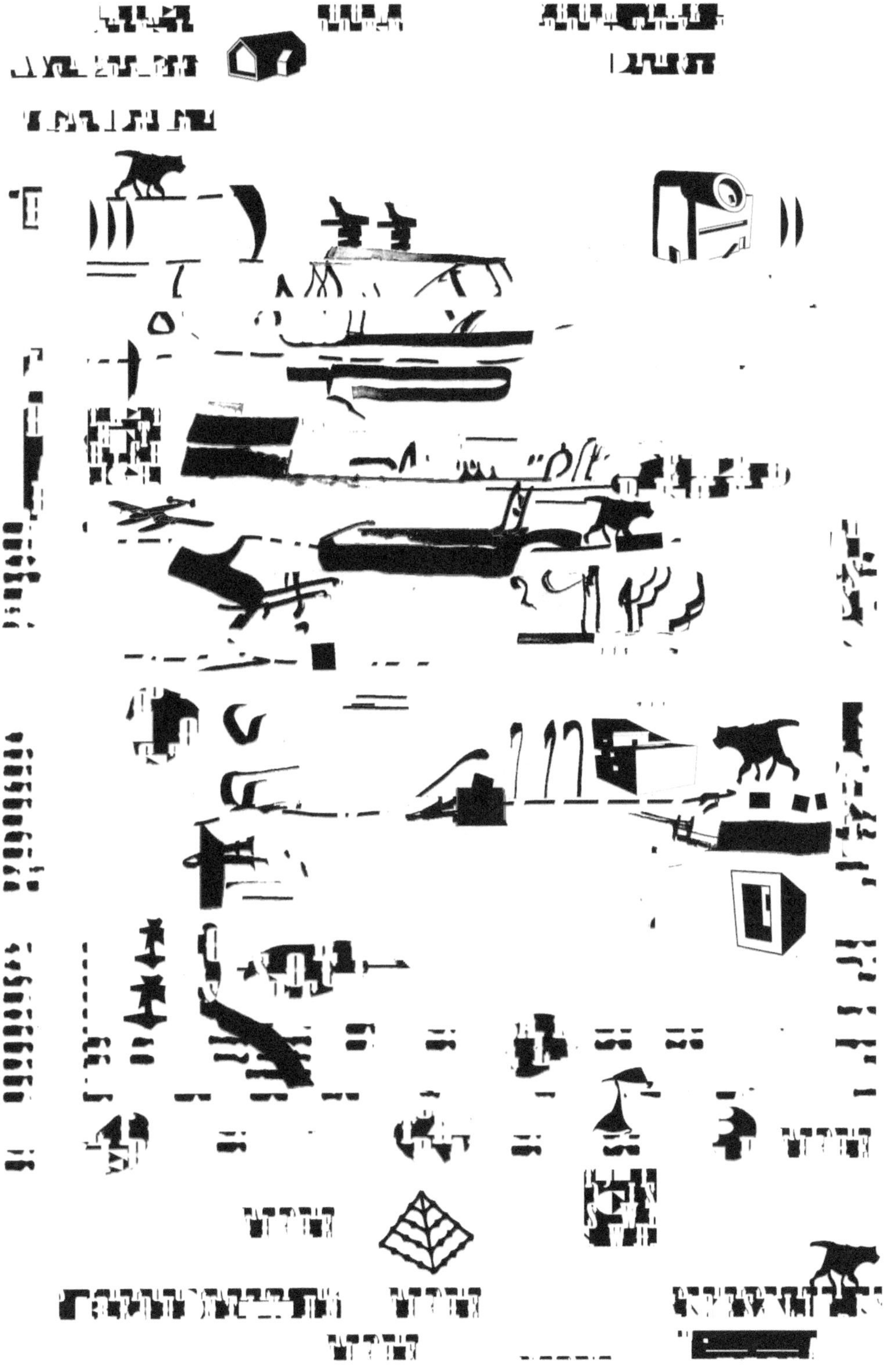

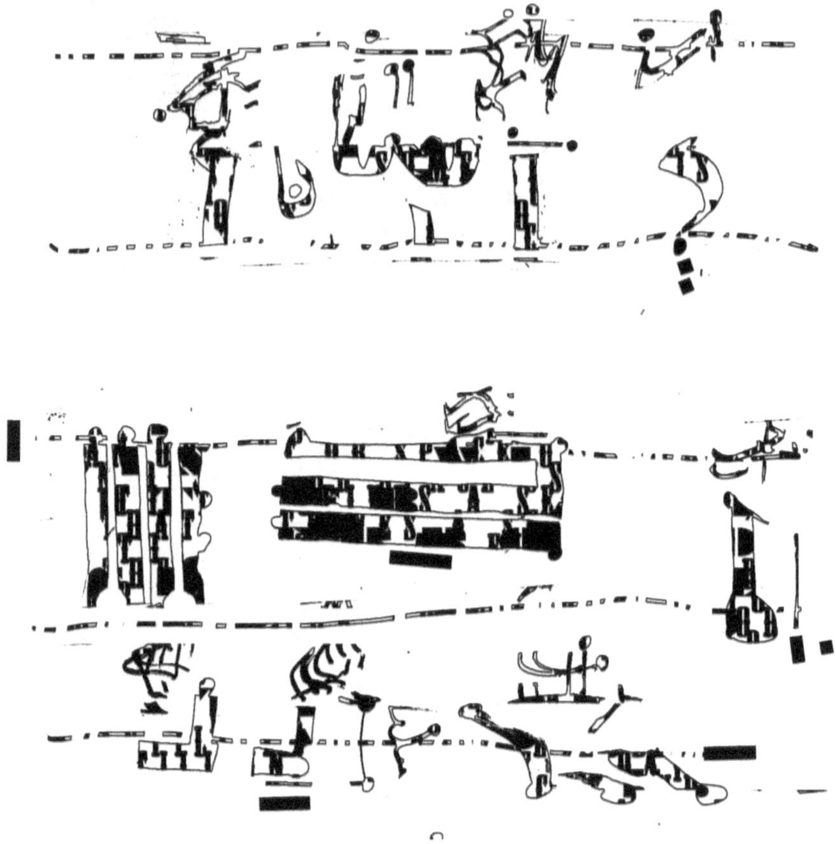

dado, wainscot, baseboard; foundation &c. (*support*) 215; substructure, *sub-stratum*, sump, ground, earth, pavement, floor, paving, flag, carpet, ground-floor, deck; footing, groundwork, basis; hold, bilge, orlop deck.

bottom, nadir, foot, sole, toe, hoof, keel, kelson, root.

Adj. bottom; under-, nether-most; fundamental; founded –, based –, grounded –, built- on.

)ping-stone, zoophorus, capi-
nce, pediment, entablature;

tory, roof.
rtop &c. (*be superior to*) 33.
); top-, upper-most; tip-top;
apital, head, polar, supreme,

– the heap.

213. Horizontality.—**N.** horizontality; flatness; level, plane; stratum &c. 204; dead -level, – flat; level plane.

recumbency; lying down &c. *v.*; reclination, decumbence; de-, discumbency; proneness &c. *adj.*; accubation, supination, resupination, prostration; azimuth.

plain, floor, platform, bowling-green; cricket-ground; court; gridiron; baseball diamond; hockey rink; tennis-, croquet-ground, – lawn; billiard table; terrace, estrade, esplanade, *parterre*, table-land, *plateau*, ledge.

spirit-, level; T-square.

V. be -horizontal &c. *adj.*; lie, recline, couch; lie -down, – flat, – prostrate; sprawl, loll; sit down.

render -horizontal &c. *adj.*; lay, – down, – out; level, flatten, even, raze, equalize, smooth, align; prostrate, knock down, floor, fell, ground.

Adj. horizontal, level, even, plane;

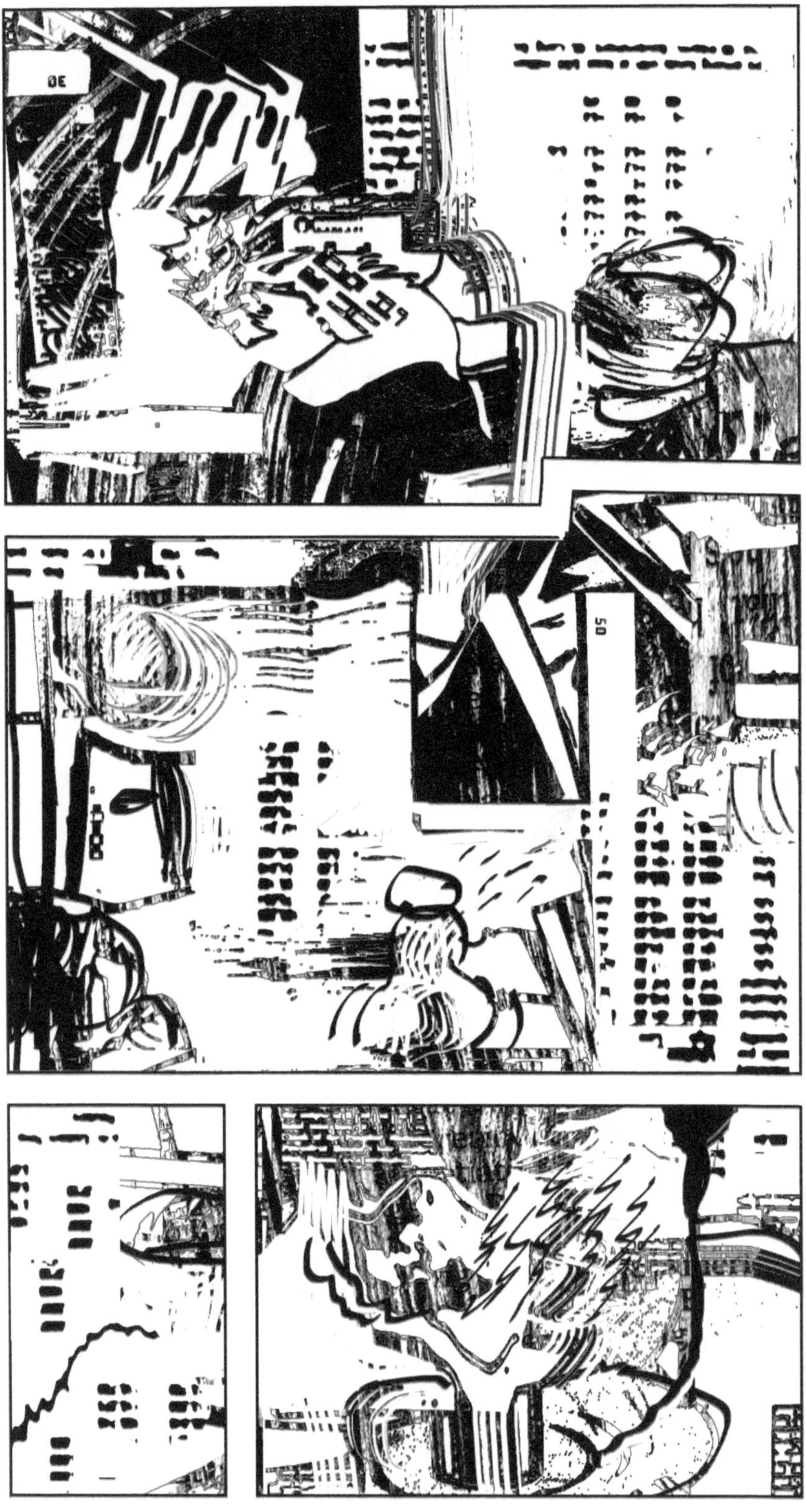

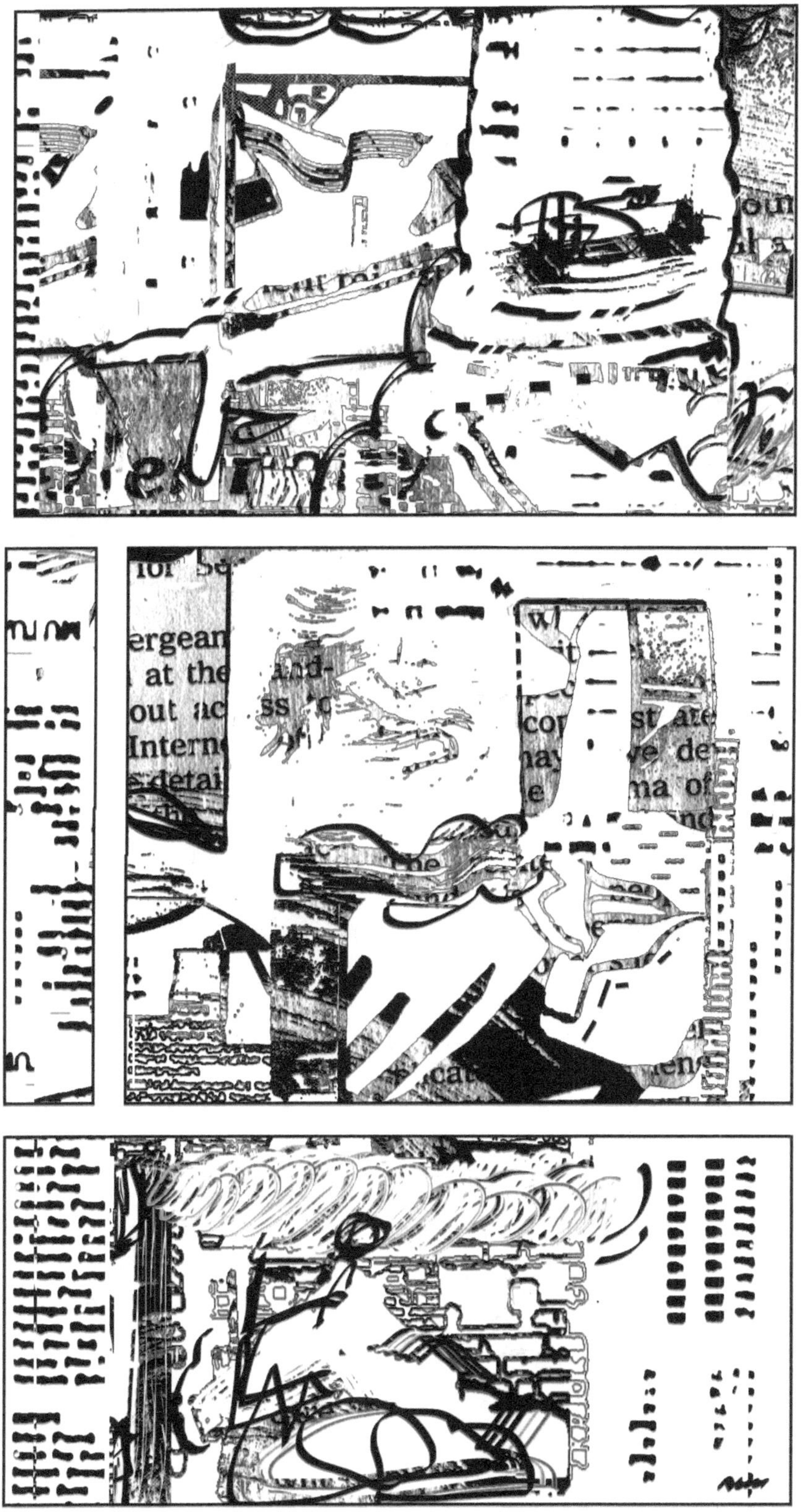
ergean
at the
and-
out ac
Interne
detai
st ate
ve de
ma of

rough.

split, *v.t.*; split *or obs.* splitted, *pt.*, *pp.*; splitting, *ppr.* [ME. *splitten*; akin to M.H.G. *splīzen.*]

1. to separate, cut, or divide into two or more parts; to cause to separate along the grain or length; to break into layers.

2. to break or tear apart by force; to burst; to rend.

3. to divide into parts or shares; to portion out; as, they *split* the cost of the trip.

4. to cause (a group, political party, etc.) to separate into divisions or factions; to disunite.

5. in chemistry, (a) to break (a molecule) into atoms; to separate the components of; (b) to produce nuclear fission in (an atom or atoms).

to split off; (a) to break off by splitting; (b) to separate or divide by or as by splitting.

to split one's sides; to burst with laughter.

to split one's vote; to vote for candidates of different parties on the same ballot.

split, *v.i.* 1. to separate or divide lengthwise into two or more parts; to separate along the grain or length.

2. to break or tear apart; to burst; to rend.

3. to separate or break up through failure to agree, etc.

4. to divide something with another or others, each taking a share; as, winners *split.* [Colloq.]

5. to burst with laughter. [Colloq.]

Each had a gravity would make you *split.*
—Pope.

6. to betray confidence; to inform on an accomplice; as, he *split* on his associate. [19th-c. Slang.]

7. to move rapidly; as, he *split* across the lot. [Colloq.]

split, *n.* 1. the act or process of splitting.

2. a crack, rent, or fissure.

3. a division or separation, as in a political party; a breach; as, there is a *split* in the cabinet.

4. a splinter; a fragment.

5. one of the short flat strips of steel, cane, etc., placed in vertical parallel order at small distances from each other in a frame to form the reed of a loom.

6. a flexible strip of wood used in basket weaving.

7. a confection made of a split banana or other fruit with ice cream, nuts, sauces, whipped cream, etc.

8. [*often pl.*] the feat of spreading the legs apart until they lie flat on the floor, the body remaining upright.

9. (a) a small bottle of carbonated water, wine, etc., half the usual size, often about six ounces; (b) a drink or portion half the usual size; (c) a half pint. [Colloq.]

10. a share, as of loot or booty. [Slang.]

11. in bowling, an arrangement of pins after the first bowl, so separated as to make a spare almost impossible.

12. in leather manufacturing, any part of divided skins which have been separated into two sections by the cutting machine.

13. in the game of faro, a division of a stake occurring when two cards of the same value turn up together, the person making the bet losing half of his stake.

split, *a.* 1. divided; rent; separated.

2. divided or separated along the length or grain; broken into parts.

3. in the stock market, given in sixteenths, and not in eighths: said of a quotation smaller than the normal trading unit.

4. in botany, cleft; deeply divided into segments.

split dynamometer; a dynamometer employed in connection with alternating currents provided with two coils, so arranged that separate currents of the same frequency can be passed independently through each other.

split infinitive; in grammar, an infinitive with the verbal and the *to* separated by an adverb. Example: he decided *to gradually change* his procedure. Despite the objections of some people to this construction, many writers use split infinitives where ambiguity or awkwardness would otherwise result.

split moss; a moss of the family *Andreæaceæ*: so named from the way in which its capsules split.

split peas; peas husked and split for making soup, pudding, etc.

split phase; in electricity, a difference produced between the phases of two or more alternating currents into which a single-phase alternating current has divided.

split-phase motor; a multiphase motor operated from a single-phase alternating-current circuit by the introduction of a phase-splitting device.

split pin; a pin or cotter with a head at one end and a split at the other. The split ends diverging after passing through an object prevent the accidental retraction of the pin.

split ring; a ring which practically consists of two turns of a spiral, thus admitting of other rings being threaded upon it: the split key ring is an example.

split ticket; see under *ticket*.

split'bēak, *n.* the plantain eater.

split'mouth, *n.* a sucker found in the Mississippi River, *Lagochila lacera.*

split'tāil, *n.* 1. a fish found in California, *Pogonichthys macrolepidotus.*

2. the pintail duck.

split'tēr, *n.* one who or that which splits.

split'ting, *a.* 1. that splits.

2. (a) aching severely: said of the head; (b) severe or sharp, as a headache.

3. very quick; as, a *splitting* pace. [Colloq.]

splōre, *n.* [etym. unknown.] a frolic; also, a carouse. [Scot.]

splotch, *n.* [prob. a fusion of *spot* and *blotch.*] a spot; a stain; a daub; a smear, especially one that is irregular.

splotch, *v.t.* to mark or soil with a splotch or splotches.

splotch'y, *a.*; *comp.* splotchier; *superl* splotchiest, having splotches; marked with splotches.

splŭrġe, *n.* [imitative.] any very showy display or effort; an ostentatious demonstration. [Colloq.]

splŭrġe, *v.i.*; splurged, *pt.*, *pp.*; splurging, *ppr.* to make a showy display, for the purpose of attracting attention; to show off. [Colloq.]

splut'tēr, *v.i.*; spluttered, *pt.*, *pp.*; spluttering, *ppr.* [variant of *sputter.*]

1. to speak hastily and confusedly, as when excited or embarrassed.

A huge Cyclops that hissed and *spluttered.*
—W. A. Fraser.

lev′el, *n.* [ME. *level, livel;* OFr. *livel;* L. *libella,* a level, dim. of *libra,* a balance, level.]

1. an instrument for determining whether a surface is on an even horizontal plane or for adjusting a surface to such a plane: it has a glass tube partly filled with ether or alcohol so as to leave an air bubble that moves to the exact center of the tube when the instrument is on an even horizontal plane.

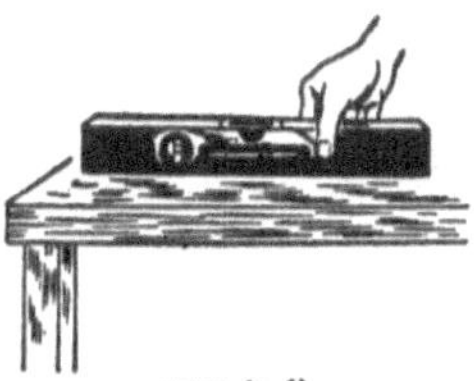

LEVEL (*n.* 1)

2. a measuring of differences in height, or altitude, with such an instrument.

3. a horizontal plane or line; especially, such a plane taken as a basis for the measurement of elevation; as, sea *level.*

4. a relatively flat and even area of land or other surface; horizontal area.

5. the same horizontal plane; as, the tops of the pictures should be on a *level.*

6. height; altitude; as, water boils more quickly at this *level.*

7. usual or normal position or height; as, water seeks its *level.*

8. position or elevation considered as one of the planes in a scale of values; as, few can rise to the *level* of a great man.

9. a horizontal walk or passageway, as between tiers of seats.

10. the line of aim or direction, as of a gun.

11. a more or less horizontal passage or drift of a mine.

lev′el, *a.* 1. even; flat; not having one part higher than another; parallel with the free surface of a liquid at rest; as, a *level* surface.

2. horizontal; not ascending or descending; as, a *level* floor; a *level* road.

3. even with, of the same height as, or on the same line or plane with something else; as, *level* with his ability.

4. equal in rank or degree; as, *level* in value.

5. even; uniform; unchanging; as, a *level* voice; a *level* hue.

6. equally advanced in development.

7. even with the top of the container; not heaping; as, a *level* teaspoonful.

8. not having or showing sudden differences or inequalities; well balanced; equable.

9. direct; straightforward; undeviating; as, a *level* story. [Rare.]

lev′el, *adv.* in a level or horizontal line; evenly; directly; steadily; as, aim it *level.*

lev′el, *v.t.;* leveled *or* levelled, *pt., pp.;* leveling *or* levelling, *ppr.* 1. to make level; specifically, (a) to make perfectly horizontal by means of a level; (b) to make even; to give a flat, horizontal surface to (often with *off*); (c) to equalize in height, importance, rank, quality, etc. (often with *down* or *up*); (d) to make even in tone, color, pitch, etc.

2. to knock to the ground; to demolish; to lay low; as, the storm *leveled* everything in its path.

3. to raise (a gun, etc.) to a level position for firing.

4. to aim.

5. in surveying, to determine the differences in altitude in (a plot of ground).

lev′el, *v.i.* 1. to aim a gun or other weapon (with *at*).

2. to select some person or thing as a target or goal.

3. to bring people or things to an equal rank, condition, etc. (usually with *down* or *up*).

at; mēte, prey, hẽr, met; pīne, marine, bīrd,

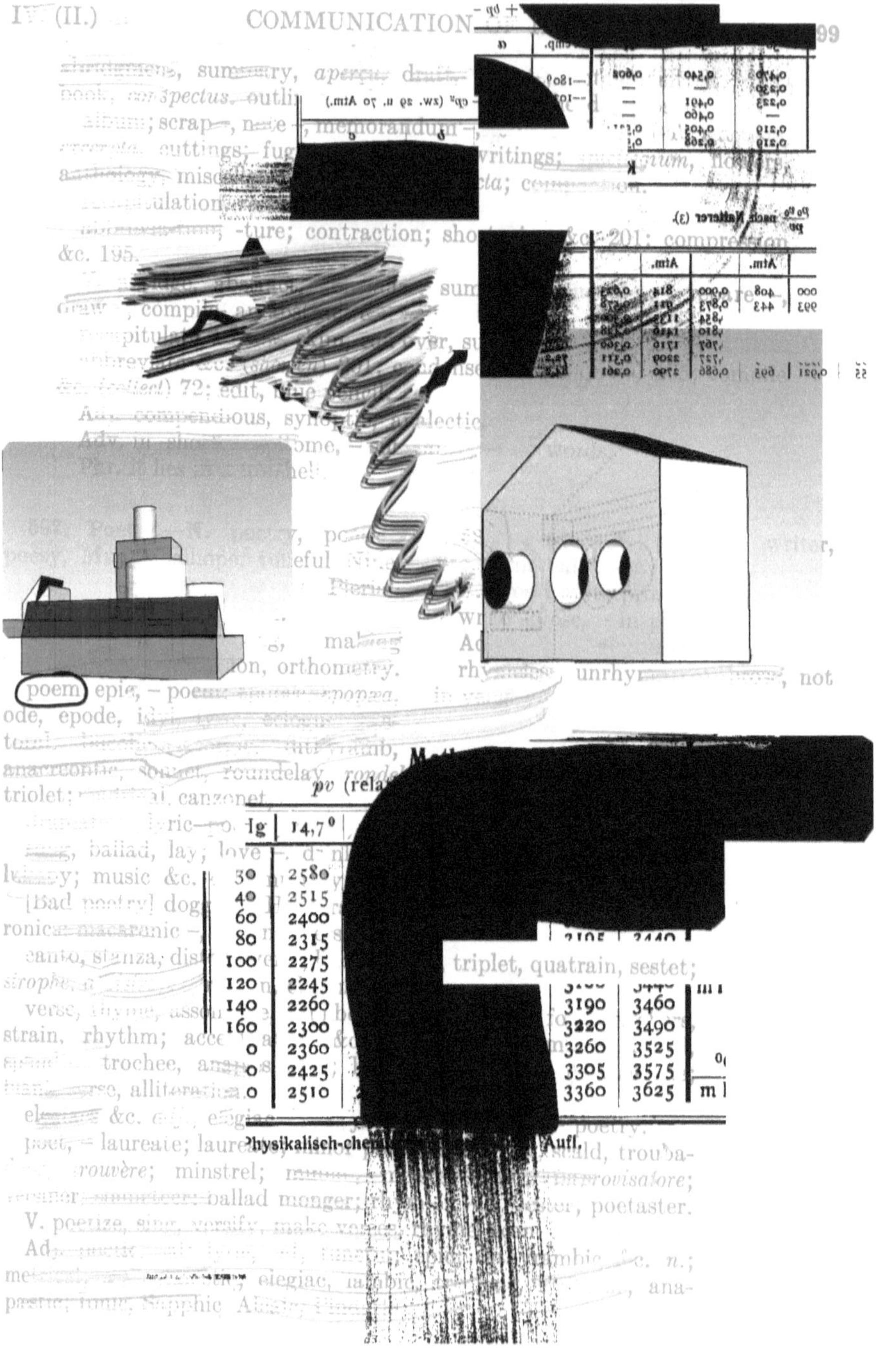
COMMUNICATION
-ture; contraction;
&c. 195.
poem
ode, epode,
triolet;
triplet, quatrain, sestet;
strain, rhythm;
trochee,
poet, – laureate;
minstrel;
ballad monger;
poetaster.
V. poetize,
elegiac,
Aufl.

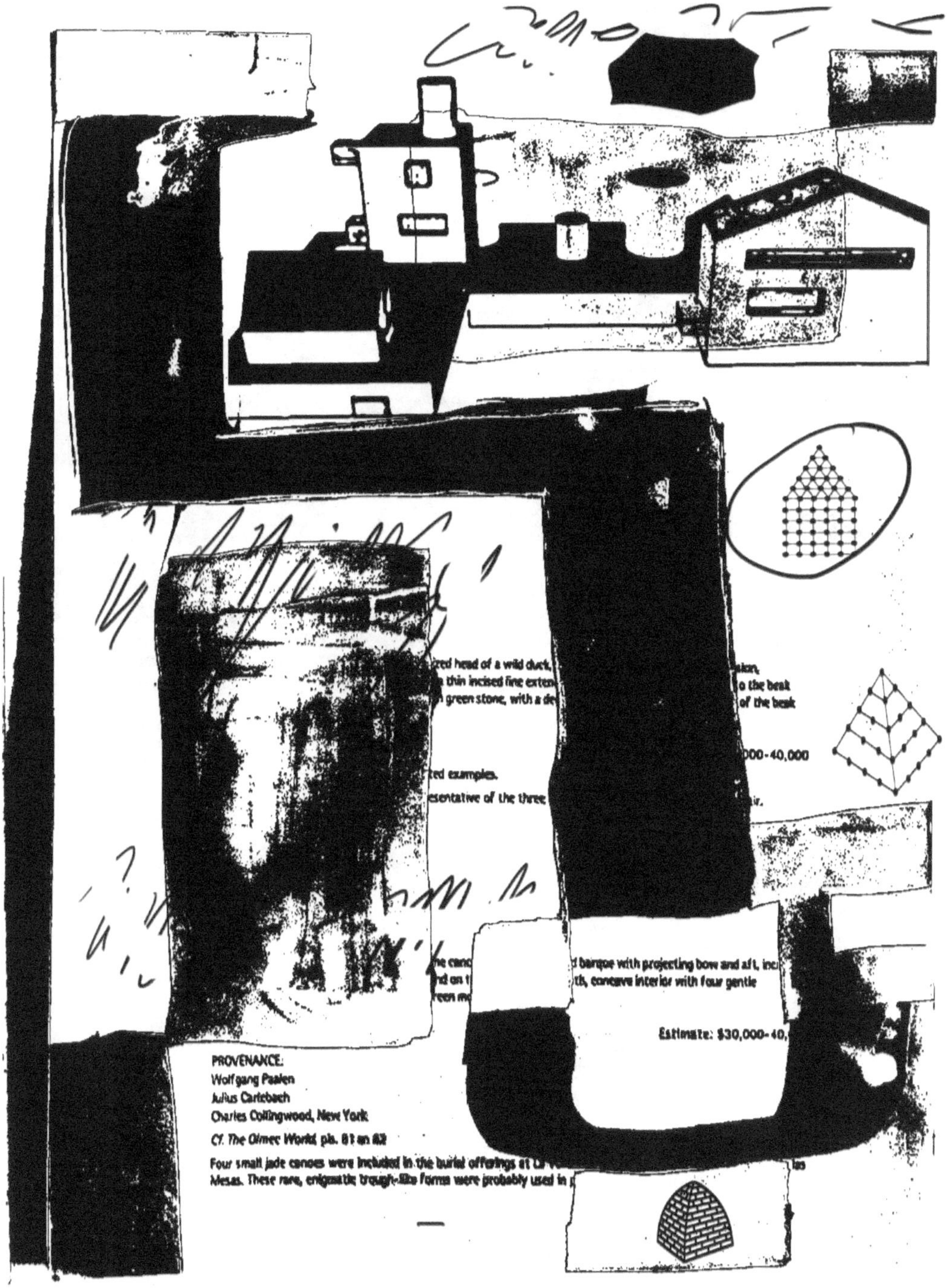
zed head of a wild duck,
a thin incised fine exten
green stone, with a de
o the beak
of the beak
000-40,000
ted examples.
esentative of the three
d barque with projecting bow and aft, inc
th, concave interior with four gentle
Estimate: $30,000-40,
PROVENANCE:
Wolfgang Paalen
Julius Carlebach
Charles Collingwood, New York
Cf. The Olmec World, pls. 81 an 82
Four small jade canoes were included in the burial offerings at
Mesas. These rare, enigmatic trough-like forms were probably used in

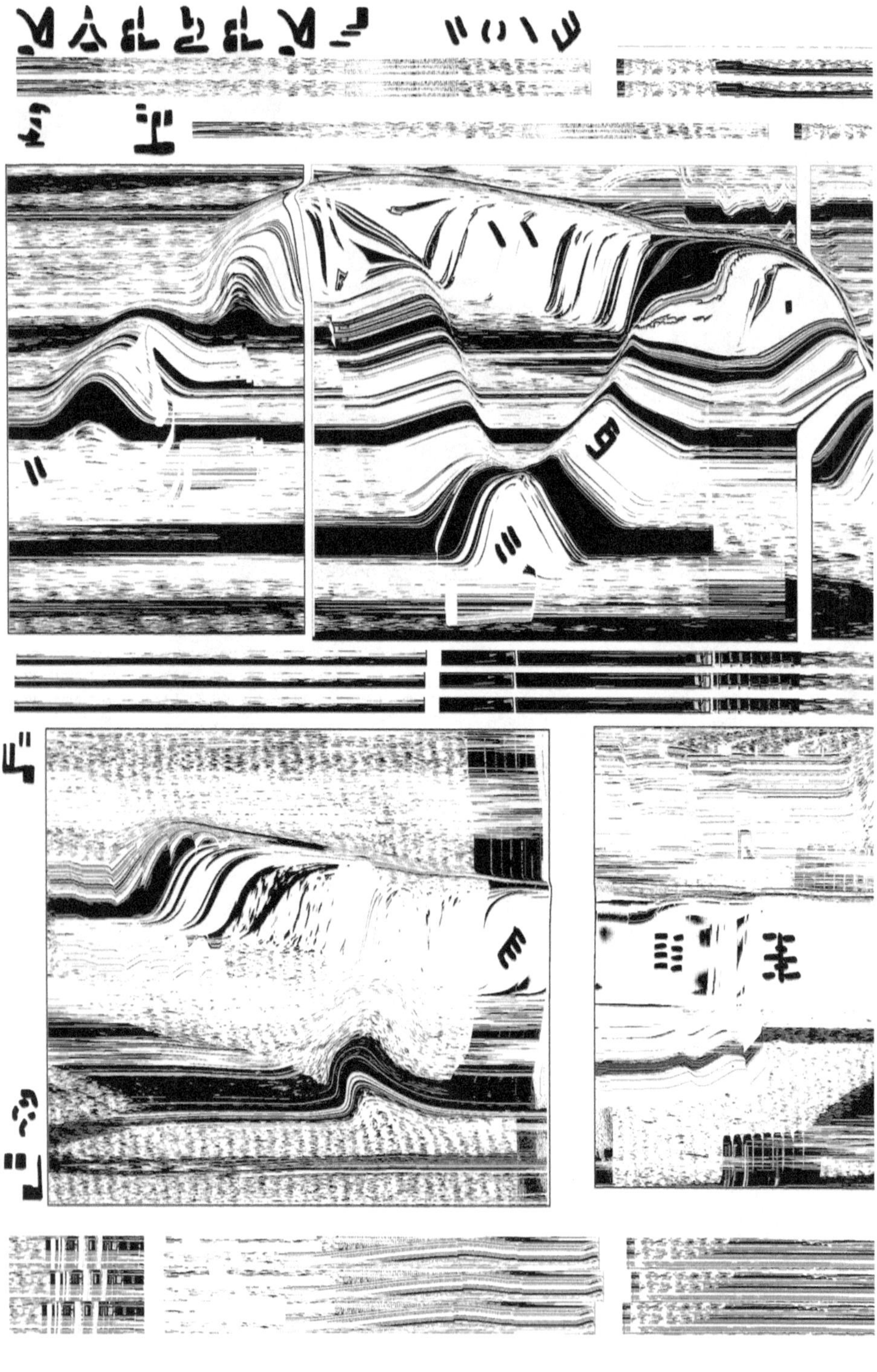

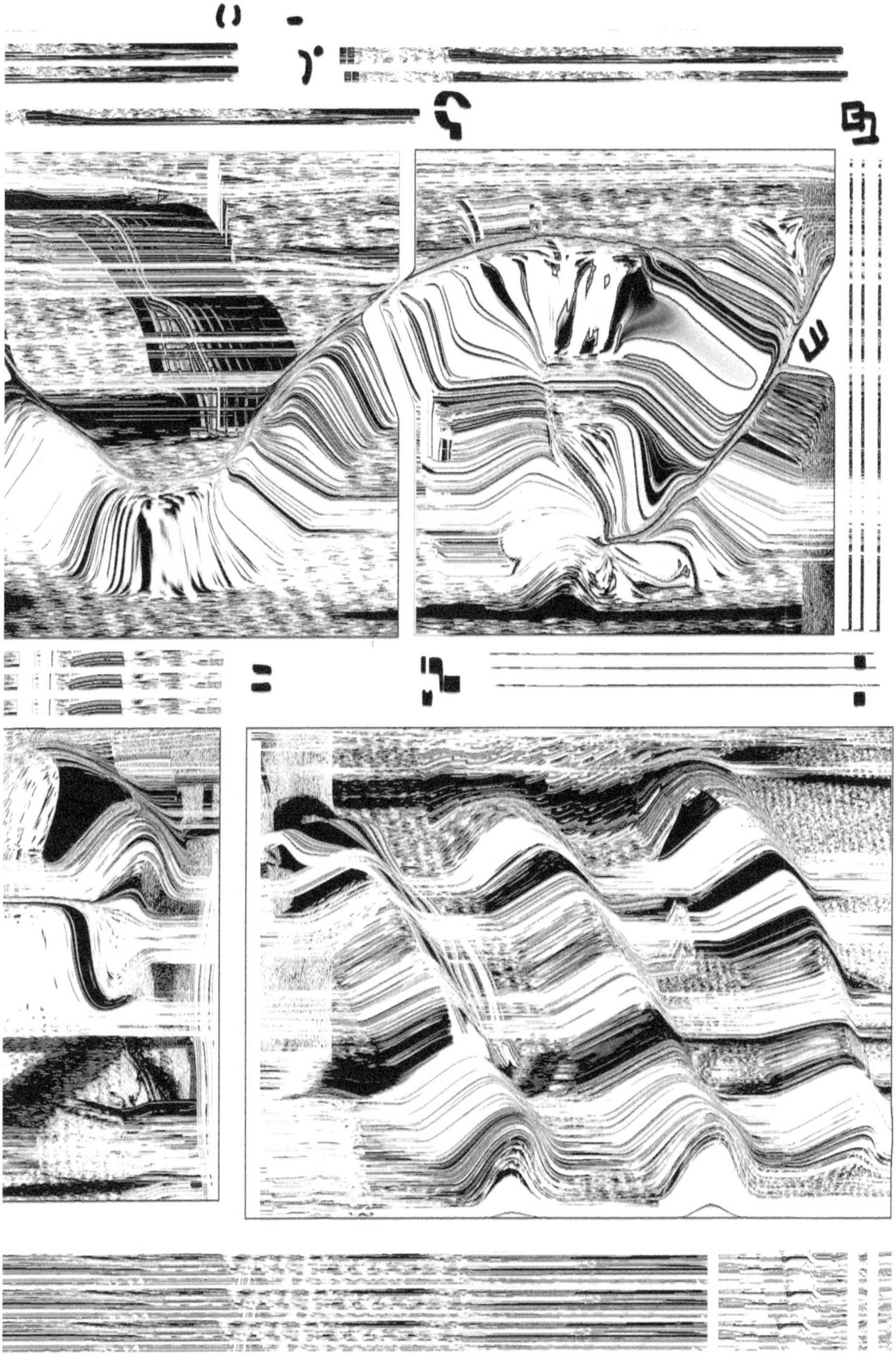

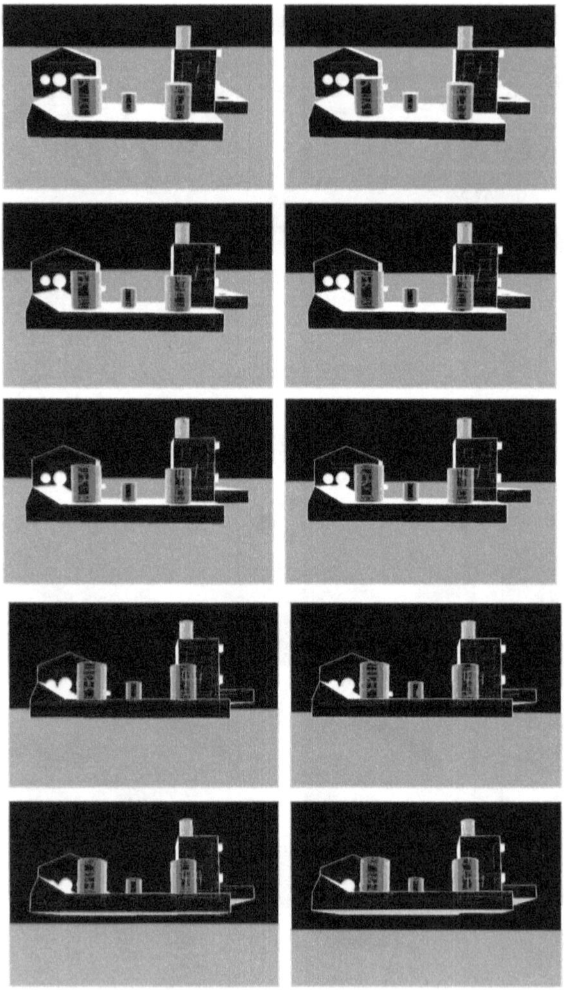

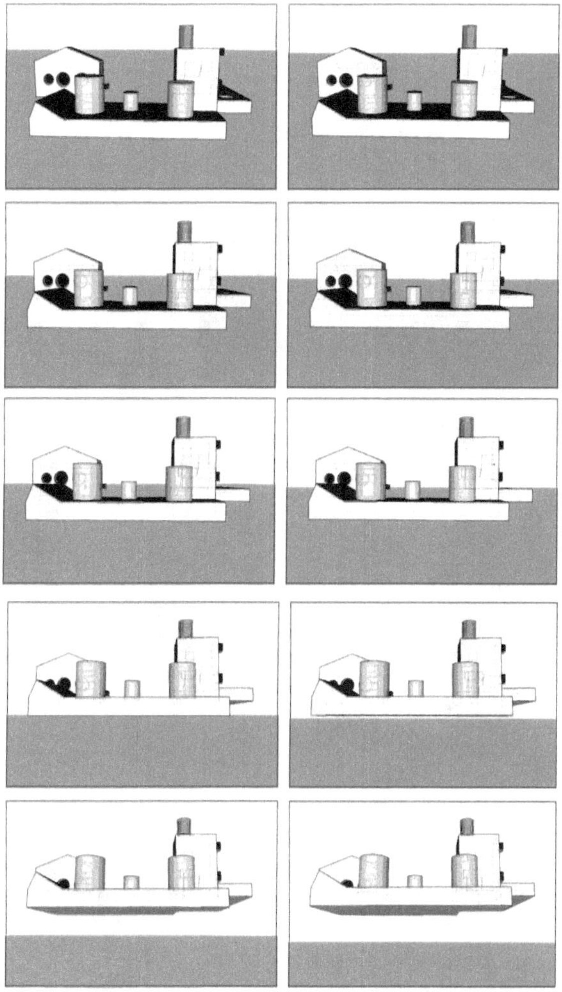

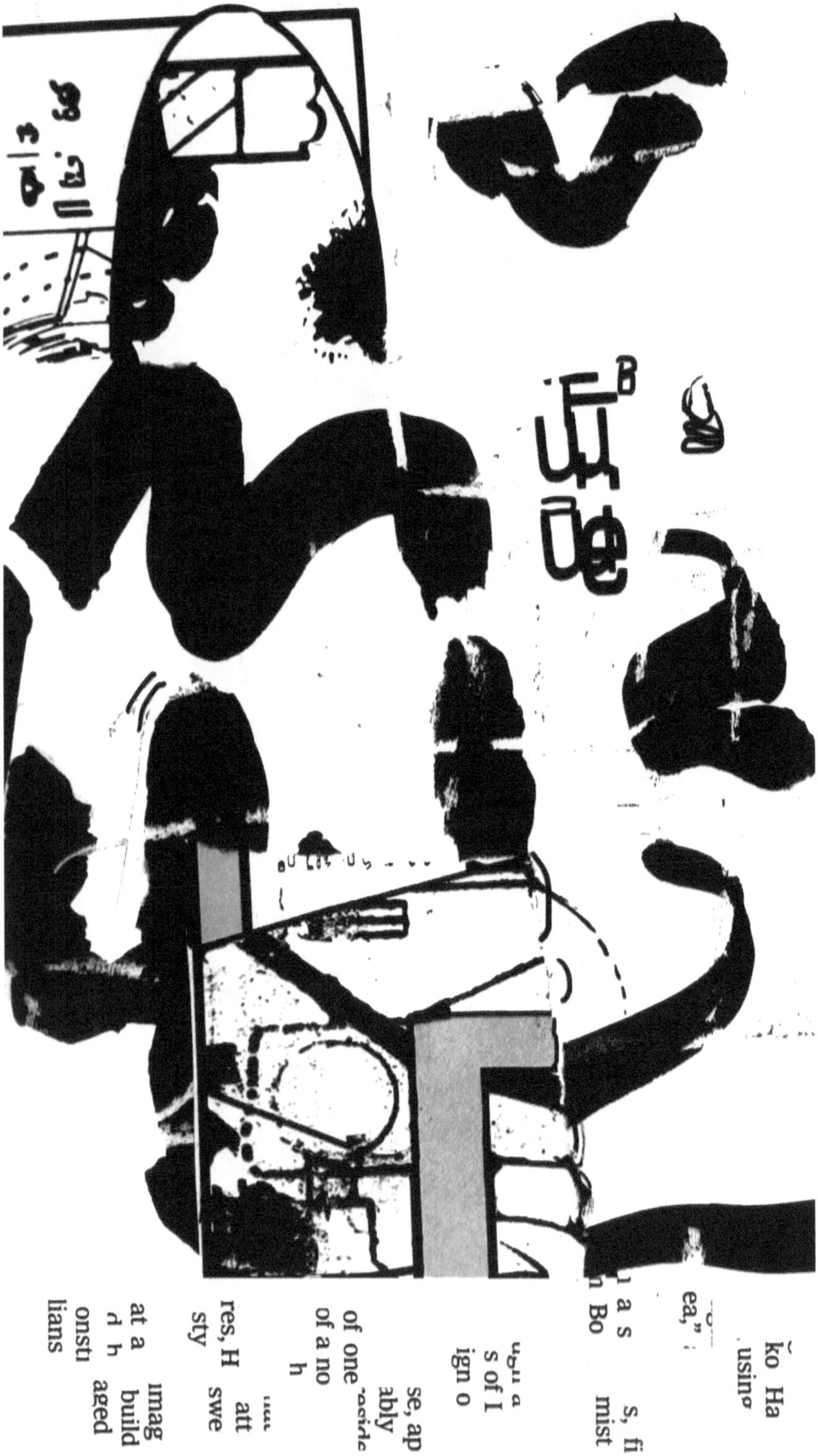

ko Ha
usin
ea,”
a s s, fi
Bo mist
s of I
ign o
se, ap
ably
of one
of a no
h
att
res, H swe
sty
imag
at a build
aged
onsti
lians

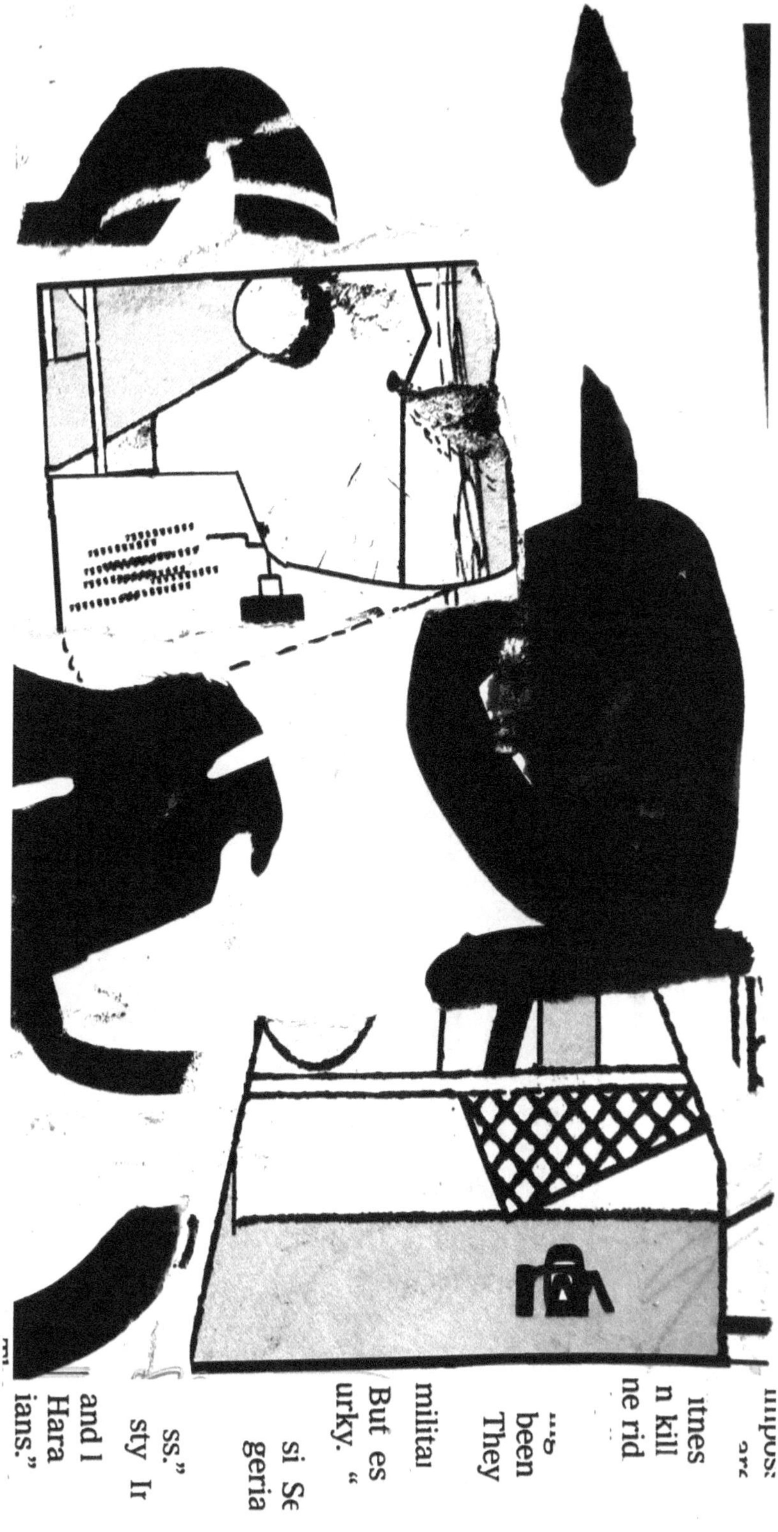
itnes
n kill
ne rid
been
They
militai
But es
urky. “
si Se
geria
ss.”
sty Ir
and l
Hara
ians.”

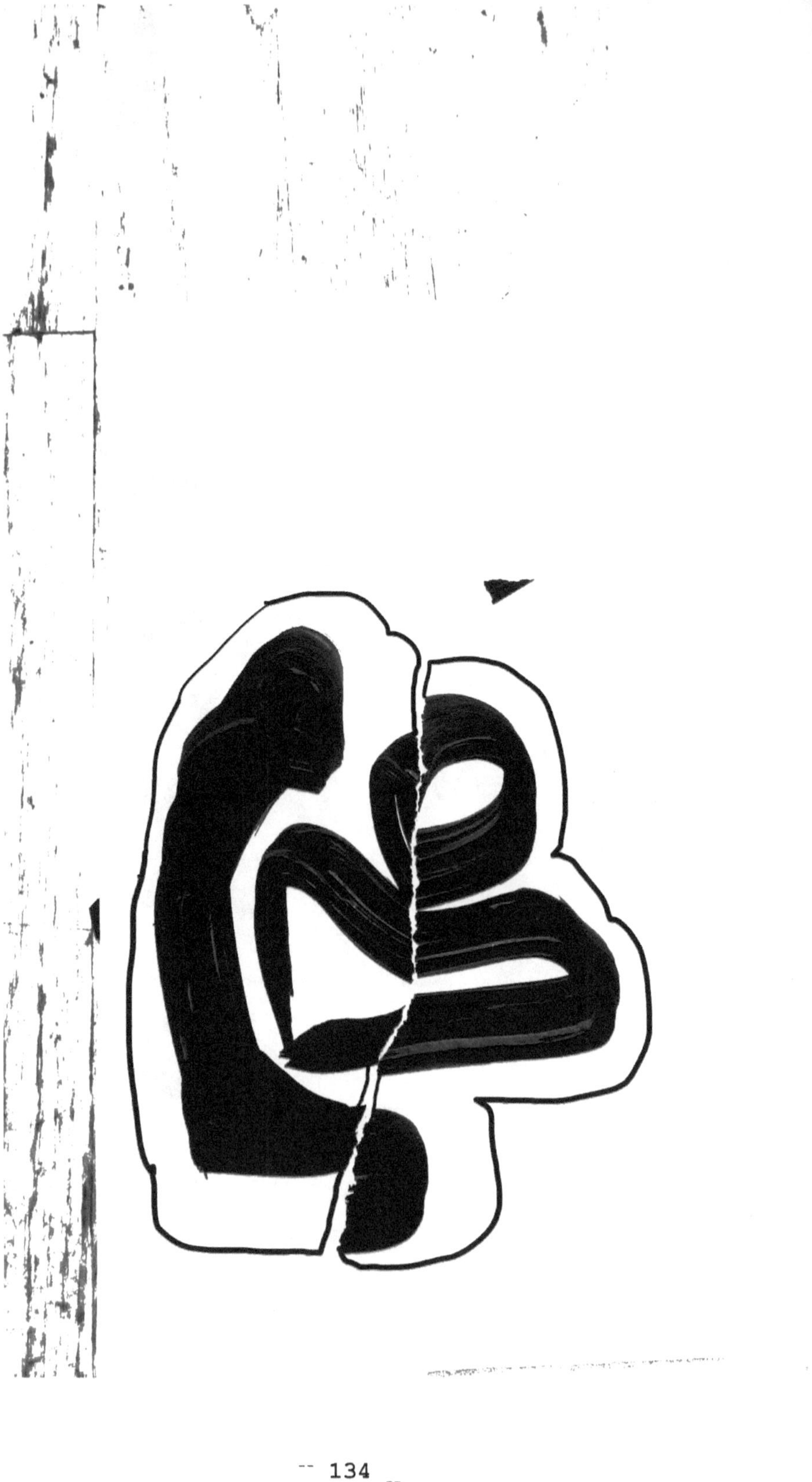

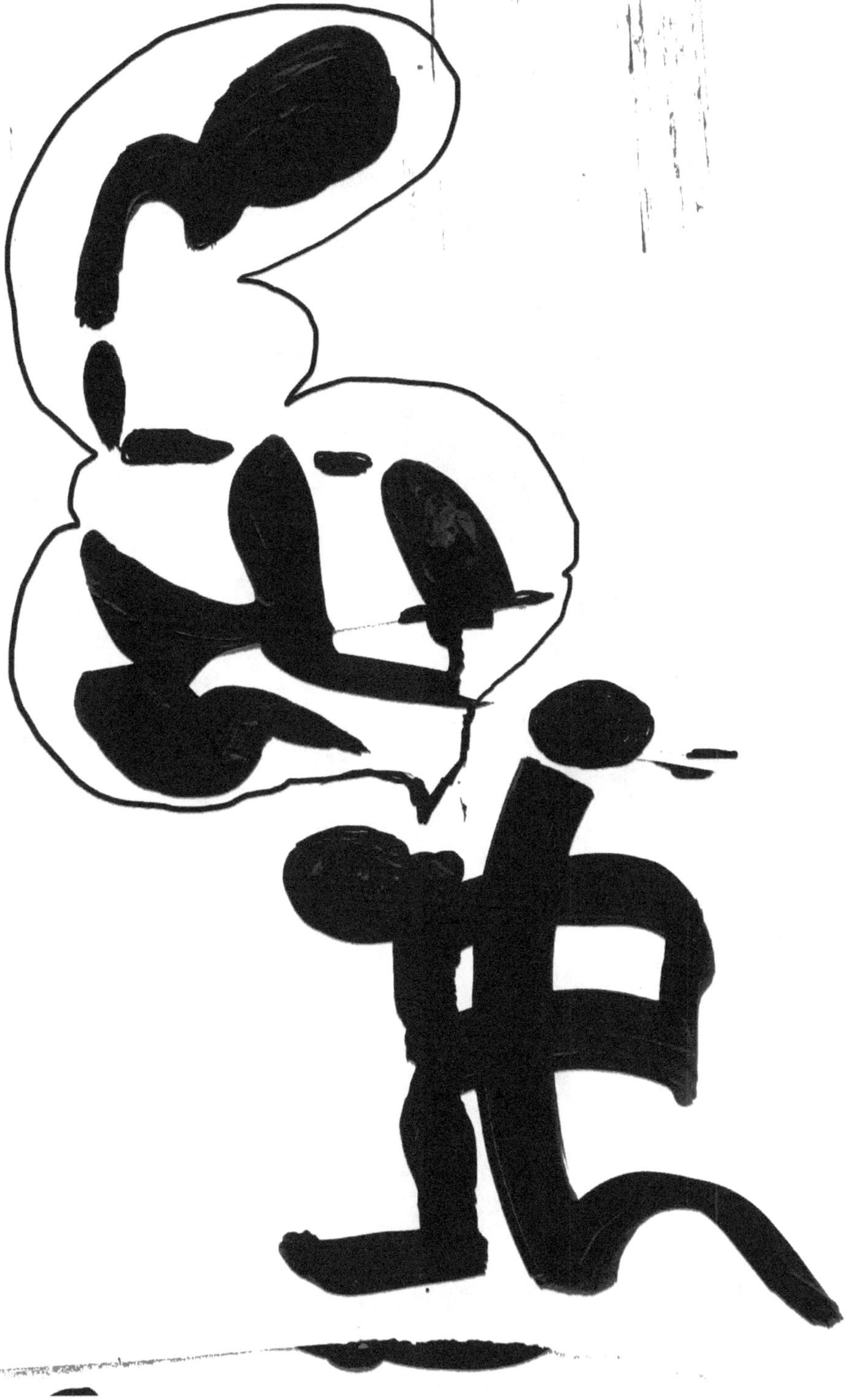

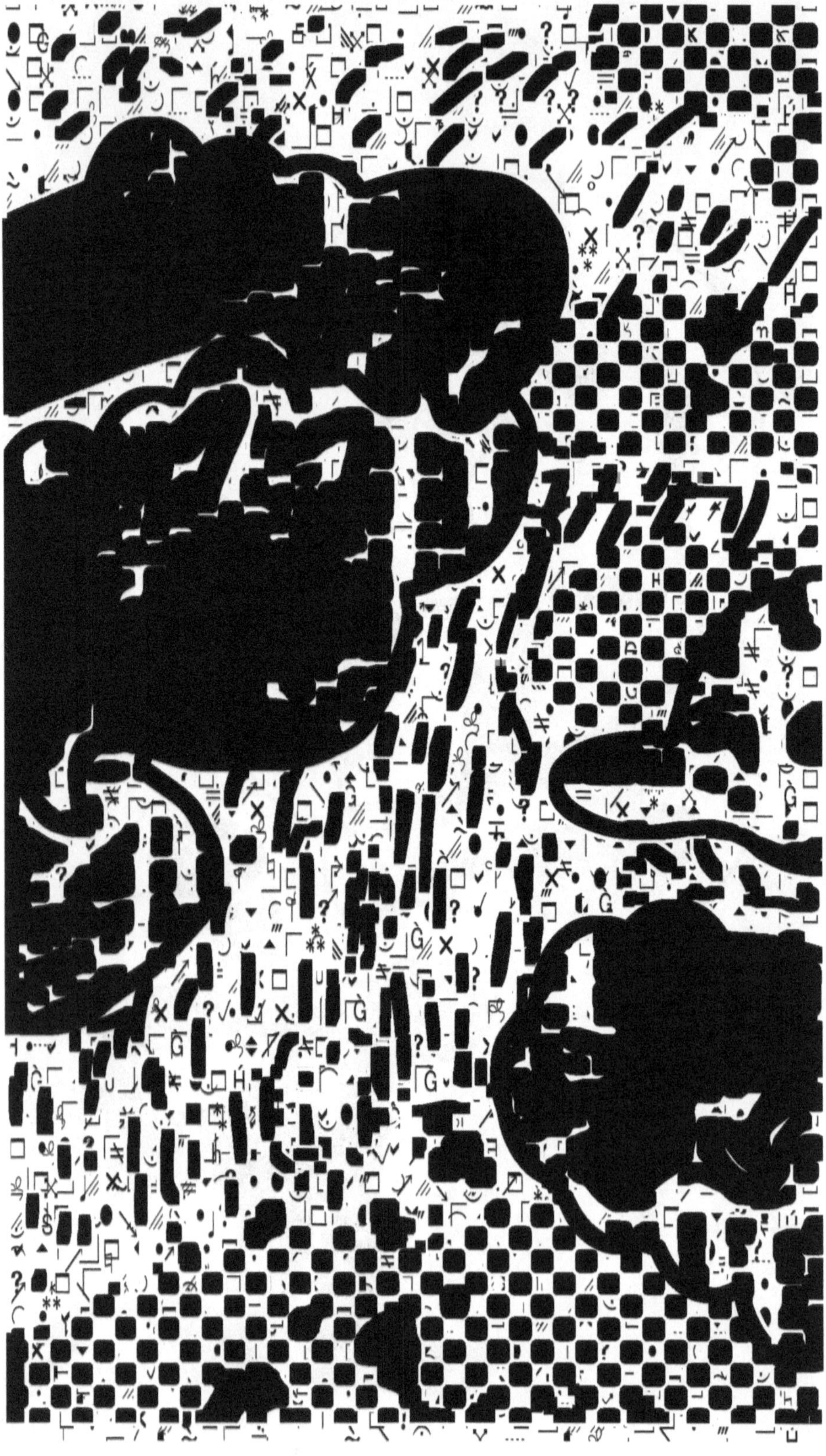

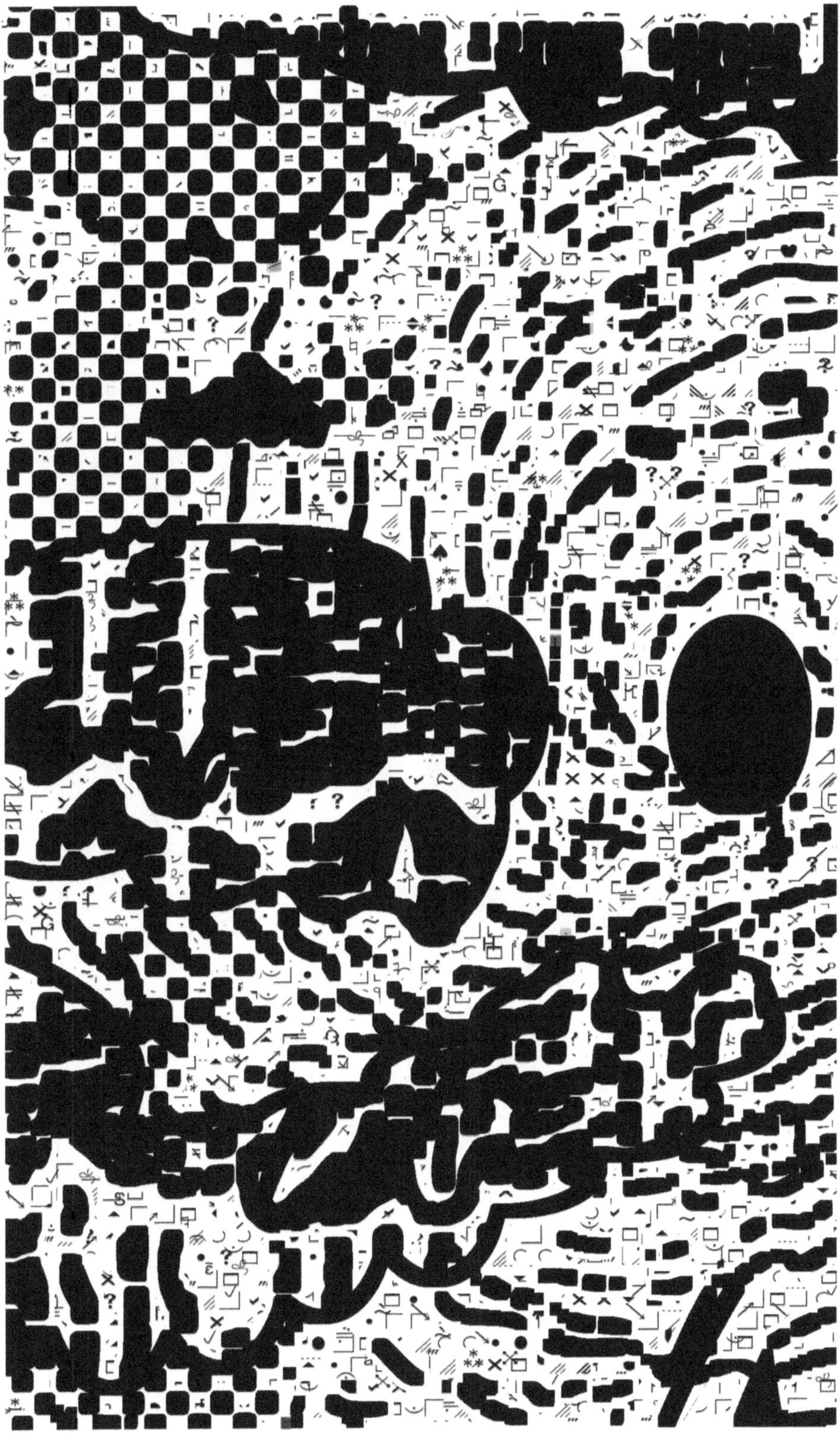

the END *n., v.* (Shaking the hands to rid them of something.) The upright "5" hands, palms facing each other, are suddenly and quickly swung around to a palm-out position. *Cf.* DONE, FINISH.

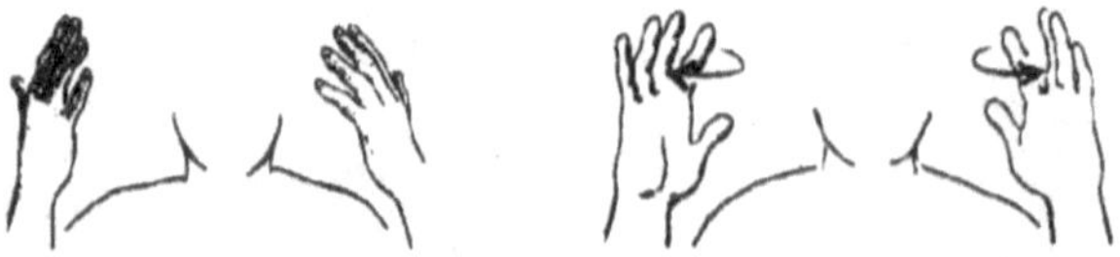

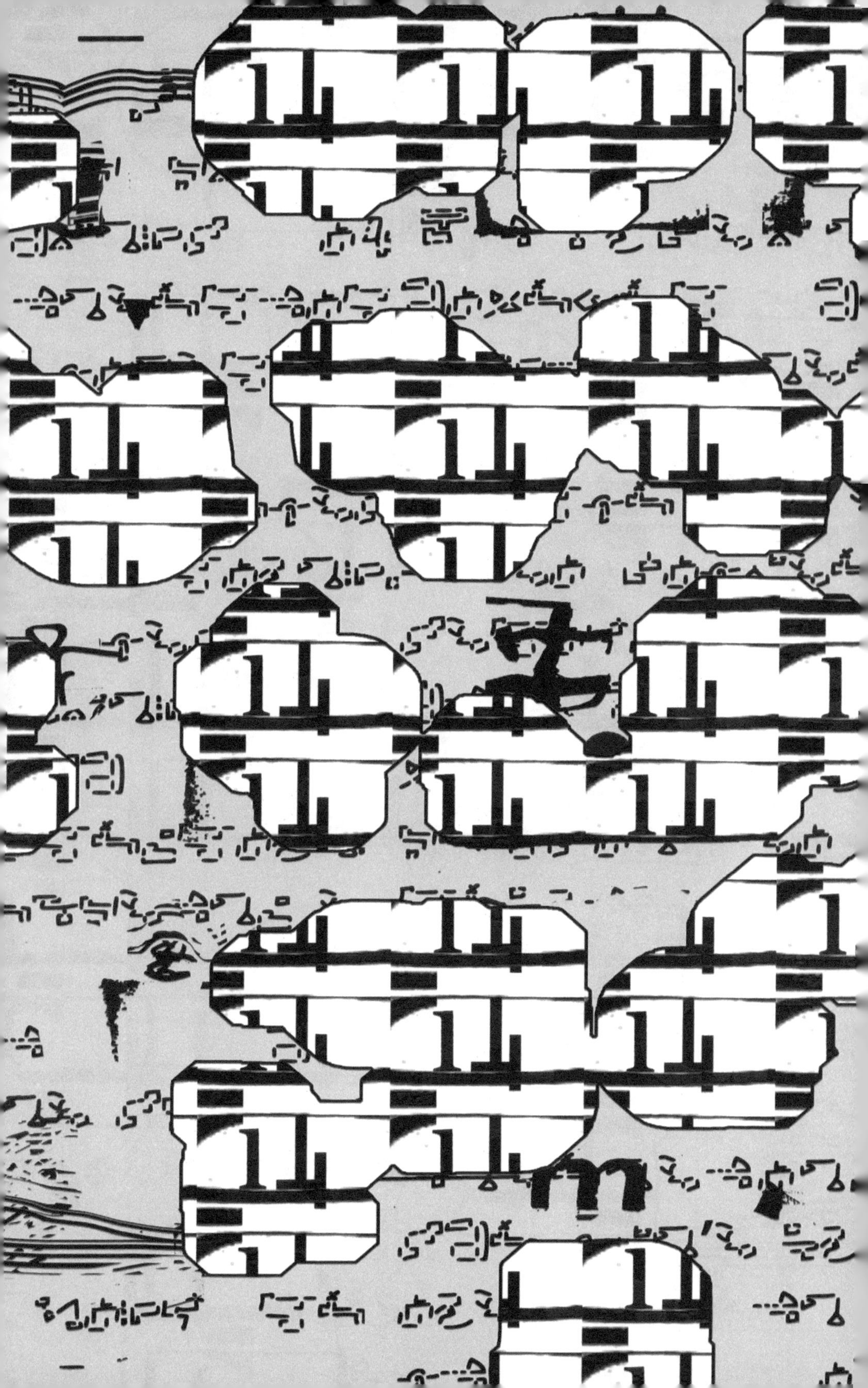

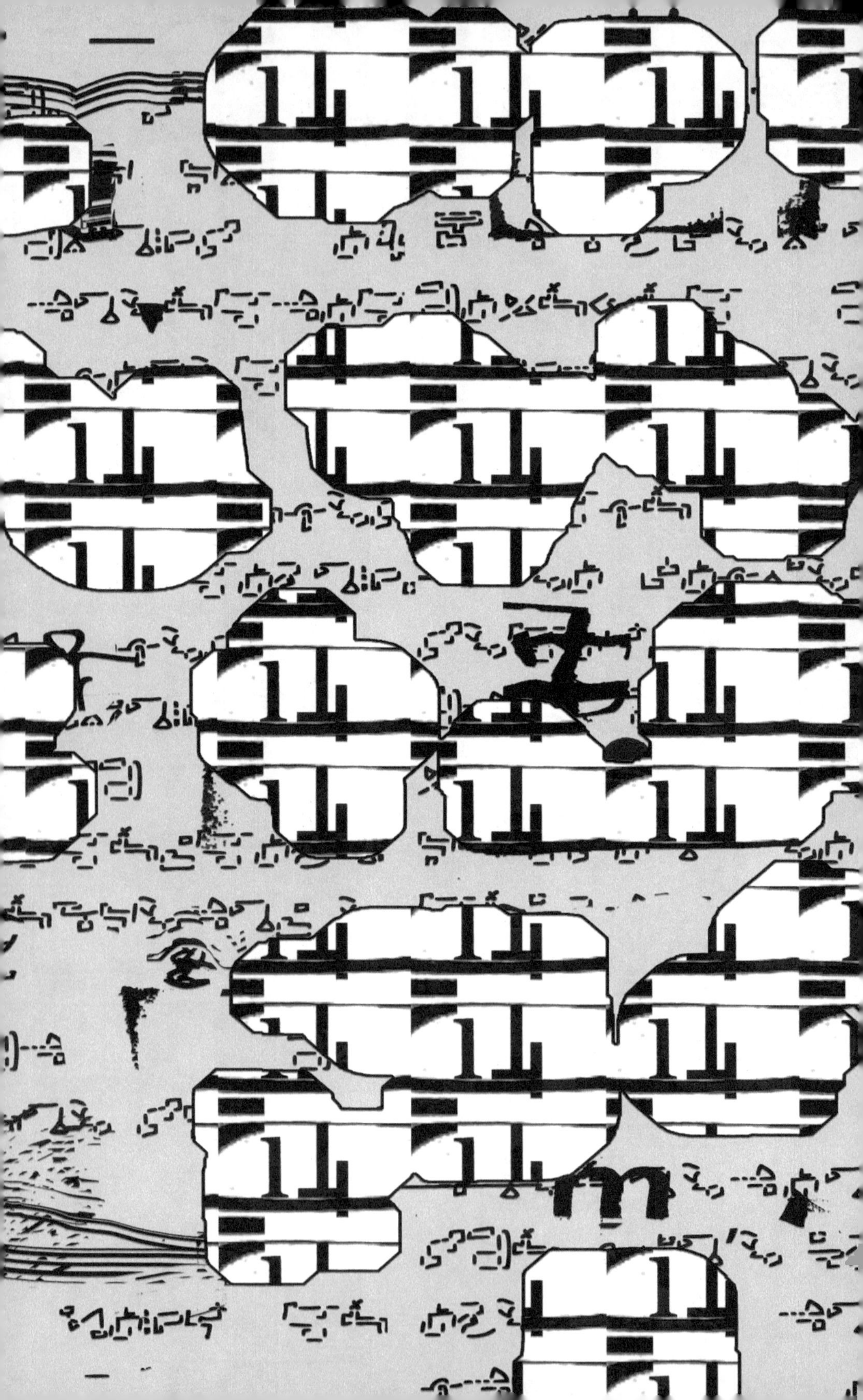

www.ingramcontent.com/pod-product-compliance
Lightning Source LLC
Chambersburg PA
CBHW021408170526
45164CB00002B/556
9781508799139